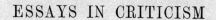
ESSAYS IN CRITICISM

MACMILLAN AND CO., Limited
LONDON · BOMBAY · CALCUTTA · MADRAS
MELBOURNE

THE MACMILLAN COMPANY
NEW YORK · BOSTON · CHICAGO
DALLAS · SAN FRANCISCO

THE MACMILLAN CO. OF CANADA, Ltd.
TORONTO

ESSAYS IN CRITICISM

FIRST SERIES

BY

MATTHEW ARNOLD

MACMILLAN AND CO., LIMITED
ST. MARTIN'S STREET, LONDON

1925

PREFACE.

(1865.)

SEVERAL of the Essays which are here collected and reprinted had the good or the bad fortune to be much criticised at the time of their first appearance. I am not now going to inflict upon the reader a reply to those criticisms; for one or two explanations which are desirable, I shall elsewhere, perhaps, be able some day to find an opportunity; but, indeed. it is not in my nature,—some of my critics would rather say, not in my power,—to dispute on behalf of any opinion, even my own, very obstinately. To try and approach truth on one side after another, not to strive or cry, nor to persist in pressing forward, on any one side, with violence and self-will,—it is only thus, it seems to me, that mortals may hope to gain any vision of the mysterious Goddess, whom we shall never see except in outline, but only thus even in outline. He who will do nothing but fight impetuously towards her on his own, one, favourite, particular line, is inevitably destined to run his head into the folds of the black robe in which she is wrapped.

So it is not to reply to my critics that I write this preface, but to prevent a misunderstanding, of which certain phrases that some of them use make me apprehensive. Mr. Wright, one of the many translators of Homer, has published a letter to the Dean of Canterbury, complaining of some remarks of mine, uttered now a long while ago, on his version of the *Iliad.* One cannot be always studying one's own works, and I was really under the impression, till I saw Mr. Wright's complaint, that I had spoken of him with all respect. The reader may judge of my astonishment, therefore, at finding, from Mr. Wright's pamphlet, that I had "declared with much solemnity that there is not any proper reason for his existing." That I never said; but, on looking back at my Lectures on translating Homer, I find that I did say, not that Mr. Wright, but that Mr. Wright's version of the *Iliad*, repeating in the main the merits and defects of Cowper's version, as Mr. Sotheby's repeated those of Pope's version, had, if I might be pardoned for saying so, no proper reason for existing. Elsewhere I expressly spoke of the merit of his version; but I confess that the phrase, qualified as I have shown, about its want of a proper reason for existing, I used. Well, the phrase had, perhaps, too much vivacity; we have all of us a right to exist, we and our works; an unpopular author should be the last person to call in question this right. So I gladly withdraw the offending phrase, and I am sorry for having used it; Mr. Wright, however, would perhaps be more indulgent to my vivacity, if he considered that we are none of us likely to be lively much longer. My vivacity is but the last sparkle of flame before we are all in the dark, the last glimpse of colour before we all go into drab,—the drab of the earnest, prosaic, practical, austerely literal future. Yes, the world will soon be the Philistines'! and then, with every voice, not of thunder, silenced, and the whole earth filled and ennobled every morning by the magnificent roaring of the young lions of the *Daily Telegraph*, we shall all yawn in one another's faces with the dismallest, the most unimpeachable gravity.

But I return to my design in writing this Preface. That design was, after apologising to Mr. Wright for my vivacity of five years ago, to beg him and others to let me bear my own burdens, without saddling the great and famous University to which I have the honour to belong with any portion of them. What I mean to deprecate is such phrases as, "his professorial assault," "his assertions issued *ex cathedrâ*," "the sanction of his name as the representative of poetry," and so on. Proud as I am of my connection with the University of Oxford,[1] I can truly say, that knowing how unpopular a task one is undertaking when one tries to pull out a few more stops in that powerful but at present somewhat narrow-toned organ, the modern Englishman, I have always sought to stand by myself, and to compromise others as little as possible. Besides this, my native modesty is such, that I have always been shy of assuming the

[1] When the above was written the author had still the Chair of Poetry at Oxford, which he has since vacated.

honourable style of Professor, because this is a title
I share with so many distinguished men,—Professor
Pepper, Professor Anderson, Professor Frickel, and
others,—who adorn it, I feel, much more than I do.

However, it is not merely out of modesty that I
prefer to stand alone, and to concentrate on myself,
as a plain citizen of the republic of letters, and not
as an office-bearer in a hierarchy, the whole responsi-
bility for all I write; it is much more out of genuine
devotion to the University of Oxford, for which I
feel, and always must feel, the fondest, the most
reverential attachment. In an epoch of dissolution
and transformation, such as that on which we are
now entered, habits, ties, and associations are inevitably broken up, the action of individuals becomes
more distinct, the shortcomings, errors, heats, disputes, which necessarily attend individual action, are
brought into greater prominence. Who would not
gladly keep clear, from all these passing clouds, an
august institution which was there before they arose,
and which will be there when they have blown over?

It is true, the *Saturday Review* maintains that our
epoch of transformation is finished; that we have
found our philosophy; that the British nation has
searched all anchorages for the spirit, and has finally
anchored itself, in the fulness of perfected knowledge,
on Benthamism. This idea at first made a great
impression on me; not only because it is so consoling
in itself, but also because it explained a phenomenon
which in the summer of last year had, I confess, a
good deal troubled me. At that time my avocations

led me travel almost daily on one of the Great Eastern Lines,—the Woodford Branch. Every one knows that the murderer, Müller, perpetrated his detestable act on the North London Railway, close by. The English middle class, of which I am myself a feeble unit, travel on the Woodford Branch in large numbers. Well, the demoralisation of our class,—the class which (the newspapers are constantly saying it, so I may repeat it without vanity) has done all the great things which have ever been done in England,—the demoralisation, I say, of our class, caused by the Bow tragedy, was something bewildering. Myself a transcendentalist (as the *Saturday Review* knows), I escaped the infection; and, day after day, I used to ply my agitated fellow-travellers with all the consolations which my transcendentalism would naturally suggest to me. I reminded them how Cæsar refused to take precautions against assassination, because life was not worth having at the price of an ignoble solicitude for it. I reminded them what insignificant atoms we all are in the life of the world. " Suppose the worst to happen," I said, addressing a portly jeweller from Cheapside; " suppose even yourself to be the victim; *il n'y a pas d'homme nécessaire.* We should miss you for a day or two upon the Woodford Branch; but the great mundane movement would still go on, the gravel walks of your villa would still be rolled, dividends would still be paid at the Bank, omnibuses would still run, there would still be the old crush at the corner of Fenchurch Street." All was of no avail. Nothing could moderate, in the bosom of the

great English middle-class, their passionate, absorbing, almost blood-thirsty clinging to life. At the
moment I thought this over-concern a little unworthy; but the *Saturday Review* suggests a touching
explanation of it. What I took for the ignoble clinging to life of a comfortable worldling, was, perhaps,
only the ardent longing of a faithful Benthamite,
traversing an age still dimmed by the last mists of
transcendentalism, to be spared long enough to see
his religion in the full and final blaze of its triumph.
This respectable man, whom I imagined to be going
up to London to serve his shop, or to buy shares, or
to attend an Exeter Hall meeting, or to assist at the
deliberations of the Marylebone Vestry, was even,
perhaps, in real truth, on a pious pilgrimage, to obtain
from Mr. Bentham's executors a secret bone of his
great, dissected master.

And yet, after all, I cannot but think that the
Saturday Review has here, for once, fallen a victim to
an idea,—a beautiful but deluding idea,—and that
the British nation has not yet, so entirely as the
reviewer seems to imagine, found the last word of its
philosophy. No, we are all seekers still! seekers
often make mistakes, and I wish mine to redound to
my own discredit only, and not to touch Oxford.
Beautiful city! so venerable, so lovely, so unravaged
by the fierce intellectual life of our century, so
serene!

"There are our young barbarians, all at play!"

And yet, steeped in sentiment as she lies, spreading

her gardens to the moonlight, and whispering from her towers the last enchantments of the Middle Age, who will deny that Oxford, by her ineffable charm, keeps ever calling us nearer to the true goal of all of us, to the ideal, to perfection,—to beauty, in a word, which is only truth seen from another side?—nearer, perhaps, than all the science of Tübingen. Adorable dreamer, whose heart has been so romantic! who hast given thyself so prodigally, given thyself to sides and to heroes not mine, only never to the Philistines! home of lost causes, and forsaken beliefs, and unpopular names, and impossible loyalties! what example could ever so inspire us to keep down the Philistine in ourselves, what teacher could ever so save us from that bondage to which we are all prone, that bondage which Goethe, in his incomparable lines on the death of Schiller, makes it his friend's highest praise (and nobly did Schiller deserve the praise) to have left miles out of sight behind him;—the bondage of "*was uns alle bändigt*, DAS GEMEINE!" She will forgive me, even if I have unwittingly drawn upon her a shot or two aimed at her unworthy son; for she is generous, and the cause in which I fight is, after all, hers. Apparitions of a day, what is our puny warfare against the Philistines, compared with the warfare which this queen of romance has been waging against them for centuries, and will wage after we are gone?

CONTENTS.

I.

THE FUNCTION OF CRITICISM AT THE PRESENT TIME.

MANY objections have been made to a proposition which, in some remarks of mine on translating Homer, I ventured to put forth; a proposition about criticism, and its importance at the present day. I said: "Of the literature of France and Germany, as of the intellect of Europe in general, the main effort, for now many years, has been a critical effort; the endeavour, in all branches of knowledge, theology, philosophy, history, art, science, to see the object as in itself it really is." I added, that owing to the operation in English literature of certain causes, "almost the last thing for which one would come to English literature is just that very thing which now Europe most desires,—criticism;" and that the power and value of English literature was thereby impaired. More than one rejoinder declared that the importance I here assigned to criticism was excessive, and asserted the inherent superiority of the creative effort of the human spirit over its critical effort.

And the other day, having been led by a Mr. Shairp's excellent notice of Wordsworth [1] to turn again to his biography, I found, in the words of this great man, whom I, for one, must always listen to with the profoundest respect, a sentence passed on the critic's business, which seems to justify every possible disparagement of it. Wordsworth says in one of his letters:—

"The writers in these publications" (the Reviews), "while they prosecute their inglorious employment, can not be supposed to be in a state of mind very favourable for being affected by the finer influences of a thing so pure as genuine poetry."

And a trustworthy reporter of his conversation quotes a more elaborate judgment to the same effect :—

"Wordsworth holds the critical power very low, infinitely lower than the inventive; and he said to-day that if the quantity of time consumed in writing critiques on the works of others were given to original composition, of whatever kind it might be, it would be much better employed; it would make a man find out sooner his own level, and it would do infinitely less mischief. A false or

---

[1] I cannot help thinking that a practice, common in England during the last century, and still followed in France, of printing a notice of this kind,—a notice by a competent critic,—to serve as an introduction to an eminent author's works, might be revived among us with advantage. To introduce all succeeding editions of Wordsworth, Mr. Shairp's notice might, it seems to me, excellently serve ; it is written from the point of view of an admirer, nay, of a disciple, and that is right ; but then the disciple must be also, as in this case he is, a critic, a man of letters, not, as too often happens, some relation or friend with no qualification for his task except affection for his author.

malicious criticism may do much injury to the minds of others, a stupid invention, either in prose or verse, is quite harmless."

It is almost too much to expect of poor human nature, that a man capable of producing some effect in one line of literature, should, for the greater good of society, voluntarily doom himself to impotence and obscurity in another. Still less is this to be expected from men addicted to the composition of the "false or malicious criticism" of which Wordsworth speaks. However, everybody would admit that a false or malicious criticism had better never have been written. Everybody, too, would be willing to admit, as a general proposition, that the critical faculty is lower than the inventive. But is it true that criticism is really, in itself, a baneful and injurious employment; is it true that all time given to writing critiques on the works of others would be much better employed if it were given to original composition, of whatever kind this may be? Is it true that Johnson had better have gone on producing more *Irenes* instead of writing his *Lives of the Poets;* nay, is it certain that Wordsworth himself was better employed in making his Ecclesiastical Sonnets than when he made his celebrated Preface, so full of criticism, and criticism of the works of others? Wordsworth was himself a great critic, and it is to be sincerely regretted that he has not left us more criticism; Goethe was one of the greatest of critics, and we may sincerely congratulate ourselves that he has left us so much criticism. Without wasting time over the exaggera

tion which Wordsworth's judgment on criticism
clearly contains, or over an attempt to trace the
causes,—not difficult, I think, to be traced,—which may
have led Wordsworth to this exaggeration, a critic
may with advantage seize an occasion for trying his
own conscience, and for asking himself of what real
service at any given moment the practice of criticism
either is or may be made to his own mind and spirit,
and to the minds and spirits of others.

The critical power is of lower rank than the creative.   True; but in assenting to this proposition, one
or two things are to be kept in mind.   It is undeniable that the exercise of a creative power, that a free
creative activity, is the highest function of man; it is
proved to be so by man's finding in it his true happiness.   But it is undeniable, also, that men may have
the sense of exercising this free creative activity in
other ways than in producing great works of literature or art; if it were not so, all but a very few men
would be shut out from the true happiness of all men.
They may have it in well-doing, they may have it in
learning, they may have it even in criticising.   This
is one thing to be kept in mind.   Another is, that
the exercise of the creative power in the production
of great works of literature or art, however high this
exercise of it may rank, is not at all epochs and under
all conditions possible; and that therefore labour may
be vainly spent in attempting it, which might with
more fruit be used in preparing for it, in rendering
it possible.   This creative power works with elements,
with materials; what if it has not those materials

those elements, ready for its use? In that case it
must surely wait till they are ready. Now, in
literature,—I will limit myself to literature, for it
is about literature that the question arises,—the
elements with which the creative power works are
ideas; the best ideas on every matter which literature touches, current at the time. At any rate we
may lay it down as certain that in modern literature
no manifestation of the creative power not working
with these can be very important or fruitful. And I
say *current* at the time, not merely accessible at the
time; for creative literary genius does not princi-
pally show itself in discovering new ideas, that is
rather the business of the philosopher. The grand
work of literary genius is a work of synthesis and
exposition, not of analysis and discovery; its gift
lies in the faculty of being happily inspired by a
certain intellectual and spiritual atmosphere, by a
certain order of ideas, when it finds itself in them;
of dealing divinely with these ideas, presenting them
in the most effective and attractive combinations,—
making beautiful works with them, in short. But it
must have the atmosphere, it must find itself amidst
the order of ideas, in order to work freely; and these
it is not so easy to command. This is why great
creative epochs in literature are so rare, this is why
there is so much that is unsatisfactory in the productions of many men of real genius; because, for the
creation of a master-work of literature two powers
must concur, the power of the man and the power of
the moment, and the man is not enough without the

moment; the creative power has, for its happy exercise, appointed elements, and those elements are not
in its own control.

Nay, they are more within the control of the
critical power. It is the business of the critical
power, as I said in the words already quoted, "in
all branches of knowledge, theology, philosophy,
history, art, science, to see the object as in itself it
really is." Thus it tends, at last, to make an intellectual situation of which the creative power can
profitably avail itself. It tends to establish an order
of ideas, if not absolutely true, yet true by comparison with that which it displaces; to make the
best ideas prevail. Presently these new ideas reach
society, the touch of truth is the touch of life, and
there is a stir and growth everywhere; out of this
stir and growth come the creative epochs of literature.

Or, to narrow our range, and quit these considerations of the general march of genius and of society,—
considerations which are apt to become too abstract
and impalpable,—every one can see that a poet, for
instance, ought to know life and the world before
dealing with them in poetry; and life and the world
being in modern times very complex things, the creation of a modern poet, to be worth much, implies a
great critical effort behind it; else it must be a comparatively poor, barren, and short-lived affair. This
is why Byron's poetry had so little endurance in it,
and Goethe's so much; both Byron and Goethe had
a great productive power, but Goethe's was nourished
by a great critical effort providing the true materials

for it, and Byron's was not; Goethe knew life and
the world, the poet's necessary subjects, much more
comprehensively and thoroughly than Byron.   He
knew a great deal more of them, and he knew them
much more as they really are.

It has long seemed to me that the burst of creative
activity in our literature, through the first quarter of
this century, had about it in fact something premature; and that from this cause its productions are
doomed, most of them, in spite of the sanguine hopes
which accompanied and do still accompany them, to
prove hardly more lasting than the productions of far
less splendid epochs.   And this prematureness comes
from its having proceeded without having its proper
data, without sufficient materials to work with.   In
other words, the English poetry of the first quarter
of this century, with plenty of energy, plenty of creative force, did not know enough.   This makes Byron
so empty of matter, Shelley so incoherent, Wordsworth even, profound as he is, yet so wanting in completeness and variety.   Wordsworth cared little for
books, and disparaged Goethe.   I admire Wordsworth,
as he is, so much that I cannot wish him different;
and it is vain, no doubt, to imagine such a man
different from what he is, to suppose that he *could*
have been different.   But surely the one thing wanting to make Wordsworth an even greater poet than
he is,—his thought richer, and his influence of wider
application,—was that he should have read more
books, among them, no doubt, those of that Goethe
whom he disparaged without reading him.

But to speak of books and reading may easily lead to a misunderstanding here. It was not really books and reading that lacked to our poetry at this epoch; Shelley had plenty of reading, Coleridge had immense reading. Pindar and Sophocles—as we all say so glibly, and often with so little discernment of the real import of what we are saying—had not many books; Shakspeare was no deep reader. True; but in the Greece of Pindar and Sophocles, in the England of Shakspeare, the poet lived in a current of ideas in the highest degree animating and nourishing to the creative power; society was, in the fullest measure, permeated by fresh thought, intelligent and alive. And this state of things is the true basis for the creative power's exercise, in this it finds its data, its materials, truly ready for its hand; all the books and reading in the world are only valuable as they are helps to this. Even when this does not actually exist, books and reading may enable a man to construct a kind of semblance of it in his own mind, a world of knowledge and intelligence in which he may live and work. This is by no means an equivalent to the artist for the nationally diffused life and thought of the epochs of Sophocles or Shakspeare; but, besides that it may be a means of preparation for such epochs, it does really constitute, if many share in it, a quickening and sustaining atmosphere of great value. Such an atmosphere the many-sided learning and the long and widely-combined critical effort of Germany formed for Goethe, when he lived and worked. There was no national glow of life and thought there as in the Athens of Pericles or the England of Elizabeth. That was the poet's weakness. But there was a sort of equivalent for it in the complete culture and unfettered thinking of a large body of Germans. That was his strength. In the England of the first quarter of this century there was neither a national glow of life and thought, such as we had in the age of Elizabeth, nor yet a culture and a force of learning and criticism such as were to be found in Germany. Therefore the creative power of poetry wanted, for success in the highest sense, materials and a basis; a thorough interpretation of the world was necessarily denied to it.

At first sight it seems strange that out of the immense stir of the French Revolution and its age should not have come a crop of works of genius equal to that which came out of the stir of the great productive time of Greece, or out of that of the Renascence, with its powerful episode the Reformation. But the truth is that the stir of the French Revolution took a character which essentially distinguished it from such movements as these. These were, in the main, disinterestedly intellectual and spiritual movements; movements in which the human spirit looked for its satisfaction in itself and in the increased play of its own activity. The French Revolution took a political, practical character. The movement which went on in France under the old *régime*, from 1700 to 1789, was far more really akin than that of the Revolution itself to the movement of the Renascence; the France of Voltaire and Rousseau told far more powerfully upon the mind of Europe than the France of the Revolution. Goethe reproached this last expressly with having "thrown quiet culture back." Nay, and the true key to how much in our Byron, even in our Wordsworth, is this!—that they had their source in a great movement of feeling, not in a great movement of mind. The French Revolution, however,—that object of so much blind love and so much blind hatred,—found undoubtedly its motive-power in the intelligence of men, and not in their practical sense; this is what distinguishes it from the English Revolution of Charles the First's time. This is what makes it a more spiritual event than our Revolution, an event of much more powerful and world-wide interest, though practically less successful; it appeals to an order of ideas which are universal, certain, permanent. 1789 asked of a thing, Is it rational? 1642 asked of a thing, Is it legal? or, when it went furthest, Is it according to conscience? This is the English fashion, a fashion to be treated, within its own sphere, with the highest respect; for its success, within its own sphere, has been prodigious. But what is law in one place is not law in another, what is law here to-day is not law even here to-morrow; and as for conscience, what is binding on one man's conscience is not binding on another's. The old woman who threw her stool at the head of the surpliced minister in St. Giles's Church at Edinburgh obeyed an impulse to which millions of the human race may be permitted to remain strangers. But the prescriptions of reason are absolute, unchang ing, of universal validity; *to count by tens is the easiest way of counting*—that is a proposition of which every one, from here to the Antipodes, feels the force; at least I should say so if we did not live in a country where it is not impossible that any morning we may find a letter in the *Times* declaring that a decimal coinage is an absurdity. That a whole nation should have been penetrated with an enthusiasm for pure reason, and with an ardent zeal for making its pre-scriptions triumph, is a very remarkable thing, when we consider how little of mind, or anything so worthy and quickening as mind, comes into the motives which alone, in general, impel great masses of men. In spite of the extravagant direction given to this enthusiasm, in spite of the crimes and follies in which it lost itself, the French Revolution derives from the force, truth, and universality of the ideas which it took for its law, and from the passion with which it could inspire a multitude for these ideas, a unique and still living power; it is—it will probably long remain—the greatest, the most animating event in history. And as no sincere passion for the things of the mind, even though it turn out in many respects an unfortunate passion, is ever quite thrown away and quite barren of good, France has reaped from hers one fruit—the natural and legitimate fruit, though not precisely the grand fruit she expected: she is the country in Europe where *the people* is most alive.

But the mania for giving an immediate political and practical application to all these fine ideas of the

reason was fatal. Here an Englishman is in his
element: on this theme we can all go on for hours.
And all we are in the habit of saying on it has undoubtedly a great deal of truth. Ideas cannot be too
much prized in and for themselves, cannot be too
much lived with; but to transport them abruptly into
the world of politics and practice, violently to revolu-
tionise this world to their bidding,—that is quite
another thing. There is the world of ideas and there
is the world of practice; the French are often for
suppressing the one and the English the other; but
neither is to be suppressed. A member of the House
of Commons said to me the other day : "That a thing
is an anomaly, I consider to be no objection to it
whatever." I venture to think he was wrong; that
a thing is an anomaly *is* an objection to it, but absolutely and in the sphere of ideas : it is not necessarily,
under such and such circumstances, or at such and
such a moment, an objection to it in the sphere of
politics and practice. Joubert has said beautifully :
" C'est la force et le droit qui règlent toutes choses
dans le monde ; la force en attendant le droit."
(Force and right are the governors of this world;
force till right is ready.) *Force till right is ready ;* and
till right is ready, force, the existing order of things,
is justified, is the legitimate ruler. But right is something moral, and implies inward recognition, free
assent of the will; we are not ready for right,—*right*,
so far as we are concerned, *is not ready*,—until we have
attained this sense of seeing it and willing it. The
way in which for us it may change and transform

force, the existing order of things, and become, in its turn, the legitimate ruler of the world, should depend on the way in which, when our time comes, we see it and will it. Therefore for other people enamoured of their own newly discerned right, to attempt to impose it upon us as ours, and violently to substitute their right for our force, is an act of tyranny, and to be resisted. It sets at nought the second great half of our maxim, *force till right is ready.* This was the grand error of the French Revolution; and its move- ment of ideas, by quitting the intellectual sphere and rushing furiously into the political sphere, ran, indeed, a prodigious and memorable course, but produced no such intellectual fruit as the movement of ideas of the Renascence, and created, in opposition to itself, what I may call an *epoch of concentration.* The great force of that epoch of concentration was England; and the great voice of that epoch of concentration was Burke. It is the fashion to treat Burke's writings on the French Revolution as superannuated and conquered by the event; as the eloquent but unphilosophical tirades of bigotry and prejudice. I will not deny that they are often disfigured by the violence and passion of the moment, and that in some directions Burke's view was bounded, and his observation there- fore at fault. But on the whole, and for those who can make the needful corrections, what distinguishes these writings is their profound, permanent, fruitful, philosophical truth. They contain the true philosophy of an epoch of concentration, dissipate the heavy atmosphere which its own nature is apt to engender round it, and make its resistance rational instead of mechanical.

But Burke is so great because, almost alone in England, he brings thought to bear upon politics, he saturates politics with thought. It is his accident that his ideas were at the service of an epoch of concentration, not of an epoch of expansion; it is his characteristic that he so lived by ideas, and had such a source of them welling up within him, that he could float even an epoch of concentration and English Tory politics with them. It does not hurt him that Dr. Price and the Liberals were enraged with him; it does not even hurt him that George the Third and the Tories were enchanted with him. His greatness is that he lived in a world which neither English Liberalism nor English Toryism is apt to enter;—the world of ideas, not the world of catchwords and party habits. So far is it from being really true of him that he " to party gave up what was meant for mankind," that at the very end of his fierce struggle with the French Revolution, after all his invectives against its false pretensions, hollowness, and madness, with his sincere conviction of its mischievousness, he can close a memorandum on the best means of combating it, some of the last pages he ever wrote,—the *Thoughts on French Affairs*, in December 1791,—with these striking words :—

" The evil is stated, in my opinion, as it exists The remedy must be where power, wisdom, and information, I hope, are more united with good intentions than they can be with me. I have done with this subject, I believe, for ever. It has given me many anxious moments for the last two years. *If a great change is to be made in human affairs, the minds of men will be fitted to it ; the general opinions and feelings will draw that way. Every fear, every hope will forward it ; and then they who persist in opposing this mighty current in human affairs, will appear rather to resist the decrees of Providence itself, than the mere designs of men. They will not be resolute and firm, but perverse and obstinate.*"

That return of Burke upon himself has always seemed to me one of the finest things in English literature, or indeed in any literature. That is what I call living by ideas : when one side of a question has long had your earnest support, when all your feelings are engaged, when you hear all round you no language but one, when your party talks this language like a steam-engine and can imagine no other,—still to be able to think, still to be irresistibly carried, if so it be, by the current of thought to the opposite side of the question, and, like Balaam, to be unable to speak anything *but what the Lord has put in your mouth.* I know nothing more striking, and I must add that I know nothing more un-English.

For the Englishman in general is like my friend the Member of Parliament, and believes, point-blank, that for a thing to be an anomaly is absolutely no objection to it whatever. He is like the Lord Auckland of Burke's day, who, in a memorandum on the French Revolution, talks of "certain miscreants, assuming the name of philosophers, who have pre sumed themselves capable of establishing a new system of society." The Englishman has been called a political animal, and he values what is political and practical so much that ideas easily become objects of dislike in his eyes, and thinkers " miscreants," because ideas and thinkers have rashly meddled with politics and practice. This would be all very well if the dislike and neglect confined themselves to ideas transported out of their own sphere, and meddling rashly with practice; but they are inevitably extended to ideas as such, and to the whole life of intelligence; practice is everything, a free play of the mind is nothing. The notion of the free play of the mind upon all subjects being a pleasure in itself, being an object of desire, being an essential provider of elements without which a nation's spirit, whatever compensations it may have for them, must, in the long run, die of inanition, hardly enters into an Englishman's thoughts. It is noticeable that the word *curiosity*, which in other languages is used in a good sense, to mean, as a high and fine quality of man's nature, just this disinterested love of a free play of the mind on all subjects, for its own sake,—it is noticeable, I say, that this word has in our language no sense of the kind, no sense but a rather bad and disparaging one. But criticism, real criticism, is essentially the exercise of this very quality. It obeys an instinct prompting it to try to know the best that is known and thought in the world, irrespectively of practice, politics, and everything of the kind; and to value knowledge and thought as they approach this best, without the intrusion of any other considera tions whatever. This is an instinct for which there is, I think, little original sympathy in the practical English nature, and what there was of it has undergone a long benumbing period of blight and suppression in the epoch of concentration which followed the French Revolution.

But epochs of concentration cannot well endure for ever; epochs of expansion, in the due course of things, follow them. Such an epoch of expansion seems to be opening in this country. In the first place all danger of a hostile forcible pressure of foreign ideas upon our practice has long disappeared; like the traveller in the fable, therefore, we begin to wear our cloak a little more loosely. Then, with a long peace, the ideas of Europe steal gradually and amicably in, and mingle, though in infinitesimally small quantities at a time, with our own notions. Then, too, in spite of all that is said about the absorbing and brutalising influence of our passionate material progress, it seems to me indisputable that this progress is likely, though not certain, to lead in the end to an apparition of intellectual life; and that man, after he has made himself perfectly comfortable and has now to determine what to do with himself next, may begin to remember that he has a mind, and that the mind may be made the source of great pleasure. I grant it is mainly the privilege of faith, at present, to discern this end to our railways, our business, and our fortune-making; but we shall see if, here as elsewhere, faith is not in the end the true prophet. Our ease, our travelling, and our unbounded liberty to hold just as hard and securely as we please to the practice to which our notions have given birth, all tend to beget an inclination to deal a little more freely with these notions themselves, to canvass them a little, to penetrate a little into their real nature. Flutterings of curiosity, in the foreign sense of the word, appear amongst us, and it is in these that criticism must look to find its account. Criticism first; a time of true creative activity, perhaps,—which, as I have said, must inevitably be preceded amongst us by a time of criticism,—hereafter, when criticism has done its work.

It is of the last importance that English criticism should clearly discern what rule for its course, in order to avail itself of the field now opening to it, and to produce fruit for the future, it ought to take. The rule may be summed up in one word,—*disinterestedness.* And how is criticism to show disinterestedness? By keeping aloof from what is called "the practical view of things;" by resolutely following the law of its own nature, which is to be a free play of the mind on all subjects which it touches. By steadily refusing to lend itself to any of those ulterior, political, practical considerations about ideas, which plenty of people will be sure to attach to them, which perhaps ought often to be attached to them, which in this country at any rate are certain to be attached to them quite sufficiently, but which criticism has really nothing to do with. Its business is, as I have said, simply to know the best that is known and thought in the world, and by in its turn making this known, to create

a current of true and fresh ideas. Its business is to
do this with inflexible honesty, with due ability; but
its business is to do no more, and to leave alone all
questions of practical consequences and applications,
questions which will never fail to have due prominence
given to them. Else criticism, besides being really
false to its own nature, merely continues in the old
rut which it has hitherto followed in this country, and
will certainly miss the chance now given to it. For
what is at present the bane of criticism in this country?
It is that practical considerations cling to it and stifle
it. It subserves interests not its own. Our organs
of criticism are organs of men and parties having
practical ends to serve, and with them those practical
ends are the first thing and the play of mind the
second; so much play of mind as is compatible with
the prosecution of those practical ends is all that is
wanted. An organ like the *Revue des Deux Mondes*,
having for its main function to understand and utter
the best that is known and thought in the world,
existing, it may be said, as just an organ for a free
play of the mind, we have not. But we have the
Edinburgh Review, existing as an organ of the old
Whigs, and for as much play of the mind as may suit
its being that; we have the *Quarterly Review*, existing
as an organ of the Tories, and for as much play of
mind as may suit its being that; we have the *British
Quarterly Review*, existing as an organ of the political
Dissenters, and for as much play of mind as may suit
its being that; we have the *Times*, existing as an
organ of the common, satisfied, well-to-do English

man, and for as much play of mind as may suit its
being that. And so on through all the various fractions, political and religious, of our society; every
fraction has, as such, its organ of criticism, but the
notion of combining all fractions in the common pleasure of a free disinterested play of mind meets with
no favour. Directly this play of mind wants to have
more scope, and to forget the pressure of practical
considerations a little, it is checked, it is made to feel
the chain. We saw this the other day in the extinc-
tion, so much to be regretted, of the *Home and Foreign
Review.* Perhaps in no organ of criticism in this
country was there so much knowledge, so much play
of mind; but these could not save it. The *Dublin
Review* subordinates play of mind to the practical
business of English and Irish Catholicism, and lives.
It must needs be that men should act in sects and
parties, that each of these sects and parties should
have its organ, and should make this organ subserve
the interests of its action; but it would be well, too,
that there should be a criticism, not the minister of
these interests, not their enemy, but absolutely and
entirely independent of them. No other criticism
will ever attain any real authority or make any real
way towards its end,—the creating a current of true
and fresh ideas.

It is because criticism has so little kept in the pure
intellectual sphere, has so little detached itself from
practice, has been so directly polemical and controversial, that it has so ill accomplished, in this country,
its best spiritual work; which is to keep man from a

self-satisfaction which is retarding and vulgarising, to lead him towards perfection, by making his mind dwell upon what is excellent in itself, and the absolute beauty and fitness of things.   A polemical practical criticism makes men blind even to the ideal imperfection of their practice, makes them willingly assert its ideal perfection, in order the better to secure it against attack ; and clearly this is narrowing and baneful for them.   If they were reassured on the practical side, speculative considerations of ideal perfection they might be brought to entertain, and their spiritual horizon would thus gradually widen. Sir Charles Adderley says to the Warwickshire farmers :—

"Talk of the improvement of breed ! Why, the race we ourselves represent, the men and women, the old Anglo-Saxon race, are the best breed in the whole world. . . . The absence of a too enervating climate, too unclouded skies, and a too luxurious nature, has produced so vigorous a race of people, and has rendered us so superior to all the world."

Mr. Roebuck says to the Sheffield cutlers :—

"I look around me and ask what is the state of England ? Is not property safe ? Is not every man able to say what he likes ? Can you not walk from one end of England to the other in perfect security ? I ask you whether, the world over or in past history, there is anything like it ? Nothing. I pray that our unrivalled happiness may last."

Now obviously there is a peril for poor human nature in words and thoughts of such exuberant self-satisfaction, until we find ourselves safe in the streets of the Celestial City.

> " Das wenige verschwindet leicht dem Blicke
> Der vorwärts sieht, wie viel noch übrig bleibt—"

says Goethe ; " the little that is done seems nothing when we look forward and see how much we have yet to do." Clearly this is a better line of reflection for weak humanity, so long as it remains on this earthly field of labour and trial.

But neither Sir Charles Adderley nor Mr. Roebuck is by nature inaccessible to considerations of this sort. They only lose sight of them owing to the controversial life we all lead, and the practical form which all speculation takes with us. They have in view opponents whose aim is not ideal, but practical ; and in their zeal to uphold their own practice against these innovators, they go so far as even to attribute to this practice an ideal perfection. Somebody has been wanting to introduce a six-pound franchise, or to abolish church-rates, or to collect agricultural statistics by force, or to diminish local self-government How natural, in reply to such proposals, very likely improper or ill-timed, to go a little beyond the mark, and to say stoutly, " Such a race of people as we stand, so superior to all the world ! The old Anglo-Saxon race, the best breed in the whole world ! I pray that our unrivalled happiness may last ! I ask you whether, the world over or in past history, there is anything like it ?" And so long as criticism answers this dithyramb by insisting that the old Anglo-Saxon race

would be still more superior to all others if it had no
church-rates, or that our unrivalled happiness would
last yet longer with a six-pound franchise, so long will
the strain, "The best breed in the whole world!"
swell louder and louder, everything ideal and refining
will be lost out of sight, and both the assailed and
their critics will remain in a sphere, to say the truth,
perfectly unvital, a sphere in which spiritual pro-
gression is impossible. But let criticism leave church-
rates and the franchise alone, and in the most candid
spirit, without a single lurking thought of practical
innovation, confront with our dithyramb this para-
graph on which I stumbled in a newspaper immediately after reading Mr. Roebuck :—

"A shocking child murder has just been committed
at Nottingham. A girl named Wragg left the workhouse there on Saturday morning with her young
illegitimate child. The child was soon afterwards
found dead on Mapperly Hills, having been strangled.
Wragg is in custody."

Nothing but that ; but, in juxtaposition with the
absolute eulogies of Sir Charles Adderley and Mr.
Roebuck, how eloquent, how suggestive are those few
lines ! "Our old Anglo-Saxon breed, the best in the
whole world !"—how much that is harsh and ill-
favoured there is in this best ! *Wragg !* If we are
to talk of ideal perfection, of "the best in the whole
world," has any one reflected what a touch of gross-
ness in our race, what an original shortcoming in the
more delicate spiritual perceptions, is shown by the
natural growth amongst us of such hideous names.

Higginbottom, Stiggins, Bugg! In Ionia and Attica they were luckier in this respect than "the best race in the world;" by the Ilissus there was no Wragg, poor thing! And "our unrivalled happiness;"— what an element of grimness, bareness, and hideousness mixes with it and blurs it; the workhouse, the dismal Mapperly Hills,—how dismal those who have seen them will remember;—the gloom, the smoke, the cold, the strangled illegitimate child! "I ask you whether, the world over or in past history, there is anything like it?" Perhaps not, one is inclined to answer; but at any rate, in that case, the world is very much to be pitied. And the final touch,—short, bleak, and inhuman: *Wragg is in custody.* The sex lost in the confusion of our unrivalled happiness; or (shall I say?) the superfluous Christian name lopped off by the straightforward vigour of our old Anglo-Saxon breed! There is profit for the spirit in such contrasts as this; criticism serves the cause of perfection by establishing them. By eluding sterile conflict, by refusing to remain in the sphere where alone narrow and relative conceptions have any worth and validity, criticism may diminish its momentary importance, but only in this way has it a chance of gaining admittance for those wider and more perfect conceptions to which all its duty is really owed. Mr. Roebuck will have a poor opinion of an adversary who replies to his defiant songs of triumph only by murmuring under his breath, *Wragg is in custody;* but in no other way will these songs of triumph be induced gradually to moderate themselves, to get rid of what in them is excessive and offensive, and to fall into a softer and truer key. /

It will be said that it is a very subtle and indirect action which I am thus prescribing for criticism, and that, by embracing in this manner the Indian virtue of detachment and abandoning the sphere of practical life, it condemns itself to a slow and obscure work. Slow and obscure it may be, but it is the only proper work of criticism. The mass of mankind will never have any ardent zeal for seeing things as they are; very inadequate ideas will always satisfy them. On these inadequate ideas reposes, and must repose, the general practice of the world. That is as much as saying that whoever sets himself to see things as they are will find himself one of a very small circle; but it is only by this small circle resolutely doing its own work that adequate ideas will ever get current at all. The rush and roar of practical life will always have a dizzying and attracting effect upon the most collected spectator, and tend to draw him into its vortex; most of all will this be the case where that life is so powerful as it is in England. But it is only by re- maining collected, and refusing to lend himself to the point of view of the practical man, that the critic can do the practical man any service; and it is only by the greatest sincerity in pursuing his own course, and by at last convincing even the practical man of his sincerity, that he can escape misunderstandings which perpetually threaten him.

For the practical man is not apt for fine distinc- tions, and yet in these distinctions truth and the highest culture greatly find their account. But it is not easy to lead a practical man,—unless you reassure him as to your practical intentions, you have no chance of leading him,—to see that a thing which he has always been used to look at from one side only, which he greatly values, and which, looked at from that side, quite deserves, perhaps, all the prizing and admiring which he bestows upon it,—that this thing, looked at from another side, may appear much less beneficent and beautiful, and yet retain all its claims to our practical allegiance. Where shall we find language innocent enough, how shall we make the spotless purity of our intentions evident enough, to enable us to say to the political Englishman that the British Constitution itself, which, seen from the practical side, looks such a magnificent organ of progress and virtue, seen from the speculative side,—with its compromises, its love of facts, its horror of theory, its studied avoidance of clear thoughts,—that, seen from this side, our august Constitution sometimes looks,— forgive me, shade of Lord Somers !—a colossal machine for the manufacture of Philistines? How is Cobbett to say this and not be misunderstood, blackened as he is with the smoke of a lifelong conflict in the field of political practice ? how is Mr. Carlyle to say it and not be misunderstood, after his furious raid into this field with his *Latter-day Pamphlets* ? how is Mr. Ruskin, after his pugnacious political economy? I say, the critic must keep out of the region of immediate practice in the political, social, humanitarian sphere, if he wants to make a beginning for that more free specu-

lative treatment of things, which may perhaps one
day make its benefits felt even in this sphere, but in
a natural and thence irresistible manner.

Do what he will, however, the critic will still remain exposed to frequent misunderstandings, and
nowhere so much as in this country. For here people
are particularly indisposed even to comprehend that
without this free disinterested treatment of things,
truth and the highest culture are out of the question.
So immersed are they in practical life, so accustomed
to take all their notions from this life and its processes, that they are apt to think that truth and
culture themselves can be reached by the processes
of this life, and that it is an impertinent singularity
to think of reaching them in any other. "We are
all *terræ filii*," cries their eloquent advocate; "all
Philistines together. Away with the notion of proceeding by any other course than the course dear to
the Philistines; let us have a social movement, let us
organise and combine a party to pursue truth and new
thought, let us call it *the liberal party*, and let us all
stick to each other, and back each other up. Let us
have no nonsense about independent criticism, and
intellectual delicacy, and the few and the many.
Don't let us trouble ourselves about foreign thought;
we shall invent the whole thing for ourselves as we
go along. If one of us speaks well, applaud him; if
one of us speaks ill, applaud him too; we are all in
the same movement, we are all liberals, we are all in
pursuit of truth." In this way the pursuit of truth
becomes really a social, practical, pleasurable affair,

almost requiring a chairman, a secretary, and adver-
tisements; with the excitement of an occasional
scandal, with a little resistance to give the happy
sense of difficulty overcome; but, in general, plenty
of bustle and very little thought. To act is so easy,
as Goethe says; to think is so hard! It is true that the
critic has many temptations to go with the stream, to
make one of the party movement, one of these *terræ
filii;* it seems ungracious to refuse to be a *terræ filius,*
when so many excellent people are; but the critic's
duty is to refuse, or, if resistance is vain, at least to
cry with Obermann : *Périssons en résistant.*

How serious a matter it is to try and resist, I had
ample opportunity of experiencing when I ventured
some time ago to criticise the celebrated first volume
of Bishop Colenso.[1] The echoes of the storm which
was then raised I still, from time to time, hear grumbling round me. That storm arose out of a misunderstanding almost inevitable. It is a result of no little
culture to attain to a clear perception that science and
religion are two wholly different things. The multi-

---

[1] So sincere is my dislike to all personal attack and controversy, that I abstain from reprinting, at this distance of time
from the occasion which called them forth, the essays in which
I criticised Dr. Colenso's book; I feel bound, however, after all
that has passed, to make here a final declaration of my sincere
impenitence for having published them. Nay, I cannot forbear
repeating yet once more, for his benefit and that of his readers,
this sentence from my original remarks upon him : *There is
truth of science and truth of religion; truth of science does not
become truth of religion till it is made religious.* And I will add :
Let us have all the science there is from the men of science;
from the men of religion let us have religion.

tude will for ever confuse them; but happily that is of no great real importance, for while the multitude imagines itself to live by its false science, it does really live by its true religion. Dr. Colenso, however, in his first volume did all he could to strengthen the confusion,[1] and to make it dangerous. He did this with the best intentions, I freely admit, and with the most candid ignorance that this was the natural effect of what he was doing; but, says Joubert, "Ignorance, which in matters of morals extenuates the crime, is itself, in intellectual matters, a crime of the first order." I criticised Bishop Colenso's speculative confusion. Immediately there was a cry raised: "What is this? here is a liberal attacking a liberal. Do not you belong to the movement? are not you a friend of truth? Is not Bishop Colenso in pursuit of truth? then speak with proper respect of his book. Dr. Stanley is another friend of truth, and you speak with proper respect of his book; why make these invidious differences? both books are excellent, admirable, liberal; Bishop Colenso's perhaps the most so, because it is the boldest, and will have the best practical consequences for the liberal cause. Do you want to encourage to the attack of a brother liberal his, and your, and our implacable enemies, the *Church and State Review* or the *Record*,—the High Church rhinoceros and the Evangelical hyæna? Be silent, there-

---

[1] It has been said I make it "a crime against literary criticism and the higher culture to attempt to inform the ignorant." Need I point out that the ignorant are not informed by being confirmed in a confusion?

fore; or rather speak, speak as loud as ever you can I and go into ecstasies over the eighty and odd pigeons."

But criticism cannot follow this coarse and indiscriminate method. It is unfortunately possible for a man in pursuit of truth to write a book which reposes upon a false conception. Even the practical consequences of a book are to genuine criticism no recommendation of it, if the book is, in the highest sense, blundering. I see that a lady who herself, too, is in pursuit of truth, and who writes with great ability, but a little too much, perhaps, under the influence of the practical spirit of the English liberal movement, classes Bishop Colenso's book and M. Renan's together, in her survey of the religious state of Europe, as facts of the same order, works, both of them, of " great importance ;" " great ability, power, and skill;" Bishop Colenso's, perhaps, the most powerful; at least, Miss Cobbe gives special expression to her gratitude that to Bishop Colenso "has been given the strength to grasp, and the courage to teach, truths of such deep import." In the same way, more than one popular writer has compared him to Luther. Now it is just this kind of false estimate which the critical spirit is, it seems to me, bound to resist. It is really the strongest possible proof of the low ebb at which, in England, the critical spirit is, that while the critical hit in the religious literature of Germany is Dr. Strauss's book, in that of France M. Renan's book, the book of Bishop Colenso is the critical hit in the religious literature of England. Bishop Colenso's book reposes on a total misconception of the essential elements of the religious problem, as that problem is now presented for solution.   To criticism, therefore, which seeks to have the best that is known and thought on this problem, it is, however well meant, of no importance whatever.   M. Renan's book attempts a new synthesis of the elements furnished to us by the Four Gospels.   It attempts, in my opinion, a synthesis, perhaps premature, perhaps impossible, certainly not successful.   Up to the present time, at any rate, we must acquiesce in Fleury's sentence on such recastings of the Gospel-story : *Quiconque s'imagine la pouvoir mieux écrire, ne l'entend pas.*   M. Renan had himself passed by anticipation a like sentence on his own work, when he said : " If a new presentation of the character of Jesus were offered to me, I would not have it ; its very clearness would be, in my opinion, the best proof of its insufficiency."   His friends may with perfect justice rejoin that at the sight of the Holy Land, and of the actual scene of the Gospel-story, all the current of M. Renan's thoughts may have naturally changed, and a new casting of that story irresistibly suggested itself to him ; and that this is just a case for applying Cicero's maxim : Change of mind is not inconsistency—*nemo doctus unquam mutationem consilii inconstantiam dixit esse.*   Nevertheless, for criticism, M. Renan's first thought must still be the truer one, as long as his new casting so fails more fully to commend itself, more fully (to use Coleridge's happy phrase about the Bible) to *find* us.   Still M. Renan's attempt is, for criticism, of the most real interest and importance,

since, with all its difficulty, a fresh synthesis of the
New Testament *data*,—not a making war on them, in
Voltaire's fashion, not a leaving them out of mind, in
the world's fashion, but the putting a new construction
upon them, the taking them from under the old,
traditional, conventional point of view and placing
them under a new one,—is the very essence of the
religious problem, as now presented ; and only by
efforts in this direction can it receive a solution.

Again, in the same spirit in which she judges
Bishop Colenso, Miss Cobbe, like so many earnest
liberals of our practical race, both here and in
America, herself sets vigorously about a positive re-
construction of religion, about making a religion of
the future out of hand, or at least setting about
making it. We must not rest, she and they are
always thinking and saying, in negative criticism, we
must be creative and constructive ; hence we have
such works as her recent *Religious Duty*, and works
still more considerable, perhaps, by others, which will
be in every one's mind. These works often have
much ability ; they often spring out of sincere con-
victions, and a sincere wish to do good ; and they
sometimes, perhaps, do good. Their fault is (if I
may be permitted to say so) one which they have in
common with the British College of Health, in the
New Road. Every one knows the British College of
Health ; it is that building with the lion and the
statue of the Goddess Hygeia before it ; at least I
am sure about the lion, though I am not absolutely
certain about the Goddess Hygeia. This building

does credit, perhaps, to the resources of Dr. Morrison and his disciples; but it falls a good deal short of one's idea of what a British College of Health ought to be. In England, where we hate public interference and love individual enterprise, we have a whole crop of places like the British College of Health; the grand name without the grand thing. Unluckily, creditable to individual enterprise as they are, they tend to impair our taste by making us forget what more grandiose, noble, or beautiful character properly belongs to a public institution. The same may be said of the religions of the future of Miss Cobbe and others. Creditable, like the British College of Health, to the resources of their authors, they yet tend to make us forget what more grandiose, noble, or beautiful character properly belongs to religious constructions. The historic religions, with all their faults, have had this; it certainly belongs to the religious sentiment, when it truly flowers, to have this; and we impoverish our spirit if we allow a religion of the future without it. What then is the duty of criticism here? To take the practical point of view, to applaud the liberal movement and all its works,—its New Road religions of the future into the bargain,—for their general utility's sake? By no means; but to be perpetually dissatisfied with these works, while they perpetually fall short of a high and perfect ideal.

For criticism, these are elementary laws; but they never can be popular, and in this country they have been very little followed, and one meets with immense obstacles in following them. That is a reason for asserting them again and again. Criticism must maintain its independence of the practical spirit and its aims. Even with well-meant efforts of the practical spirit it must express dissatisfaction, if in the sphere of the ideal they seem impoverishing and limiting. It must not hurry on to the goal because of its practical importance. It must be patient, and know how to wait; and flexible, and know how to attach itself to things and how to withdraw from them. It must be apt to study and praise elements that for the fulness of spiritual perfection are wanted, even though they belong to a power which in the practical sphere may be maleficent. It must be apt to discern the spiritual shortcomings or illusions of powers that in the practical sphere may be beneficent. And this without any notion of favouring or injuring, in the practical sphere, one power or the other; without any notion of playing off, in this sphere, one power against the other. When one looks, for instance, at the English Divorce Court,—an institution which perhaps has its practical conveniences, but which in the ideal sphere is so hideous; an institution which neither makes divorce impossible nor makes it decent, which allows a man to get rid of his wife, or a wife of her husband, but makes them drag one another first, for the public edification, through a mire of unutterable infamy,—when one looks at this charming institution, I say, with its crowded trials, its newspaper reports, and its money compensations, this institution in which the gross unregenerate British Philistine has indeed stamped an image of himself,—

one may be permitted to find the marriage theory of
Catholicism refreshing and elevating. Or when Protestantism, in virtue of its supposed rational and
intellectual origin, gives the law to criticism too
magisterially, criticism may and must remind it that
its pretensions, in this respect, are illusive and do it
harm ; that the Reformation was a moral rather than
an intellectual event ; that Luther's theory of grace
no more exactly reflects the mind of the spirit than
Bossuet's philosophy of history reflects it ; and that
there is no more antecedent probability of the Bishop
of Durham's stock of ideas being agreeable to perfect
reason than of Pope Pius the Ninth's.   But criticism
will not on that account forget the achievements of
Protestantism in the practical and moral sphere ; nor
that, even in the intellectual sphere, Protestantism,
though in a blind and stumbling manner, carried forward the Renascence, while Catholicism threw itself
violently across its path.

I lately heard a man of thought and energy contrasting the want of ardour and movement which he
now found amongst young men in this country with
what he remembered in his own youth, twenty years
ago.   "What reformers we were then !" he exclaimed ; "what a zeal we had ! how we canvassed
every institution in Church and State, and were prepared to remodel them all on first principles !" He
was inclined to regret, as a spiritual flagging, the lull
which he saw.   I am disposed rather to regard it as
a pause in which the turn to a new mode of spiritual
progress is being accomplished.   Everything was

long seen, by the young and ardent amongst us, in inseparable connection with politics and practical life. We have pretty well exhausted the benefits of seeing things in this connection, we have got all that can be got by so seeing them. Let us try a more disinterested mode of seeing them; let us betake ourselves more to the serener life of the mind and spirit. This life, too, may have its excesses and dangers; but they are not for us at present. Let us think of quietly enlarging our stock of true and fresh ideas, and not, as soon as we get an idea or half an idea, be running out with it into the street, and trying to make it rule there. Our ideas will, in the end, shape the world all the better for maturing a little. Perhaps in fifty years' time it will in the English House of Commons be an objection to an institution that it is an anomaly, and my friend the Member of Parliament will shudder in his grave. But let us in the meanwhile rather endeavour that in twenty years' time it may, in English literature, be an objection to a proposition that it is absurd. That will be a change so vast, that the imagination almost fails to grasp it. *Ab integro sæclorum nascitur ordo.*

If I have insisted so much on the course which criticism must take where politics and religion are concerned, it is because, where these burning matters are in question, it is most likely to go astray. I have wished, above all, to insist on the attitude which criticism should adopt towards things in general; on its right tone and temper of mind. But then comes another question as to the subject-matter which

literary criticism should most seek.   Here, in general,
its course is determined for it by the idea which is
the law of its being; the idea of a disinterested endeavour to learn and propagate the best that is
known and thought in the world, and thus to establish a current of fresh and true ideas.   By the very
nature of things, as England is not all the world,
much of the best that is known and thought in the
world cannot be of English growth, must be foreign ;
by the nature of things, again, it is just this that we
are least likely to know, while English thought is
streaming in upon us from all sides, and takes excellent care that we shall not be ignorant of its
existence.   The English critic of literature, therefore,
must dwell much on foreign thought, and with particular heed on any part of it, which, while significant
and fruitful in itself, is for any reason specially likely
to escape him.   Again, judging is often spoken of as
the critic's one business, and so in some sense it is ;
but the judgment which almost insensibly forms itself
in a fair and clear mind, along with fresh knowledge,
is the valuable one ; and thus knowledge, and ever
fresh knowledge, must be the critic's great concern
for himself.   And it is by communicating fresh
knowledge, and letting his own judgment pass along
with it,—but insensibly, and in the second place, not
the first, as a sort of companion and clue, not as an
abstract lawgiver,—that the critic will generally do
most good to his readers.   Sometimes, no doubt, for
the sake of establishing an author's place in literature,
and his relation to a central standard (and if this is

not done, how are we to get at our *best in the world ?*
criticism may have to deal with a subject-matter so
familiar that fresh knowledge is out of the question,
and then it must be all judgment; an enunciation
and detailed application of principles.   Here the
great safeguard is never to let oneself become abstract,
always to retain an intimate and lively consciousness
of the truth of what one is saying, and, the moment
this fails us, to be sure that something is wrong.
Still, under all circumstances, this mere judgment
and application of principles is, in itself, not the most
satisfactory work to the critic; like mathematics, it
is tautological, and cannot well give us, like fresh
learning, the sense of creative activity.

But stop, some one will say; all this talk is of no
practical use to us whatever; this criticism of yours
is not what we have in our minds when we speak of
criticism; when we speak of critics and criticism, we
mean critics and criticism of the current English
literature of the day; when you offer to tell criticism
its function, it is to this criticism that we expect you to
address yourself.   I am sorry for it, for I am afraid I
must disappoint these expectations.   I am bound by
my own definition of criticism : *a disinterested endeavour to learn and propagate the best that is known and
thought in the world.*   How much of current English
literature comes into this " best that is known and
thought in the world ? "   Not very much, I fear;
certainly less, at this moment, than of the current
literature of France or Germany.   Well, then, am
I to alter my definition of criticism, in order to meet

the requirements of a number of practising English critics, who, after all, are free in their choice of a business? That would be making criticism lend itself just to one of those alien practical considerations, which, I have said, are so fatal to it. One may say, indeed, to those who have to deal with the mass—so much better disregarded—of current English litera-ture, that they may at all events endeavour, in dealing with this, to try it, so far as they can, by the standard of the best that is known and thought in the world; one may say, that to get anywhere near this standard, every critic should try and possess one great litera-ture, at least, besides his own; and the more unlike his own, the better. But, after all, the criticism I am really concerned with,—the criticism which alone can much help us for the future, the criticism which, throughout Europe, is at the present day meant, when so much stress is laid on the importance of criticism and the critical spirit,—is a criticism which regards Europe as being, for intellectual and spiritual pur-poses, one great confederation, bound to a joint action and working to a common result; and whose members have, for their proper outfit, a knowledge of Greek, Roman, and Eastern antiquity, and of one another. Special, local, and temporary advantages being put out of account, that modern nation will in the intel-lectual and spiritual sphere make most progress, which most thoroughly carries out this programme. And what is that but saying that we too, all of us, as in-dividuals, the more thoroughly we carry it out, shall make the more progress?

There is so much inviting us!—what are we to take? what will nourish us in growth towards perfection? That is the question which, with the immense field of life and of literature lying before him, the critic has to answer; for himself first, and afterwards for others. In this idea of the critic's business the essays brought together in the following pages have had their origin; in this idea, widely different as are their subjects, they have, perhaps, their unity.

I conclude with what I said at the beginning: to have the sense of creative activity is the great happiness and the great proof of being alive, and it is not denied to criticism to have it; but then criticism must be sincere, simple, flexible, ardent, ever widening its knowledge. Then it may have, in no contemptible measure, a joyful sense of creative activity; a sense which a man of insight and conscience will prefer to what he might derive from a poor, starved, fragmentary, inadequate creation. And at some epochs no other creation is possible.

Still, in full measure, the sense of creative activity belongs only to genuine creation; in literature we must never forget that. But what true man of letters ever can forget it? It is no such common matter for a gifted nature to come into possession of a current of true and living ideas, and to produce amidst the inspiration of them, that we are likely to underrate it. The epochs of Æschylus and Shakspeare make us feel their pre-eminence. In an epoch like those is, no doubt, the true life of literature; there is the promised land, towards which criticism can only beckon.

That promised land it will not be ours to enter, and we shall die in the wilderness : but to have desired to enter it, to have saluted it from afar, is already, perhaps, the best distinction among contemporaries; it will certainly be the best title to esteem with posterity.

THE LITERARY INFLUENCE OF ACADEMIES.

IT is impossible to put down a book like the history of the French Academy, by Pellisson and D'Olivet, which M. Charles Livet has lately re-edited, without being led to reflect upon the absence, in our own country, of any institution like the French Academy, upon the probable causes of this absence, and upon its results. A thousand voices will be ready to tell us that this absence is a signal mark of our national superiority; that it is in great part owing to this absence that the exhilarating words of Lord Macaulay, lately given to the world by his very clever nephew, Mr. Trevelyan, are so profoundly true: "It may safely be said that the literature now extant in the English language is of far greater value than all the literature which three hundred years ago was extant in all the languages of the world together." I dare-say this is so; only, remembering Spinoza's maxim that the two great banes of humanity are self-conceit and the laziness coming from self-conceit, I think it

may do us good, instead of resting in our pre-eminence
with perfect security, to look a little more closely
why this is so, and whether it is so without any
limitations.

But first of all I must give a very few words to the
outward history of the French Academy.   About the
year 1629, seven or eight persons in Paris, fond of
literature, formed themselves into a sort of little club
to meet at one another's houses and discuss literary
matters.   Their meetings got talked of, and Cardinal
Richelieu, then minister and all-powerful, heard of
them.   He himself had a noble passion for letters,
and for all fine culture; he was interested by what he
heard of the nascent society. · Himself a man in the
grand style, if ever man was, he had the insight to
perceive what a potent instrument of the grand style
was here to his hand.   It was the beginning of a
great century for France, the seventeenth ; men's
minds were working, the French language was forming.   Richelieu sent to ask the members of the new
society whether they would be willing to become a
body with a public character, holding regular meetings.   Not without a little hesitation,—for apparently
they found themselves very well as they were, and
these seven or eight gentlemen of a social and literary
turn were not perfectly at their ease as to what the
great and terrible minister could want with them,—
they consented.   The favours of a man like Richelieu
are not easily refused, whether they are honestly
meant or no ; but this favour of Richelieu's was meant
quite honestly.   The Parliament, however, had its

doubts of this. The Parliament had none of Richelieu's enthusiasm about letters and culture; it was
jealous of the apparition of a new public body in the
State; above all, of a body called into existence by
Richelieu. The King's letters-patent, establishing
and authorising the new society, were granted early
in 1635; but, by the old constitution of France, these
letters-patent required the verification of the Parliament. It was two years and a half—towards the
autumn of 1637—before the Parliament would give
it; and it then gave it only after pressing solicitations,
and earnest assurances of the innocent intentions of
the young Academy. Jocose people said that this
society, with its mission to purify and embellish the
language, filled with terror a body of lawyers like the
French Parliament, the stronghold of barbarous jargon
and of chicane.

This improvement of the language was in truth
the declared grand aim for the operations of the
Academy. Its statutes of foundation, approved by
Richelieu before the royal edict establishing it was
issued, say expressly: "The Academy's principal
function shall be to work with all the care and all
the diligence possible at giving sure rules to our language, and rendering it pure, eloquent, and capable
of treating the arts and sciences." This zeal for
making a nation's great instrument of thought,—its
language,—correct and worthy, is undoubtedly a sign
full of promise,—a weighty earnest of future power.
It is said that Richelieu had it in his mind that French
should succeed Latin in its general ascendency, as

Latin had succeeded Greek; if it was so, even this wish has to some extent been fulfilled. But, at any rate, the *ethical* influences of style in language,—its close relations, so often pointed out, with character, —are most important. Richelieu, a man of high culture, and, at the same time, of great character, felt them profoundly; and that he should have sought to regularise, strengthen, and perpetuate them by an institution for perfecting language, is alone a striking proof of his governing spirit and of his genius.

This was not all he had in his mind, however. The new Academy, now enlarged to a body of forty members, and meant to contain all the chief literary men of France, was to be a *literary tribunal*. The works of its members were to be brought before it previous to publication, were to be criticised by it, and finally, if it saw fit, to be published with its declared approbation. The works of other writers, not members of the Academy, might also, at the request of these writers themselves, be passed under the Academy's review. Besides this, in essays and discussions the Academy examined and judged works already published, whether by living or dead authors, and literary matters in general. The celebrated opinion on Corneille's *Cid*, delivered in 1637 by the Academy at Richelieu's urgent request, when this poem, which strongly occupied public attention, had been attacked by M. de Scudéry, shows how fully Richelieu designed his new creation to do duty as a supreme court of literature, and how early it in fact began to exercise this function. One[1] who had known Richelieu declared, after the Cardinal's death, that he had projected a yet greater institution than the Academy, a sort of grand European college of art, science, and literature, a Prytaneum, where the chief authors of all Europe should be gathered together in one central home, there to live in security, leisure, and honour ;—that was a dream which will not bear to be pulled about too roughly. But the project of forming a high court of letters for France was no dream ; Richelieu in great measure fulfilled it. This is what the Academy, by its idea, really is ; this is what it has always tended to become ; this is what it has, from time to time, really been ; by being, or tending to be this, far more than even by what it has done for the language, it is of such importance in France. To give the law, the tone to literature, and that tone a high one, is its business. "Richelieu meant it," says M. Sainte-Beuve, "to be a *haut jury*," —a jury the most choice and authoritative that could be found on all important literary matters in question before the public ; to be, as it in fact became in the latter half of the eighteenth century, "a sovereign organ of opinion." "The duty of the Academy is," says M. Renan, "*maintenir la délicatesse de l'esprit fran-çais*"—to keep the fine quality of the French spirit unimpaired ; it represents a kind of "*maîtrise en fait de bon ton*"—the authority of a recognised master in matters of tone and taste. "All ages," says M. Renan again, "have had their inferior literature ; but the

[1] La Mesnardière.

great danger of our time is that this inferior literature tends more and more to get the upper place. No one has the same advantage as the Academy for fighting against this mischief;" the Academy, which, as he says elsewhere, has even special facilities for " creating a form of intellectual culture *which shall impose itself on all around.*" M. Sainte-Beuve and M. Renan are, both of them, very keen-sighted critics; and they show it signally by seizing and putting so prominently forward this character of the French Academy.

Such an effort to set up a recognised authority, imposing on us a high standard in matters of intellect and taste, has many enemies in human nature. We all of us like to go our own way, and not to be forced out of the atmosphere of commonplace habitual to most of us ;—" *was uns alle bändigt,*" says Goethe, " *das Gemeine.*" We like to be suffered to lie comfortably in the old straw of our habits, especially of our intellectual habits, even though this straw may not be very clean and fine. But if the effort to limit this freedom of our lower nature finds, as it does and must find, enemies in human nature, it finds also auxiliaries in it. Out of the four great parts, says Cicero, of the *honestum,* or good, which forms the matter on which *officium,* or human duty, finds employment, one is the fixing of a *modus* and an *ordo,* a measure and an order, to fashion and wholesomely constrain our action, in order to lift it above the level it keeps if left to itself, and to bring it nearer to perfection. Man alone of living creatures, he says, goes feeling after " *quid sit ordo, quid sit quod deceat, in factis dictisque qui modus*

—the discovery of an *order*, a law of *good taste*, a *measure* for his words and actions." Other creatures submissively follow the law of their nature; man alone has an impulse leading him to set up some other law to control the bent of his nature.

This holds good, of course, as to moral matters, as well as intellectual matters : and it is of moral matters that we are generally thinking when we affirm it. But it holds good as to intellectual matters too. Now, probably, M. Sainte-Beuve had not these words of Cicero in his mind when he made, about the French nation, the assertion I am going to quote; but, for all that, the assertion leans for support, one may say, upon the truth conveyed in those words of Cicero, and wonderfully illustrates and confirms them. " In France," says M. Sainte-Beuve, " the first consideration for us is not whether we are amused and pleased by a work of art or mind, nor is it whether we are touched by it. What we seek above all to learn is, whether *we were right* in being amused with it, and in applauding it, and in being moved by it." Those are very remarkable words, and they are, I believe, in the main quite true. A Frenchman has, to a considerable degree, what one may call a conscience in intellectual matters ; he has an active belief that there is a right and a wrong in them, that he is bound to honour and obey the right, that he is disgraced by cleaving to the wrong. All the world has, or professes to have, this conscience in moral matters. The word *conscience* has become almost confined, in popular use, to the moral sphere, because this lively susceptibility of feeling is, in the moral sphere, so far more common than in the intellectual sphere; the livelier, in the moral sphere, this susceptibility is, the greater becomes a man's readiness to admit a high standard of action, an ideal authoritatively correcting his everyday moral habits; here, such willing admission of authority is due to sensitiveness of conscience. And a like deference to a standard higher than one's own habitual standard in intellectual matters, a like respectful recognition of a superior ideal, is caused, in the intellectual sphere, by sensitiveness of intelligence. Those whose intelligence is quickest, openest, most sensitive, are readiest with this deference; those whose intelligence is less delicate and sensitive are less disposed to it. Well, now we are on the road to see why the French have their Academy and we have nothing of the kind.

What are the essential characteristics of the spirit of our nation? Not, certainly, an open and clear mind, not a quick and flexible intelligence. Our greatest admirers would not claim for us that we have these in a pre-eminent degree; they might say that we had more of them than our detractors gave us credit for; but they would not assert them to be our essential characteristics. They would rather allege, as our chief spiritual characteristics, energy and honesty; and, if we are judged favourably and positively, not invidiously and negatively, our chief characteristics are, no doubt, these:—energy and honesty, not an open and clear mind, not a quick and flexible intelligence. Openness of mind and flexibility of intelligence were very signal characteristics of the

Athenian people in ancient times ; everybody will feel that. Openness of mind and flexibility of intelligence are remarkable characteristics of the French people in modern times ; at any rate, they strikingly characterise them as compared with us ; I think everybody, or almost everybody, will feel that. I will not now ask what more the Athenian or the French spirit has than this, nor what shortcomings either of them may have as a set-off against this ; all I want now to point out is that they have this, and that we have it in a much lesser degree.

Let me remark, however, that not only in the moral sphere, but also in the intellectual and spiritual sphere, energy and honesty are most important and fruitful qualities ; that, for instance, of what we call genius energy is the most essential part. So, by assigning to a nation energy and honesty as its chief spiritual characteristics,—by refusing to it, as at all eminent characteristics, openness of mind and flexibility of intelligence,—we do not by any means, as some people might at first suppose, relegate its importance and its power of manifesting itself with effect from the intellectual to the moral sphere. We only indicate its probable special line of successful activity in the intellectual sphere, and, it is true, certain imperfections and failings to which, in this sphere, it will always be subject. Genius is mainly an affair of energy, and poetry is mainly an affair of genius ; therefore, a nation whose spirit is characterised by energy may well be eminent in poetry ;—and we have Shakspeare. Again, the highest reach of science is,

one may say, an inventive power, a faculty of divination, akin to the highest power exercised in poetry ;
therefore, a nation whose spirit is characterised by
energy may well be eminent in science ;—and we have
Newton.   Shakspeare and Newton : in the intellectual
sphere there can be no higher names.   And what that
energy, which is the life of genius, above everything
demands and insists upon, is freedom ; entire independence of all authority, prescription, and routine,—
the fullest room to expand as it will.   Therefore, a
nation whose chief spiritual characteristic is energy,
will not be very apt to set up, in intellectual matters,
a fixed standard, an authority, like an academy.   By
this it certainly escapes certain real inconveniences
and dangers, and it can, at the same time, as we have
seen, reach undeniably splendid heights in poetry and
science.   On the other hand, some of the requisites
of intellectual work are specially the affair of quick-
ness of mind and flexibility of intelligence.   The
form, the method of evolution, the precision, the proportions, the relations of the parts to the whole, in
an intellectual work, depend mainly upon them.   And
these are the elements of an intellectual work which
are really most communicable from it, which can most
be learned and adopted from it, which have, therefore, the greatest effect upon the intellectual performance of others.   Even in poetry, these requisites
are very important ; and the poetry of a nation, not
eminent for the gifts on which they depend, will,
more or less, suffer by this shortcoming.   In poetry,
however, they are, after all, secondary, and energy is

the first thing; but in prose they are of first-rate im
portance.   In its prose literature, therefore, and in
the routine of intellectual work generally, a nation
with no particular gifts for these will not be so successful.   These are what, as I have said, can to a
certain degree be learned and appropriated, while the
free activity of genius cannot.   Academies consecrate
and maintain them, and, therefore, a nation with an
eminent turn for them naturally establishes academies.
So far as routine and authority tend to embarrass
energy and inventive genius, academies may be said
to be obstructive to energy and inventive genius, and,
to this extent, to the human spirit's general advance.
But then this evil is so much compensated by the
propagation, on a large scale, of the mental aptitudes
and demands which an open mind and a flexible intelligence naturally engender, genius itself, in the
long run, so greatly finds its account in this propagation, and bodies like the French Academy have such
power for promoting it, that the general advance of
the human spirit is perhaps, on the whole, rather
furthered than impeded by their existence.

How much greater is our nation in poetry than
prose! how much better, in general, do the productions of its spirit show in the qualities of genius than
in the qualities of intelligence!   One may constantly
remark this in the work of individuals; how much
more striking, in general, does any Englishman,—of
some vigour of mind, but by no means a poet,—seem
in his verse than in his prose! His verse partly
suffers from his not being really a poet, partly, no

doubt, from the very same defects which impair his prose, and he cannot express himself with thorough success in it. But how much more powerful a personage does he appear in it, by dint of feeling, and of originality and movement of ideas, than when he is writing prose! With a Frenchman of like stamp, it is just the reverse : set him to write poetry, he is limited, artificial, and impotent; set him to write prose, he is free, natural, and effective. The power of French literature is in its prose-writers, the power of English literature is in its poets. Nay, many of the celebrated French poets depend wholly for their fame upon the qualities of intelligence which they exhibit,—qualities which are the distinctive support of prose; many of the celebrated English prose-writers depend wholly for their fame upon the qualities of genius and imagination which they exhibit,—qualities which are the distinctive support of poetry. But, as I have said, the qualities of genius are less transferable than the qualities of intelligence; less can be immediately learned and appropriated from their product; they are less direct and stringent intellectual agencies, though they may be more beautiful and divine. Shakspeare and our great Elizabethan group were certainly more gifted writers than Corneille and his group; but what was the sequel to this great literature, this literature of genius, as we may call it, stretching from Marlowe to Milton ? What did it lead up to in English literature ? To our provincial and second-rate literature of the eighteenth century. What on the other hand, was the sequel to the litera-

ture of the French "great century," to this literature
of intelligence, as, by comparison with our Elizabethan
literature, we may call it; what did it lead up to?
To the French literature of the eighteenth century,
one of the most powerful and pervasive intellectual
agencies that have ever existed,—the greatest European force of the eighteenth century. In science,
again, we had Newton, a genius of the very highest
order, a type of genius in science, if ever there was
one. On the continent, as a sort of counterpart to
Newton, there was Leibnitz; a man, it seems to me
(though on these matters I speak under correction),
of much less creative energy of genius, much less
power of divination than Newton, but rather a man
of admirable intelligence, a type of intelligence in
science, if ever there was one. Well, and what did
they each directly lead up to in science? What was
the intellectual generation that sprang from each of
them? I only repeat what the men of science have
themselves pointed out. The man of genius was continued by the English analysts of the eighteenth
century, comparatively powerless and obscure followers
of the renowned master. The man of intelligence
was continued by successors like Bernouilli, Euler,
Lagrange, and Laplace, the greatest names in modern
mathematics.

What I want the reader to see is, that the question
as to the utility of academies to the intellectual life
of a nation is not settled when we say, for instance:
"Oh, we have never had an academy, and yet we
have, confessedly, a very great literature." It still

remains to be asked : "What sort of a great literature ?
a literature great in the special qualities of genius, or
great in the special qualities of intelligence ?" If
in the former, it is by no means sure that either our
literature, or the general intellectual life of our nation,
has got already, without academies, all that academies
can give.   Both the one and the other may very well
be somewhat wanting in those qualities of intelligence
out of a lively sense for which a body like the French
Academy, as I have said, springs, and which such a
body does a great deal to spread and confirm.   Our
literature, in spite of the genius manifested in it, may
fall short in form, method, precision, proportions,
arrangement,—all of them, I have said, things where
intelligence proper comes in.   It may be comparatively
weak in prose, that branch of literature where intelligence proper is, so to speak, all in all.   In this branch
it may show many grave faults to which the want of
a quick, flexible intelligence, and of the strict standard
which such an intelligence tends to impose, makes it
liable ; it may be full of hap-hazard, crudeness, pro-
vincialism, eccentricity, violence, blundering.   It may
be a less stringent and effective intellectual agency,
both upon our own nation and upon the world at
large, than other literatures which show less genius,
perhaps, but more intelligence.

The right conclusion certainly is that we should
try, so far as we can, to make up our shortcomings ;
and that to this end, instead of always fixing our
thoughts upon the points in which our literature, and
our intellectual life generally, are strong, we should,

from time to time, fix them upon those in which they are weak, and so learn to perceive clearly what we have to amend. What is our second great spiritual characteristic,—our honesty,—good for, if it is not good for this? But it will,—I am sure it will,—more and more, as time goes on, be found good for this.

Well, then, an institution like the French Academy, —an institution owing its existence to a national bent towards the things of the mind, towards culture, towards clearness, correctness, and propriety in thinking and speaking, and, in its turn, promoting this bent,—sets standards in a number of directions, and creates, in all these directions, a force of educated opinion, checking and rebuking those who fall below these standards, or who set them at nought. Educated opinion exists here as in France; but in France the Academy serves as a sort of centre and rallying-point to it, and gives it a force which it has not got here. Why is all the *journeyman-work* of literature, as I may call it, so much worse done here than it is in France? I do not wish to hurt any one's feelings; but surely this is so. Think of the difference between our books of reference and those of the French, between our biographical dictionaries (to take a striking instance) and theirs; think of the difference between the translations of the classics turned out for Mr. Bohn's library and those turned out for M. Nisard's collection! As a general rule, hardly any one amongst us, who knows French and German well, would use an English book of reference when he could get a French or German one; or would look at an English prose translation of an ancient author when he could get a French or German one. It is not that there do not exist in England, as in France, a number of people perfectly well able to discern what is good, in these things, from what is bad, and preferring what is good ; but they are isolated, they form no powerful body of opinion, they are not strong enough to set a standard, up to which even the journeyman-work of literature must be brought, if it is to be vendible. Ignorance and charlatanism in work of this kind are always trying to pass off their wares as excellent, and to cry down criticism as the voice of an insignificant, over-fastidious minority ; they easily persuade the multitude that this is so when the minority is scattered about as it is here ; not so easily when it is banded together as in the French Academy. So, again, with freaks in dealing with language ; certainly all such freaks tend to impair the power and beauty of language ; and how far more common they are with us than with the French ! To take a very familiar instance. Every one has noticed the way in which the *Times* chooses to spell the word " diocese ;" it always spells it diocess,[1] deriving it, I suppose, from *Zeus* and *census*. The *Journal des Débats* might just as well write " diocess " instead of " diocèse," but imagine the *Journal des Débats* doing so ! Imagine an educated Frenchman indulging himself in an orthographical antic of this sort, in face of the grave respect with which the Academy and its dictionary invest the French language ! Some

---

[1] The *Times* has now (1868) abandoned this spelling and adopted the ordinary one.

people will say these are little things; they are not; they are of bad example. They tend to spread the baneful notion that there is no such thing as a high, correct standard in intellectual matters; that every one may as well take his own way; they are at variance with the severe discipline necessary for all real culture; they confirm us in habits of wilfulness and eccentricity, which hurt our minds, and damage our credit with serious people. The late Mr. Donaldson was certainly a man of great ability, and I, who am not an Orientalist, do not pretend to judge his *Jashar:* but let the reader observe the form which a foreign Orientalist's judgment of it naturally takes. M. Renan calls it a *tentative malheureuse*, a failure, in short; this it may be, or it may not be; I am no judge. But he goes on: "It is astonishing that a recent article" (in a French periodical, he means) "should have brought forward as the last word of German exegesis a work like this, composed by a doctor of the University of Cambridge, and universally condemned by German critics." You see what he means to imply : an extravagance of this sort could never have come from Germany, where there is a great force of critical opinion controlling a learned man's vagaries, and keeping him straight; it comes from the native home of intellectual eccentricity of all kinds,[1]—from England, from a doctor of the

---

[1] A critic declares I am wrong in saying that M. Renan's language implies this. I still think that there is a shade, a *nuance* of expression, in M. Renan's language, which does imply this ; but, I confess, the only person who can really settle such a question is M. Renan himself.

University of Cambridge :—and I daresay he would
not expect much better things from a doctor of the
University of Oxford. Again, after speaking of what
Germany and France have done for the history of
Mahomet: "America and England," M. Renan goes
on, "have also occupied themselves with Mahomet."
He mentions Washington Irving's *Life of Mahomet*,
which does not, he says, evince much of an historical
sense, a *sentiment historique fort élevé ;* "but," he proceeds, "this book shows a real progress, when one
thinks that in 1829 Mr. Charles Forster published
two thick volumes, which enchanted the English
révérends, to make out that Mahomet was the little
horn of the he-goat that figures in the eighth chapter
of Daniel, and that the Pope was the great horn.
Mr. Forster founded on this ingenious parallel a
whole philosophy of history, according to which the
Pope represented the Western corruption of Christianity, and Mahomet the Eastern ; thence the striking resemblances between Mahometanism and Popery."
And in a note M. Renan adds : "This is the same
Mr. Charles Forster who is the author of a mystifica-
tion about the Sinaitic inscriptions, in which he
declares he finds the primitive language." As much
as to say : "It is an Englishman, be surprised at no
extravagance." If these innuendoes had no ground,
and were made in hatred and malice, they would not
be worth a moment's attention ; but they come from
a grave Orientalist, on his own subject, and they
point to a real fact ;—the absence, in this country, of
any force of educated literary and scientific opinion.

making aberrations like those of the author of *The One Primeval Language* out of the question.   Not only the author of such aberrations, often a very clever man, suffers by the want of check, by the not being kept straight, and spends force in vain on a false road, which, under better discipline, he might have used with profit on a true one ; but all his adherents, both "reverends" and others, suffer too, and the general rate of information and judgment is in this way kept low.

In a production which we have all been reading lately, a production stamped throughout with a literary quality very rare in this country, and of which I shall have a word to say presently—*urbanity ;* in this production, the work of a man never to be named by any son of Oxford without sympathy, a man who alone in Oxford of his generation, alone of many generations, conveyed to us in his genius that same charm, that same ineffable sentiment which this exquisite place itself conveys,—I mean Dr. Newman,—an expression is frequently used which is more common in theological than in literary language, but which seems to me fitted to be of general service ; the *note* of so and so, the note of catholicity, the note of antiquity, the note of sanctity, and so on.   Adopting this expressive word, I say that in the bulk of the intellectual work of a nation which has no centre, no intellectual metropolis like an academy, like M. Sainte-Beuve's "sovereign organ of opinion," like M. Renan's "recognised authority in matters of tone and taste,"—there is observable a *note of provinciality.* Now to get rid of provinciality is a certain stage of culture ; a stage the positive result of which we must not make of too much importance, but which is, nevertheless, indispensable, for it brings us on to the platform where alone the best and highest intellectual work can be said fairly to begin.   Work done after men have reached this platform is *classical ;* and that is the only work which, in the long run, can stand. All the *scoriæ* in the work of men of great genius who have not lived on this platform are due to their not having lived on it.   Genius raises them to it by moments, and the portions of their work which are immortal are done at these moments ; but more of it would have been immortal if they had not reached this platform at moments only, if they had had the culture which makes men live there.

The less a literature has felt the influence of a supposed centre of correct information, correct judgment, correct taste, the more we shall find in it this note of provinciality.   I have shown the note of provinciality as caused by remoteness from a centre of correct information.   Of course the note of provinciality from the want of a centre of correct taste is still more visible, and it is also still more common. For here great—even the greatest—powers of mind most fail a man.   Great powers of mind will make him inform himself thoroughly, great powers of mind will make him think profoundly, even with ignorance and platitude all round him ; but not even great powers of mind will keep his taste and style perfectly sound and sure, if he is left too much to himself, with no "sovereign organ of opinion" in these matters

near him.   Even men like Jeremy Taylor and Burke
suffer here.   Take this passage from Taylor's funeral
sermon on Lady Carbery :—

"So have I seen a river, deep and smooth, passing
with a still foot and a sober face, and paying to the
fiscus, the great exchequer of the sea, a tribute large
and full ; and hard by it a little brook, skipping and
making a noise upon its unequal and neighbour
bottom ; and after all its talking and bragged motion,
it paid to its common audit no more than the revenues
of a little cloud or a contemptible vessel : so have I
sometimes compared the issues of her religion to the
solemnities and famed outsides of another's piety."

That passage has been much admired, and, indeed,
the genius in it is undeniable.   I should say, for my
part, that genius, the ruling divinity of poetry, had
been too busy in it, and intelligence, the ruling
divinity of prose, not busy enough.   But can any
one, with the best models of style in his head, help
feeling the note of provinciality there, the want of
simplicity, the want of measure, the want of just the
qualities that make prose classical ?   If he does not
feel what I mean, let him place beside the passage of
Taylor this passage from the Panegyric of St. Paul,
by Taylor's contemporary, Bossuet :—

"Il ira, cet ignorant dans l'art de bien dire, avec cette
locution rude, avec cette phrase qui sent l'étranger il
ira en cette Grèce polie, la mère des philosophes et
des orateurs ; et malgré la résistance du monde, il y
établira plus d'Eglises que Platon n'y a gagné de
disciples par cette éloquence qu'on a crue divine."

There we have prose without the note of provinciality—classical prose, prose of the centre.

Or take Burke, our greatest English prose-writer, as I think ; take expressions like this :—

"Blindfold themselves, like bulls that shut their eyes when they push, they drive, by the point of their bayonets, their slaves, blindfolded, indeed, no worse than their lords, to take their fictions for currencies, and to swallow down paper pills by thirty-four millions sterling at a dose."

Or this :—

"They used it" (the royal name) "as a sort of navel-string, to nourish their unnatural offspring from the bowels of royalty itself. Now that the monster can purvey for its own subsistence, it will only carry the mark about it, as a token of its having torn the womb it came from."

Or this :—

"Without one natural pang, he" (Rousseau) "casts away, as a sort of offal and excrement, the spawn of his disgustful amours, and sends his children to the hospital of foundlings."

Or this :—

" I confess I never liked this continual talk of resistance and revolution, or the practice of making the extreme medicine of the constitution its daily bread. It renders the habit of society dangerously valetudinary ; it is taking periodical doses of mercury sublimate, and swallowing down repeated provocatives of cantharides to our love of liberty."

I say that is extravagant prose ; prose too much

suffered to indulge its caprices; prose at too great a
distance from the centre of good taste; prose, in
short, with the note of provinciality. People may
reply, it is rich and imaginative; yes, that is just it,
it is *Asiatic* prose, as the ancient critics would have
said; prose somewhat barbarously rich and over-
loaded. But the true prose is Attic prose.

Well, but Addison's prose is Attic prose. Where,
then, it may be asked, is the note of provinciality in
Addison? I answer, in the commonplace of his ideas.[1]
This is a matter worth remarking. Addison claims
to take leading rank as a moralist. To do that, you
must have ideas of the first order on your subject—
the best ideas, at any rate, attainable in your time—
as well as be able to express them in a perfectly
sound and sure style. Else you show your distance
from the centre of ideas by your matter; you are
provincial by your matter, though you may not be

---

[1] A critic says this is paradoxical, and urges that many
second-rate French academicians have uttered the most commonplace ideas possible. I agree that many second-rate French
academicians have uttered the most commonplace ideas possible;
but Addison is not a second-rate man. He is a man of the
order, I will not say of Pascal, but at any rate of La Bruyère
and Vauvenargues; why does he not equal them? I say because of the medium in which he finds himself, the atmosphere
in which he lives and works; an atmosphere which tells unfavourably, or rather *tends* to tell unfavourably (for that is the
truer way of putting it) either upon style or else upon ideas;
tends to make even a man of great ability either a Mr. Carlyle
or else a Lord Macaulay.

It is to be observed, however, that Lord Macaulay's style has
in its turn suffered by his failure in ideas, and this cannot be
said of Addison's.

provincial by your style.   It is comparatively a small
matter to express oneself well, if one will be content
with not expressing much, with expressing only trite
ideas; the problem is to express new and profound
ideas in a perfectly sound and classical style.   He is
the true classic, in every age, who does that.   Now
Addison has not, on his subject of morals, the force
of ideas of the moralists of the first class—the classical
moralists; he has not the best ideas attainable in or
about his time, and which were, so to speak, in the
air then, to be seized by the finest spirits; he is not
to be compared for power, searchingness, or delicacy
of thought to Pascal or La Bruyère or Vauvenargues;
he is rather on a level, in this respect, with a man
like Marmontel.   Therefore, I say, he has the note of
provinciality as a moralist; he is provincial by his
matter, though not by his style.

To illustrate what I mean by an example.   Addison,
writing as a moralist on fixedness in religious faith,
says :—

" Those who delight in reading books of controversy
do very seldom arrive at a fixed and settled habit of
faith.   The doubt which was laid revives again, and
shows itself in new difficulties; and that generally for
this reason,—because the mind, which is perpetually
tossed in controversies and disputes, is apt to forget
the reasons which had once set it at rest, and to
be disquieted with any former perplexity when it
appears in a new shape, or is started by a different
hand."

It may be said, that is classical English, perfect in

lucidity, measure, and propriety. I make no objec
tion; but, in my turn, I say that the idea expressed
is perfectly trite and barren, and that it is a note of
provinciality in Addison, in a man whom a nation
puts forward as one of its great moralists, to have no
profounder and more striking idea to produce on this
great subject. Compare, on the same subject, these
words of a moralist really of the first order, really at
the centre by his ideas,—Joubert :—

"L'expérience de beaucoup d'opinions donne à
l'esprit beaucoup de flexibilité et l'affermit dans celles
qu'il croit les meilleures."

With what a flash of light that touches the subject!
how it sets us thinking! what a genuine contribution
to moral science it is!

In short, where there is no centre like an academy,
if you have genius and powerful ideas, you are apt
not to have the best style going; if you have precision of style and not genius, you are apt not to have
the best ideas going.

The provincial spirit, again, exaggerates the value
of its ideas for want of a high standard at hand by
which to try them. Or rather, for want of such a
standard, it gives one idea too much prominence at
the expense of others; it orders its ideas amiss; it is
hurried away by fancies; it likes and dislikes too
passionately, too exclusively. Its admiration weeps
hysterical tears, and its disapprobation foams at the
mouth. So we get the *eruptive* and the *aggressive*
manner in literature; the former prevails most in
our criticism, the latter in our newspapers. For, not

having the lucidity of a large and centrally placed
intelligence, the provincial spirit has not its gracious-
ness; it does not persuade, it makes war; it has not
urbanity, the tone of the city, of the centre, the tone
which always aims at a spiritual and intellectual effect,
and not excluding the use of banter, never disjoins
banter itself from politeness, from felicity. But the
provincial tone is more violent, and seems to aim
rather at an effect upon the blood and senses than
upon the spirit and intellect; it loves hard-hitting
rather than persuading. The newspaper, with its
party spirit, its thorough-goingness, its resolute avoidance of shades and distinctions, its short, highly-
charged, heavy-shotted articles, its style so unlike
that style *lenis minimèque pertinax*—easy and not too
violently insisting,—which the ancients so much admired, is its true literature; the provincial spirit likes
in the newspaper just what makes the newspaper such
bad food for it,—just what made Goethe say, when he
was pressed hard about the immorality of Byron's
poems, that, after all, they were not so immoral as
the newspapers. The French talk of the *brutalité des
journaux anglais.* What strikes them comes from the
necessary inherent tendencies of newspaper-writing
not being checked in England by any centre of intelligent and urbane spirit, but rather stimulated by
coming in contact with a provincial spirit. Even a
newspaper like the *Saturday Review*, that old friend of
all of us, a newspaper expressly aiming at an immunity
from the common newspaper-spirit, aiming at being a
sort of organ of reason,—and, by thus aiming, it merits

great gratitude and has done great good,—even the *Saturday Review*, replying to some foreign criticism on our precautions against invasion, falls into a strain of this kind :—

"To do this" (to take these precautions) "seems to us eminently worthy of a great nation, and to talk of it as unworthy of a great nation, seems to us eminently worthy of a great fool."

There is what the French mean when they talk of the *brutalité des journaux anglais;* there is a style certainly as far removed from urbanity as possible,— a style with what I call the note of provinciality. And the same note may not unfrequently be observed even in the ideas of this newspaper, full as it is of thought and cleverness : certain ideas allowed to become fixed ideas, to prevail too absolutely. I will not speak of the immediate present, but, to go a little while back, it had the critic who so disliked the Emperor of the French ; it had the critic who so disliked the subject of my present remarks—academies ; it had the critic who was so fond of the German element in our nation, and, indeed, everywhere ; who ground his teeth if one said *Charlemagne* instead of *Charles the Great*, and, in short, saw all things in Teutonism, as Malebranche saw all things in God. Certainly any one may fairly find faults in the Emperor Napoleon or in academies, and merit in the German element ; but it is a note of the provincial spirit not to hold ideas of this kind a little more easily, to be so devoured by them, to suffer them to become crotchets.

In England there needs a miracle of genius like Shakspeare's to produce balance of mind, and a miracle of intellectual delicacy like Dr. Newman's to produce urbanity of style.   How prevalent all round us is the want of balance of mind and urbanity of style ! How much, doubtless, it is to be found in ourselves,—in each of us ! but, as human nature is constituted, every one can see it clearest in his contemporaries.   There, above all, we should consider it, because they and we are exposed to the same influences ; and it is in the best of one's contemporaries that it is most worth considering, because one then most feels the harm it does when one sees what they would be without it.   Think of the difference between Mr. Ruskin exercising his genius, and Mr. Ruskin exercising his intelligence consider the truth and beauty of this :—

"Go out, in the spring-time, among the meadows that slope from the shores of the Swiss lakes to the roots of their lower mountains.   There, mingled with the taller gentians and the white narcissus, the grass grows deep and free ; and as you follow the winding mountain paths, beneath arching boughs all veiled and dim with blossom,—paths that for ever droop and rise over the green banks and mounds sweeping down in scented undulation, steep to the blue water studded here and there with new-mown heaps, filling all the air with fainter sweetness, — look up towards the higher hills, where the waves of everlasting green roll silently into their long inlets among the shadows of the pines. . . . . ."

There is what the genius, the feeling, the tempera

ment in Mr. Ruskin, the original and incommunicable
part, has to do with; and how exquisite it is! All
the critic could possibly suggest, in the way of objection, would be, perhaps, that Mr. Ruskin is there
trying to make prose do more than it can perfectly
do; that what he is there attempting he will never,
except in poetry, be able to accomplish to his own
entire satisfaction : but he accomplishes so much that
the critic may well hesitate to suggest even this.
Place beside this charming passage another,—a passage
about Shakspeare's names, where the intelligence and
judgment of Mr. Ruskin, the acquired, trained, communicable part in him, are brought into play,—and
see the difference :—

"Of Shakspeare's names I will afterwards speak at
more length ; they are curiously—often barbarously—
mixed out of various traditions and languages. Three
of the clearest in meaning have been already noticed.
Desdemona—'δυσδαιμονία,' *miserable fortune*—is also
plain enough. Othello is, I believe, 'the careful;'
all the calamity of the tragedy arising from the single
flaw and error in his magnificently collected strength.
Ophelia, 'serviceableness,' the true, lost wife of Hamlet,
is marked as having a Greek name by that of her
brother, Laertes ; and its signification is once ex-
quisitely alluded to in that brother's last word of her,
where her gentle preciousness is opposed to the use-
lessness of the churlish clergy :—'A *ministering* angel
shall my sister be, when thou liest howling.' Hamlet
is, I believe, connected in some way with 'homely,'
the entire event of the tragedy turning on betrayal

of home duty. Hermione (ἕρμα), 'pillar-like' (ἡ εἶδος
ἔχε χρυσῆς Ἀφροδίτης); Titania (τιτήνη), 'the queen;'
Benedick and Beatrice, 'blessed and blessing;' Valen-
tine and Proteus, 'enduring or strong' (*valens*), and
'changeful.' Iago and Iachimo have evidently the
same root—probably the Spanish Iago, Jacob, 'the
supplanter.'"

Now, really, what a piece of extravagance all that
is! I will not say that the meaning of Shakspeare's
names (I put aside the question as to the correctness
of Mr. Ruskin's etymologies) has no effect at all, may
be entirely lost sight of; but to give it that degree of
prominence is to throw the reins to one's whim, to
forget all moderation and proportion, to lose the
balance of one's mind altogether. It is to show in
one's criticism, to the highest excess, the note of
provinciality.

Again, there is Mr. Palgrave, certainly endowed
with a very fine critical tact: his *Golden Treasury*
abundantly proves it. The plan of arrangement which
he devised for that work, the mode in which he followed his plan out, nay, one might even say, merely
the juxtaposition, in pursuance of it, of two such
pieces as those of Wordsworth and Shelley which
form the 285th and 286th in his collection, show a
delicacy of feeling in these matters which is quite
indisputable and very rare. And his notes are full of
remarks which show it too. All the more striking,
conjoined with so much justness of perception, are
certain freaks and violences in Mr. Palgrave's criticism,
mainly imputable, I think, to the critic's isolated posi-

tion in this country, to his feeling himself too much
left to take his own way, too much without any central
authority representing high culture and sound judgment, by which he may be, on the one hand, confirmed
as against the ignorant, on the other, held in respect
when he himself is inclined to take liberties. I mean
such things as this note on Milton's line,—

"The great Emathian conqueror bade spare" . . .

"When Thebes was destroyed, Alexander ordered the
house of Pindar to be spared. *He was as incapable of
appreciating the poet as Louis XIV. of appreciating Racine;
but even the narrow and barbarian mind of Alexander
could understand the advantage of a showy act of homage
to poetry.*" A note like that I call a freak or a violence;
if this disparaging view of Alexander and Louis XIV.
so unlike the current view, is wrong,—if the current
view is, after all, the truer one of them,—the note is
a freak. But, even if its disparaging view is right,
the note is a violence; for, abandoning the true mode
of intellectual action—persuasion, the instilment of
conviction,—it simply astounds and irritates the hearer
by contradicting without a word of proof or preparation, his fixed and familiar notions; and this is mere
violence. In either case, the fitness, the measure, the
centrality, which is the soul of all good criticism, is
lost, and the note of provinciality shows itself.

Thus, in the famous *Handbook*, marks of a fine
power of perception are everywhere discernible, but
so, too, are marks of the want of sure balance, of the
check and support afforded by knowing one speaks

before good and severe judges. When Mr. Palgrave
dislikes a thing, he feels no pressure constraining
him either to try his dislike closely or to express it
moderately ; he does not mince matters, he gives his
dislike all its own way ; both his judgment and his
style would gain if he were under more restraint.
" The style which has filled London with the dead
monotony of Gower or Harley Streets, or the pale
commonplace of Belgravia, Tyburnia, and Kensing-
ton ; which has pierced Paris and Madrid with the
feeble frivolities of the Rue Rivoli and the Strada de
Toledo." He dislikes the architecture of the Rue
Rivoli, and he puts it on a level with the architecture
of Belgravia and Gower Street ; he lumps them all
together in one condemnation, he loses sight of the
shade, the distinction, which is everything here ; the
distinction, namely, that the architecture of the Rue
Rivoli expresses show, splendour, pleasure,—unworthy
things, perhaps, to express alone and for their own
sakes, but it expresses them ; whereas the architecture of Gower Street and Belgravia merely expresses
the impotence of the architect to express anything.
Then, as to style : " sculpture which stands in a
contrast with Woolner hardly more shameful than
diverting." . . "passing from Davy or Faraday to
the art of the mountebank or the science of the spirit-
rapper." . . . "it is the old, old story with Marochetti, the frog trying to blow himself out to bull
dimensions. He may puff and be puffed, but he will
never do it." We all remember that shower of
amenities on poor M. Marochetti. Now, here Mr

Palgrave himself enables us to form a contrast which
lets us see just what the presence of an academy does
for style ; for he quotes a criticism by M. Gustave
Planche on this very M. Marochetti. M. Gustave
Planche was a critic of the very first order, a man of
strong opinions, which he expressed with severity ;
he, too, condemns M. Marochetti's work, and Mr.
Palgrave calls him as a witness to back what he has
himself said ; certainly Mr. Palgrave's translation will
not exaggerate M. Planche's urbanity in dealing with
M. Marochetti, but, even in this translation, see the
difference in sobriety, in measure, between the critic
writing in Paris and the critic writing in London :—

"These conditions are so elementary, that I am at
a perfect loss to comprehend how M. Marochetti has
neglected them. There are soldiers here like the
leaden playthings of the nursery : it is almost impossible to guess whether there is a body beneath the
dress. We have here no question of style, not even
of grammar ; it is nothing beyond mere matter of the
alphabet of art. To break these conditions is the
same as to be ignorant of spelling."

That is really more formidable criticism than Mr.
Palgrave's, and yet in how perfectly temperate a
style ! M. Planche's advantage is, that he feels himself to be speaking before competent judges, that
there is a force of cultivated opinion for him to appeal
to. Therefore, he must not be extravagant, and he
need not storm ; he must satisfy the reason and
taste,—that is his business. Mr. Palgrave, on the
other hand, feels himself to be speaking before a pro

miscuous multitude, with the few good judges so
scattered through it as to be powerless; therefore,
he has no calm confidence and no self-control; he
relies on the strength of his lungs; he knows that
big words impose on the mob, and that, even if he is
outrageous, most of his audience are apt to be a great
deal more so.[1]

Again, the first two volumes of Mr. Kinglake's
Invasion of the Crimea were certainly among the most
successful and renowned English books of our time
Their style was one of the most renowned things
about them, and yet how conspicuous a fault in Mr.
Kinglake's style is this over-charge of which I have
been speaking! Mr. James Gordon Bennett, of the
New York Herald, says, I believe, that the highest
achievement of the human intellect is what he calls
"a good editorial." This is not quite so; but, if it
were so, on what a height would these two volumes
by Mr. Kinglake stand! I have already spoken of
the Attic and the Asiatic styles; besides these, there
is the Corinthian style. That is the style for "a
good editorial," and Mr. Kinglake has really reached
perfection in it. It has not the warm glow, blithe
movement, and soft pliancy of life, as the Attic style
has; it has not the over-heavy richness and encum-
bered gait of the Asiatic style; it has glitter without
warmth, rapidity without ease, effectiveness without

[1] When I wrote this I had before me the first edition of Mr.
Palgrave's *Handbook*. I am bound to say that in the second
edition much strong language has been expunged, and what
remains, softened.

charm. Its characteristic is, that it has no *soul;* all
it exists for, is to get its ends, to make its points, to
damage its adversaries, to be admired, to triumph. A
style so bent on effect at the expense of soul, simplicity,
and delicacy; a style so little studious of the charm
of the great models; so far from classic truth and
grace, must surely be said to have the note of provinciality. Yet Mr. Kinglake's talent is a really eminent
one, and so in harmony with our intellectual habits and
tendencies, that, to the great bulk of English people,
the faults of his style seem its merits; all the more
needful that criticism should not be dazzled by them.

We must not compare a man of Mr. Kinglake's
literary talent with French writers like M. de Bazan-
court. We must compare him with M. Thiers. And
what a superiority in style has M. Thiers from being
formed in a good school, with severe traditions,
wholesome restraining influences! Even in this age
of Mr. James Gordon Bennett, his style has nothing
Corinthian about it, its lightness and brightness make
it almost Attic. It is not quite Attic, however; it
has not the infallible sureness of Attic taste. Sometimes his head gets a little hot with the fumes of
patriotism, and then he crosses the line, he loses
perfect measure, he declaims, he raises a momentary
smile. France condemned ' à être l'effroi du monde
dont elle pourrait être l'amour,'—Cæsar, whose exquisite
simplicity M. Thiers so much admires, would not
have written like that. There is, if I may be allowed
to say so, the slightest possible touch of fatuity in
such language,—of that failure in good sense which

comes from too warm a self-satisfaction. But compare this language with Mr. Kinglake's Marshal St. Arnaud—"dismissed from the presence" of Lord Raglan or Lord Stratford, "cowed and pressed down" under their "stern reproofs," or under "the majesty of the great Elchi's Canning brow and tight, merciless lips!" The failure in good sense and good taste there reaches far beyond what the French mean by *fatuity;* they would call it by another word, a word expressing blank defect of intelligence, a word for which we have no exact equivalent in English,—*bête.* It is the difference between a venial, momentary, good-tempered excess, in a man of the world, of an amiable and social weakness,—vanity; and a serious, settled, fierce, narrow, provincial misconception of the whole relative value of one's own things and the things of others. So baneful to the style of even the cleverest man may be the total want of checks.

In all I have said, I do not pretend that the examples given prove my rule as to the influence of academies; they only illustrate it. Examples in plenty might very likely be found to set against them; the truth of the rule depends, no doubt, on whether the balance of all the examples is in its favour or not; but actually to strike this balance is always out of the question. Here, as everywhere else, the rule, the idea, if true, commends itself to the judicious, and then the examples make it clearer still to them. This is the real use of examples, and this alone is the purpose which I have meant mine to serve. There is also another side to the whole question,—as to the

limiting and prejudicial operation which academies
may have; but this side of the question it rather
behoves the French, not us, to study.

The reader will ask for some practical conclusion
about the establishment of an Academy in this country, and perhaps I shall hardly give him the one he
expects. But nations have their own modes of acting,
and these modes are not easily changed; they are
even consecrated, when great things have been done
in them. When a literature has produced Shakspeare
and Milton, when it has even produced Barrow and
Burke, it cannot well abandon its traditions; it can
hardly begin, at this late time of day, with an institution like the French Academy. I think academies
with a limited, special, scientific scope, in the various
lines of intellectual work,—academies like that of
Berlin, for instance,—we with time may, and probably
shall, establish. And no doubt they will do good;
no doubt the presence of such influential centres of
correct information will tend to raise the standard
amongst us for what I have called the *journeyman-
work* of literature, and to free us from the scandal of
such biographical dictionaries as Chalmers's, or such
translations as a recent one of Spinoza, or perhaps,
such philological freaks as Mr. Forster's about the one
primeval language. But an academy quite like the
French Academy, a sovereign organ of the highest
literary opinion, a recognised authority in matters of
intellectual tone and taste, we shall hardly have, and
perhaps we ought not to wish to have it. But then
every one amongst us with any turn for literature

will do well to remember to what shortcomings and
excesses, which such an academy tends to correct, we
are liable; and the more liable, of course, for not
having it.   He will do well constantly to try himself
in respect of these, steadily to widen his culture,
severely to check in himself the provincial spirit;
and he will do this the better the more he keeps in
mind that all mere glorification by ourselves of ourselves or our literature, in the strain of what, at the
beginning of these remarks, I quoted from Lord
Macaulay, is both vulgar, and, besides being vulgar
retarding.

III.

MAURICE DE GUÉRIN.

I WILL not presume to say that I now know the French language well; but at a time when I knew it even less well than at present,—some fifteen years ago,—I remember pestering those about me with this sentence, the rhythm of which had lodged itself in my head, and which, with the strangest pronunciation possible, I kept perpetually declaiming: "*Les dieux jaloux ont enfoui quelque part les témoignages de la descendance des choses; mais au bord de quel Océan ont-ils roulé la pierre qui les couvre, ô Macarée!*"

These words come from a short composition called the *Centaur*, of which the author, Georges-Maurice de Guérin, died in the year 1839, at the age of twenty-eight, without having published anything. In 1840, Madame Sand brought out the *Centaur* in the *Revue des Deux Mondes*, with a short notice of its author, and a few extracts from his letters. A year or two afterwards she reprinted these at the end of a volume of her novels; and there it was that I fell in with them. I was so much struck with the *Centaur* that I waited

anxiously to hear something more of its author, and
of what he had left; but it was not till the other day
—twenty years after the first publication of the *Centaur* in the *Revue des Deux Mondes*, that my anxiety
was satisfied.   At the end of 1860 appeared two
volumes with the title *Maurice de Guérin, Reliquiœ*,
containing the *Centaur*, several poems of Guérin, his
journals, and a number of his letters, collected and
edited by a devoted friend, M. Trebutien, and preceded by a notice of Guérin by the first of living
critics, M. Sainte-Beuve.

The grand power of poetry is its interpretative
power; by which I mean, not a power of drawing out
in black and white an explanation of the mystery of
the universe, but the power of so dealing with things
as to awaken in us a wonderfully full, new, and intimate sense of them, and of our relations with them.
When this sense is awakened in us, as to objects without us, we feel ourselves to be in contact with the
essential nature of those objects, to be no longer bewildered and oppressed by them, but to have their
secret, and to be in harmony with them; and this
feeling calms and satisfies us as no other can.   Poetry,
indeed, interprets in another way besides this; but
one of its two ways of interpreting, of exercising its
highest power, is by awakening this sense in us.   I
will not now inquire whether this sense is illusive,
whether it can be proved not to be illusive, whether
it does absolutely make us possess the real nature of
things; all I say is, that poetry can awaken it in us,
and that to awaken it is one of the highest powers of

poetry. The interpretations of science do not give
us this intimate sense of objects as the interpretations
of poetry give it; they appeal to a limited faculty,
and not to the whole man. It is not Linnæus or
Cavendish or Cuvier who gives us the true sense of
animals, or water, or plants, who seizes their secret
for us, who makes us participate in their life; it is
Shakspeare, with his

> "daffodils
> That come before the swallow dares, and take
> The winds of March with beauty;"

it is Wordsworth, with his

> "voice . . . . heard
> In spring-time from the cuckoo-bird,
> Breaking the silence of the seas
> Among the farthest Hebrides;"

it is Keats, with his

> "moving waters at their priestlike task
> Of pure ablution round Earth's human shores;"

it is Chateaubriand, with his, "*cime indéterminée des
forêts ;*" it is Senancour, with his mountain birch-tree :
"*Cette écorce blanche, lisse et crevassée ; cette tige agreste ;
ces branches qui s'inclinent vers la terre ; la mobilité des
feuilles, et tout cet abandon, simplicité de la nature, attitude
des déserts.*"

Eminent manifestations of this magical power of
poetry are very rare and very precious : the compositions of Guérin manifest it, I think, in singular emi-
nence. Not his poems, strictly so called,—his verse,
—so much as his prose; his poems in general take
for their vehicle that favourite metre of French poetry,

the Alexandrine; and, in my judgment, I confess they have thus, as compared with his prose, a great disadvantage to start with. In prose, the character of the vehicle for the composer's thoughts is not determined beforehand; every composer has to make his own vehicle; and who has ever done this more admirably than the great prose-writers of France,— Pascal, Bossuet, Fénelon, Voltaire? But in verse the composer has (with comparatively narrow liberty of modification) to accept his vehicle ready-made; it is therefore of vital importance to him that he should find at his disposal a vehicle adequate to convey the highest matters of poetry. We may even get a decisive test of the poetical power of a language and nation by ascertaining how far the principal poetical vehicle which they have employed, how far (in plainer words) the established national metre for high poetry, is adequate or inadequate. It seems to me that the established metre of this kind in France,—the Alexandrine,—is inadequate; that as a vehicle for high poetry it is greatly inferior to the hexameter or to the iambics of Greece (for example), or to the blank verse of England. Therefore the man of genius who uses it is at a disadvantage as compared with the man of genius who has for conveying his thoughts a more adequate vehicle, metrical or not. Racine is at a disadvantage as compared with Sophocles or Shakspeare, and he is likewise at a disadvantage as compared with Bossuet.

The same may be said of our own poets of the eighteenth century, a century which gave them as the main vehicle for their high poetry a metre inadequate (as much as the French Alexandrine, and nearly in the same way) for this poetry,—the ten-syllable couplet. It is worth remarking, that the English poet of the eighteenth century whose compositions wear best and give one the most entire satisfaction, —Gray,—hardly uses that couplet at all : this abstinence, however, limits Gray's productions to a few short compositions, and (exquisite as these are) he is a poetical nature repressed and without free issue. For English poetical production on a great scale, for an English poet deploying all the forces of his genius, the ten-syllable couplet was, in the eighteenth century, the established, one may almost say the inevitable, channel. Now this couplet, admirable (as Chaucer uses it) for story-telling not of the epic pitch, and often admirable for a few lines even in poetry of a very high pitch, is for continuous use in poetry of this latter kind inadequate. Pope, in his *Essay on Man*, is thus at a disadvantage compared with Lucretius in his poem on Nature : Lucretius has an adequate vehicle, Pope has not. Nay, though Pope's genius for didactic poetry was not less than that of Horace, while his satirical power was certainly greater, still one's taste receives, I cannot but think, a certain satisfaction when one reads the Epistles and Satires of Horace, which it fails to receive when one reads the Satires and Epistles of Pope. Of such avail is the superior adequacy of the vehicle used to compensate even an inferiority of genius in the user ! In the same way Pope is at a disadvantage as compared with

Addison. The best of Addison's composition (the "Coverley Papers" in the *Spectator*, for instance) wears better than the best of Pope's, because Addison has in his prose an intrinsically better vehicle for his genius than Pope in his couplet. But Bacon has no such advantage over Shakspeare; nor has Milton, writing prose (for no contemporary English prose-writer must be matched with Milton except Milton himself), any such advantage over Milton writing verse: indeed, the advantage here is all the other way.

It is in the prose remains of Guérin,—his journals, his letters, and the striking composition which I have already mentioned, the *Centaur*, — that his extraordinary gift manifests itself. He has a truly interpretative faculty; the most profound and delicate sense of the life of Nature, and the most exquisite felicity in finding expressions to render that sense. To all who love poetry, Guérin deserves to be something more than a name; and I shall try, in spite of the impossibility of doing justice to such a master of expression by translations, to make English readers see for themselves how gifted an organisation his was, and how few artists have received from Nature a more magical faculty of interpreting her.

In the winter of the year 1832 there was collected in Brittany, around the well-known Abbé Lamennais, a singular gathering. At a lonely place, La Chênaie, he had founded a religious retreat, to which disciples, attracted by his powers or by his reputation,

repaired. Some came with the intention of preparing
themselves for the ecclesiastical profession; others
merely to profit by the society and discourse of so
distinguished a master. Among the inmates were
men whose names have since become known to all
Europe,—Lacordaire and M. de Montalembert; there
were others, who have acquired a reputation, not
European, indeed, but considerable,—the Abbé Ger-
bet, the Abbé Rohrbacher; others, who have never
quitted the shade of private life. The winter of
1832 was a period of crisis in the religious world of
France : Lamennais's rupture with Rome, the condemnation of his opinions by the Pope, and his revolt
against that condemnation, were imminent. Some of
his followers, like Lacordaire, had already resolved
not to cross the Rubicon with their leader, not to go
into rebellion against Rome; they were preparing to
separate from him. The society of La Chênaie was
soon to dissolve ; but, such as it is shown to us for a
moment, with its voluntary character, its simple and
severe life in common, its mixture of lay and clerical
members, the genius of its chiefs, the sincerity of its
disciples,—above all, its paramount fervent interest
in matters of spiritual and religious concernment,—
it offers a most instructive spectacle. It is not the
spectacle we most of us think to find in France, the
France we have imagined from common English
notions, from the streets of Paris, from novels ; it
shows us how, wherever there is greatness like that
of France, there are, as its foundation, treasures of
fervour, pure-mindedness, and spirituality somewhere,

whether we know of them or not;—a store of that
which Goethe calls *Halt;*—since greatness can never
be founded upon frivolity and corruption.

On the evening of the 18th of December in this
year 1832, M. de Lamennais was talking to those
assembled in the sitting-room of La Chênaie of his
recent journey to Italy. He talked with all his usual
animation; "but," writes one of his hearers, a Breton
gentleman, M. de Marzan, " I soon became inattentive
and absent, being struck with the reserved attitude
of a young stranger some twenty-two years old, pale
in face, his black hair already thin over his temples,
with a southern eye, in which brightness and melancholy were mingled. He kept himself somewhat aloof,
seeming to avoid notice rather than to court it. All
the old faces of friends which I found about me at
this my re-entry into the circle of La Chênaie failed
to occupy me so much as the sight of this stranger,
looking on, listening, observing, and saying nothing."

The unknown was Maurice de Guérin. Of a noble
but poor family, having lost his mother at six years
old, he had been brought up by his father, a man
saddened by his wife's death, and austerely religious,
at the château of Le Cayla, in Languedoc. His childhood was not gay; he had not the society of other
boys; and solitude, the sight of his father's gloom,
and the habit of accompanying the curé of the parish
on his rounds among the sick and dying, made him
prematurely grave and familiar with sorrow. He
went to school first at Toulouse, then at the Collège
Stanislas at Paris, with a temperament almost as unfit

as Shelley's for common school life. His youth was ardent, sensitive, agitated, and unhappy. In 1832 he procured admission to La Chênaie to brace his spirit by the teaching of Lamennais, and to decide whether his religious feelings would determine themselves into a distinct religious vocation. Strong and deep religious feelings he had, implanted in him by nature, developed in him by the circumstances of his childhood; but he had also (and here is the key to his character) that temperament which opposes itself to the fixedness of a religious vocation, or to any vocation of which fixedness is an essential attribute; a temperament mobile, inconstant, eager, thirsting for new impressions, abhorring rules, aspiring to a "renovation without end;" a temperament common enough among artists, but with which few artists, who have it to the same degree as Guérin, unite a seriousness and a sad intensity like his. After leaving school, and before going to La Chênaie, he had been at home at Le Cayla with his sister Eugénie (a wonderfully gifted person, whose genius so competent a judge as M. Sainte-Beuve is inclined to pronounce even superior to her brother's) and his sister Eugénie's friends. With one of these friends he had fallen in love,—a slight and transient fancy, but which had already called his poetical powers into exercise; and his poems and fragments, in a certain green note-book (*le Cahier Vert*) which he long continued to make the depository of his thoughts, and which became famous among his friends, he brought with him to La Chênaie. There he found among the younger members of the

Society several who, like himself, had a secret passion
for poetry and literature; with these he became intimate, and in his letters and journal we find him occupied, now with a literary commerce established with
these friends, now with the fortunes, fast coming to
a crisis, of the Society, and now with that for the
sake of which he came to La Chênaie,—his religious
progress and the state of his soul.

On Christmas-day, 1832, having been then three
weeks at La Chênaie, he writes thus of it to a friend
of his family, M. de Bayne :—

"La Chênaie is a sort of oasis in the midst of the
steppes of Brittany.   In front of the château stretches
a very large garden cut in two by a terrace with a
lime avenue, at the end of which is a tiny chapel.   I
am extremely fond of this little oratory, where one
breathes a twofold peace,—the peace of solitude and
the peace of the Lord.   When spring comes we shall
walk to prayers between two borders of flowers.   On
the east side, and only a few yards from the château
sleeps a small mere between two woods, where the
birds in warm weather sing all day long ; and then,
—right, left, on all sides,—woods, woods, everywhere
woods.   It looks desolate just now that all is bare
and the woods are rust-colour, and under this Brittany
sky, which is always clouded and so low that it seems
as if it were going to fall on your head ; but as soon as
spring comes the sky raises itself up, the woods come
to life again, and everything will be full of charm."

Of what La Chênaie will be when spring comes he
has a foretaste on the 3d of March.

"To-day" (he writes in his journal) " has enchanted me. For the first time for a long while the sun has shown himself in all his beauty. He has made the buds of the leaves and flowers swell, and he has waked up in me a thousand happy thoughts. The clouds assume more and more their light and graceful shapes, and are sketching, over the blue sky, the most charming fancies. The woods have not yet got their leaves, but they are taking an indescribable air of life and gaiety, which gives them quite a new physiognomy. Everything is getting ready for the great festival of Nature."

Storm and snow adjourn this festival a little longer. On the 11th of March he writes :—

"It has snowed all night. I have been to look at our primroses; each of them has its small load of snow, and was bowing its head under its burden. These pretty flowers, with their rich yellow colour, had a charming effect under their white hoods. I saw whole tufts of them roofed over by a single block of snow; all these laughing flowers thus shrouded and leaning one upon another, made one think of a group of young girls surprised by a shower, and sheltering under a white apron."

The burst of spring comes at last, though late. On the 5th of April we find Guérin "sitting in the sun to penetrate himself to the very marrow with the divine spring." On the 3d of May, "one can actually *see* the progress of the green; it has made a start from the garden to the shrubberies, it is getting the upper hand all along the mere; it leaps, one may say,

from tree to tree, from thicket to thicket, in the fields
and on the hill-sides ; and I can see it already arrived
at the forest edge and beginning to spread itself over
the broad back of the forest.   Soon it will have over-
run everything as far as the eye can reach, and all
those wide spaces between here and the horizon will
be moving and sounding like one vast sea, a sea of
emerald."

Finally, on the 16th of May, he writes to M. de
Bayne that " the gloomy and bad days,—bad because
they bring temptation by their gloom,—are, thanks
to God and the spring, over ; and I see approaching a
long file of shining and happy days, to do me all the
good in the world.   This Brittany of ours," he continues, " gives one the idea of the grayest and most
wrinkled old woman possible suddenly changed back
by the touch of a fairy's wand into a girl of twenty,
and one of the loveliest in the world ; the fine weather
has so decked and beautified the dear old country."
He felt, however, the cloudiness and cold of the "dear
old country " with all the sensitiveness of a child of
the South.   " What a difference," he cries, " between
the sky of Brittany, even on the finest day, and the
sky of our South !   Here the summer has, even on
its highdays and holidays, something mournful, over-
cast, and stinted about it.   It is like a miser who is
making a show ; there is a niggardliness in his magnificence.   Give me our Languedoc sky, so bountiful
of light, so blue, so largely vaulted !"   And somewhat
later, complaining of the short and dim sunlight of a
February day in Paris. " What a sunshine," he ex-

claims, " to gladden eyes accustomed to all the wealth
of light of the South !—*aux larges et libérales effusions de
lumière du ciel du Midi.*"

In the long winter of La Chênaie his great resource
was literature.   One has often heard that an educated
Frenchman's reading seldom goes much beyond French
and Latin, and that he makes the authors in these
two languages his sole literary standard.   This may
or may not be true of Frenchmen in general, but
there can be no question as to the width of the reading
of Guérin and his friends, and as to the range of their
literary sympathies.   One of the circle, Hippolyte la
Morvonnais,—a poet who published a volume of verse,
and died in the prime of life,—had a passionate admiration for Wordsworth, and had even, it is said,
made a pilgrimage to Rydal Mount to visit him ; and
in Guérin's own reading I find, besides the French
names of Bernardin de St. Pierre, Chateaubriand,
Lamartine, and Victor Hugo, the names of Homer,
Dante, Shakspeare, Milton, and Goethe ; and he
quotes both from Greek and from English authors in
the original.   His literary tact is beautifully fine and
true.   " Every poet," he writes to his sister, " has his
own art of poetry written on the ground of his own
soul ; there is no other.   Be constantly observing
Nature in her smallest details, and then write as the
current of your thoughts guides you ;—that is all."
But with all this freedom from the bondage of forms
and rules, Guérin marks with perfect precision the
faults of the *free* French literature of his time,—the
littérature facile,—and judges the romantic school and

its prospects like a master : " that youthful literature which has put forth all its blossom prematurely, and has left itself a helpless prey to the returning frost, stimulated as it has been by the burning sun of our century, by this atmosphere charged with a perilous heat, which has over-hastened every sort of development, and will most likely reduce to a handful of grains the harvest of our age." And the popular authors,—those "whose name appears once and disappears for ever, whose books, unwelcome to all serious people, welcome to the rest of the world, to novelty-hunters and novel-readers, fill with vanity these vain souls, and then, falling from hands heavy with the languor of satiety, drop for ever into the gulf of oblivion;" and those, more noteworthy, "the writers of books celebrated, and, as works of art, deserving celebrity, but which have in them not one grain of that hidden manna, not one of those sweet and wholesome thoughts which nourish the human soul and refresh it when it is weary,"—these he treats with such severity that he may in some sense be described, as he describes himself, as "invoking with his whole heart a classical restoration." He is best described, however, not as a partisan of any school, but as an ardent seeker for that mode of expression which is the most natural, happy, and true. He writes to his sister Eugénie :—

"I want you to reform your system of composition ; it is too loose, too vague, too Lamartinian. Your verse is too sing-song ; it does not *talk* enough. Form for yourself a style of your own, which shall be your

real expression. Study the French language by
attentive reading, making it your care to remark
constructions, turns of expression, delicacies of style,
but without ever adopting the manner of any master.
In the works of these masters we must learn our language, but we must use it each in our own fashion." [1]

It was not, however, to perfect his literary judgment that Guérin came to La Chênaie. The religious
feeling, which was as much a part of his essence as
the passion for Nature and the literary instinct, shows
itself at moments jealous of these its rivals, and
alarmed at their predominance. Like all powerful
feelings, it wants to exclude every other feeling and
to be absolute. One Friday in April, after he has
been delighting himself with the shapes of the clouds
and the progress of the spring, he suddenly bethinks
himself that the day is Good Friday, and exclaims in
his diary :—

"My God, what is my soul about that it can thus
go running after such fugitive delights on Good Friday
on this day all filled with thy death and our redemption ? There is in me I know not what damnable
spirit, that awakens in me strong discontents, and is
for ever prompting me to rebel against the holy exercises and the devout collectedness of soul which are
the meet preparation for these great solemnities of
our faith. Oh how well can I trace here the old

[1] Part of these extracts date from a time a little after Guérin's
residence at La Chênaie ; but already, amidst the readings and
conversations of La Chênaie, his literary judgment was perfectly
formed.

leaven, from which I have not yet perfectly cleared my soul!"

And again, in a letter to M. de Marzan: "Of what, my God, are we made," he cries, "that a little verdure and a few trees should be enough to rob us of our tranquillity and to distract us from thy love?" And writing, three days after Easter Sunday, in his journal, he records the reception at La Chênaie of a fervent neophyte, in words which seem to convey a covert blame of his own want of fervency :—

"Three days have passed over our heads since the great festival. One anniversary the less for us yet to spend of the death and resurrection of our Saviour! Every year thus bears away with it its solemn festivals; when will the everlasting festival be here? I have been witness of a most touching sight; François has brought us one of his friends whom he has gained to the faith. This neophyte joined us in our exercises during the Holy week, and on Easter day he received the communion with us. François was in raptures. It is a truly good work which he has thus done. François is quite young, hardly twenty years old; M. de la M. is thirty, and is married. There is something most touching and beautifully simple in M. de la M. letting himself thus be brought to God by quite a young man; and to see friendship, on François's side, thus doing the work of an Apostle, is not less beautiful and touching."

Admiration for Lamennais worked in the same direction with this feeling. Lamennais never appreciated Guérin; his combative, rigid, despotic nature, of which the characteristic was energy, had no affinity with Guérin's elusive, undulating, impalpable nature, of which the characteristic was delicacy. He set little store by his new disciple, and could hardly bring himself to understand what others found so remarkable in him, his own genuine feeling towards him being one of indulgent compassion. But the intuition of Guérin, more discerning than the logic of his master, instinctively felt what there was commanding and tragic in Lamennais's character, different as this was from his own; and some of his notes are among the most interesting records of Lamennais which remain.

"'Do you know what it is,' M. Féli [1] said to us on the evening of the day before yesterday, 'which makes man the most suffering of all creatures? It is that he has one foot in the finite and the other in the infinite, and that he is torn asunder, not by four horses, as in the horrible old times, but between two worlds.' Again he said to us as we heard the clock strike : 'If that clock knew that it was to be destroyed the next instant, it would still keep striking its hour until that instant arrived. My children, be as the clock; whatever may be going to happen to you, strike always your hour.'"

Another time Guérin writes :

"To day M. Féli startled us. He was sitting behind the chapel, under the two Scotch firs; he took his stick and marked out a grave on the turf, and said to

[1] The familiar name given to M. de Lamennais by his followers at La Chênaie.

Elie, 'It is there I wish to be buried, but no tomb-stone! only a simple hillock of grass. Oh, how well I shall be there!' Elie thought he had a presentiment that his end was near. This is not the first time he has been visited by such a presentiment; when he was setting out for Rome, he said to those here: 'I do not expect ever to come back to you; you must do the good which I have failed to do.' He is im-patient for death."

Overpowered by the ascendency of Lamennais, Guérin, in spite of his hesitations, in spite of his confession to himself that, "after a three weeks' close scrutiny of his soul, in the hope of finding the pearl of a religious vocation hidden in some corner of it," he had failed to find what he sought, took, at the end of August 1833, a decisive step. He joined the re-ligious order which Lamennais had founded. But at this very moment the deepening displeasure of Rome with Lamennais determined the Bishop of Rennes to break up, in so far as it was a religious congregation, the Society of La Chênaie, to transfer the novices to Ploërmel, and to place them under other superintend-ence. In September, Lamennais, "who had not yet ceased," writes M. de Marzan, a fervent Catholic, "to be a Christian and a priest, took leave of his beloved colony of La Chênaie, with the anguish of a general who disbands his army down to the last recruit, and withdraws annihilated from the field of battle." Guérin went to Ploërmel. But here, in the seclusion of a real religious house, he instantly perceived how alien to a spirit like his,—a spirit which, as he himself says somewhere, "had need of the open air, wanted to see the sun and the flowers,"—was the constraint and monotony of a monastic life, when Lamennais's genius was no longer present to enliven this life for him. On the 7th of October he renounced the novitiate, believing himself a partisan of Lamennais in his quarrel with Rome, reproaching the life he had left with demanding passive obedience instead of trying "to put in practice the admirable alliance of order with liberty, and of variety with unity," and declaring that, for his part, he preferred taking the chances of a life of adventure to submitting himself to be " *garotté par un réglement*,—tied hand and foot by a set of rules." In real truth, a life of adventure, or rather a life free to wander at its own will, was that to which his nature irresistibly impelled him.

For a career of adventure, the inevitable field was Paris. But before this career began, there came a stage, the smoothest, perhaps, and the most happy in the short life of Guérin. M. la Morvonnais, one of his La Chênaie friends,—some years older than Guérin, and married to a wife of singular sweetness and charm, —had a house by the seaside at the mouth of one of the beautiful rivers of Brittany, the Arguenon. He asked Guérin, when he left Ploërmel, to come and stay with him at this place, called Le Val de l'Arguenon, and Guérin spent the winter of 1833-4 there. I grudge every word about Le Val and its inmates which is not Guérin's own, so charming is the picture he draws of them, so truly does his talent find itself in its best vein as he draws it.

"How full of goodness" (he writes in his journal of the 7th of December) "is Providence to me! For fear the sudden passage from the mild and temperate air of a religious life to the torrid clime of the world should be too trying for my soul, it has conducted me, after I have left my sacred shelter, to a house planted on the frontier between the two regions, where, without being in solitude, one is not yet in the world; a house whose windows look on the one side towards the plain where the tumult of men is rocking, on the other towards the wilderness where the servants of God are chanting. I intend to write down the record of my sojourn here, for the days here spent are full of happiness, and I know that in the time to come I shall often turn back to the story of these past felicities. A man, pious, and a poet; a woman, whose spirit is in such perfect sympathy with his that you would say they had but one being between them; a child, called Marie like her mother, and who sends, like a star, the first rays of her love and thought through the white cloud of infancy; a simple life in an old-fashioned house; the ocean, which comes morning and evening to bring us its harmonies; and lastly, a wanderer who descends from Carmel and is going on to Babylon, and who has laid down at this threshold his staff and his sandals, to take his seat at the hospitable table;— here is matter to make a biblical poem of, if I could only describe things as I can feel them!"

Every line written by Guérin during this stay at Le Val is worth quoting, but I have only room for one extract more :—

"Never" (he writes, a fortnight later, on the 20th of December), "never have I tasted so inwardly and deeply the happiness of home-life. All the little details of this life, which in their succession make up the day, are to me so many stages of a continuous charm carried from one end of the day to the other. The morning greeting, which in some sort renews the pleasure of the first arrival, for the words with which one meets are almost the same, and the separation at night, through the hours of darkness and uncertainty, does not ill represent longer separations; then breakfast, during which you have the fresh enjoyment of having met together again; the stroll afterwards, when we go out and bid Nature good-morning; the return and setting to work in an old panelled chamber looking out on the sea, inaccessible to all the stir of the house, a perfect sanctuary of labour; dinner, to which we are called, not by a bell, which reminds one too much of school or a great house, but by a pleasant voice; the gaiety, the merriment, the talk flitting from one subject to another and never dropping so long as the meal lasts; the crackling fire of dry branches to which we draw our chairs directly afterwards, the kind words that are spoken round the warm flame which sings while we talk; and then, if it is fine, the walk by the seaside, when the sea has for its visitors a mother with her child in her arms, this child's father and a stranger, each of these two last with a stick in his hand; the rosy lips of the little girl, which keep talking at the same time with the waves,—now and then tears shed by her and cries of childish fright at the edge of the sea; our thoughts, the father's and mine, as we stand and look at the mother and child smiling at one another, or at the child in tears and the mother trying to comfort it by her caresses and exhortations; the Ocean, going on all the while rolling up his waves and noises; the dead boughs which we go and cut, here and there, out of the copse-wood, to make a quick and bright fire when we get home,—this little taste of the woodman's calling which brings us closer to Nature and makes us think of M. Féli's eager fondness for the same work; the hours of study and poetical flow which carry us to supper-time; this meal, which summons us by the same gentle voice as its predecessor, and which is passed amid the same joys, only less loud, because evening sobers everything, tones everything down; then our evening, ushered in by the blaze of a cheerful fire, and which with its alternations of reading and talking brings us at last to bed-time:—to all the charms of a day so spent add the dreams which follow it, and your imagination will still fall far short of these home-joys in their delightful reality."

I said the foregoing should be my last extract, but who could resist this picture of a January evening on the coast of Brittany?—

"All the sky is covered over with gray clouds just silvered at the edges. The sun, who departed a few minutes ago, has left behind him enough light to temper for awhile the black shadows, and to soften down, as it were, the approach of night. The winds

are hushed, and the tranquil ocean sends up to me,
when I go out on the doorstep to listen, only a melodious murmur, which dies away in the soul like a
beautiful wave on the beach.   The birds, the first to
obey the nocturnal influence, make their way towards the woods, and you hear the rustle of their
wings in the clouds.   The copses which cover the
whole hill-side of Le Val, which all the day-time are
alive with the chirp of the wren, the laughing whistle
of the woodpecker,[1] and the different notes of a
multitude of birds, have no longer any sound in their
paths and thickets, unless it be the prolonged high
call of the blackbirds at play with one another and
chasing one another, after all the other birds have
their heads safe under their wings.   The noise of
man, always the last to be silent, dies gradually out
over the face of the fields.   The general murmur
fades away, and one hears hardly a sound except
what comes from the villages and hamlets, in which,
up till far into the night, there are cries of children
and barking of dogs.   Silence wraps me round:
everything seeks repose except this pen of mine,
which perhaps disturbs the rest of some living atom
asleep in a crease of my note-book, for it makes its
light scratching as it puts down these idle thoughts.
Let it stop, then! for all I write, have written, or
shall write, will never be worth setting against the
sleep of an atom."

On the 1st of February we find him in a lodging

[1] "The woodpecker *laughs*," says White of Selborne ; and
here is Guérin, in Brittany, confirming his testimony.

at Paris. "I enter the world" (such are the last words written in his journal at Le Val) "with a secret horror." His outward history for the next five years is soon told. He found himself in Paris, poor, fastidious, and with health which already, no doubt, felt the obscure presence of the malady of which he died—consumption. One of his Brittany acquaintances introduced him to editors, tried to engage him in the periodical literature of Paris; and so unmistakable was Guérin's talent that even his first essays were immediately accepted. But Guérin's genius was of a kind which unfitted him to get his bread in this manner. At first he was pleased with the notion of living by his pen; "*je n'ai qu'à écrire*," he says to his sister,—"I have only got to write." But to a nature like his, endued with the passion for perfection, the necessity to produce, to produce constantly, to produce whether in the vein or out of the vein, to produce something good or bad or middling, as it may happen, but at all events *something*,—is the most intolerable of tortures. To escape from it he betook himself to that common but most perfidious refuge of men of letters, that refuge to which Goldsmith and poor Hartley Coleridge had betaken themselves before him,—the profession of teaching. In September 1834 he procured an engagement at the Collège Stanislas, where he had himself been educated. It was vacation-time, and all he had to do was to teach a small class composed of boys who did not go home for the holidays,—in his own words, "scholars left like sick sheep in the fold, while the rest of the flock are frisking in the fields." After the vacation he was kept on at the college as a supernumerary. "The master of the fifth class has asked for a month's leave of absence; I am taking his place, and by this work I get one hundred francs (£4). I have been looking about for pupils to give private lessons to, and I have found three or four. Schoolwork and private lessons together fill my day from half-past seven in the morning till half-past nine at night. The college dinner serves me for breakfast, and I go and dine in the evening at twenty-four *sous*, as a young man beginning life should." To better his position in the hierarchy of public teachers it was necessary that he should take the degree of *agrégé ès-lettres*, corresponding to our degree of Master of Arts; and to his heavy work in teaching, there was thus added that of preparing for a severe examination. The drudgery of this life was very irksome to him, although less insupportable than the drudgery of the profession of letters; inasmuch as to a sensitive man like Guérin, to silence his genius is more tolerable than to hackney it. Still the yoke wore him deeply, and he had moments of bitter revolt; he continued, however, to bear it with resolution, and on the whole with patience, for four years. On the 15th of November 1838 he married a young Creole lady of some fortune, Mademoiselle Caroline de Gervain, "whom," to use his own words, "Destiny, who loves these surprises, has wafted from the farthest Indies into my arms." The marriage was happy, and it ensured to Guérin liberty and leisure; but now "the blind

Fury with the abhorred shears" was hard at hand.
Consumption declared itself in him: "I pass my life,"
he writes, with his old playfulness and calm, to his
sister on the 8th of April 1839, "within my bed-
curtains, and wait patiently enough, thanks to Caro's[1]
goodness, books, and dreams, for the recovery which
the sunshine is to bring with it." In search of this
sunshine he was taken to his native country, Languedoc, but in vain. He died at Le Cayla on the 19th
of July 1839.

The vicissitudes of his inward life during these
five years were more considerable. His opinions and
tastes underwent great, or what seem to be great,
changes. He came to Paris the ardent partisan of
Lamennais: even in April 1834, after Rome had
finally condemned Lamennais,—"To-night there will
go forth from Paris," he writes, "with his face set to
the west, a man whose every step I would fain follow,
and who returns to the desert for which I sigh. M.
Féli departs this evening for La Chênaie." But in
October 1835,—"I assure you," he writes to his
sister, "I am at last weaned from M. de Lamennais;
one does not remain a babe and suckling for ever; I
am perfectly freed from his influence." There was a
greater change than this. In 1834 the main cause of
Guérin's aversion to the literature of the French
romantic school, was that this literature, having had
a religious origin, had ceased to be religious: "it has
forgotten," he says, "the house and the admonitions
of its Father." But his friend M. de Marzan tells us

---

[1] His wife.

of a "deplorable revolution" which, by 1836, had taken place in him. Guérin had become intimate with the chiefs of this very literature; he no longer went to church; "the bond of a common faith, in which our friendship had its birth, existed between us no longer." Then, again, "this interregnum was not destined to last." Reconverted to his old faith by suffering and by the pious efforts of his sister Eugénie, Guérin died a Catholic. His feelings about society underwent a like change. After "entering the world with a secret horror," after congratulating himself when he had been some months at Paris on being "disengaged from the social tumult, out of the reach of those blows which, when I live in the thick of the world, bruise me, irritate me, or utterly crush me," M. Sainte-Beuve tells us of him, two years afterwards, appearing in society "a man of the world, elegant, even fashionable; a talker who could hold his own against the most brilliant talkers of Paris."

In few natures, however, is there really such essential consistency as in Guérin's. He says of himself, in the very beginning of his journal: "I owe everything to poetry, for there is no other name to give to the sum total of my thoughts; I owe to it whatever I now have pure, lofty, and solid in my soul; I owe to it all my consolations in the past; I shall probably owe to it my future." Poetry, the poetical instinct, was indeed the basis of his nature; but to say so thus absolutely is not quite enough. One aspect of poetry fascinated Guérin's imagination and held it prisoner. Poetry is the interpretress of the natural world, and she is the interpretress of the moral world; it was as the interpretress of the natural world that she had Guérin for her mouthpiece. To make magically near and real the life of Nature, and man's life only so far as it is a part of that Nature, was his faculty; a faculty of naturalistic, not of moral interpretation. This faculty always has for its basis a peculiar temperament, an extraordinary delicacy of organisation and susceptibility to impressions; in exercising it the poet is in a great degree passive (Wordsworth thus speaks of a *wise passiveness*); he aspires to be a sort of human Æolian harp, catching and rendering every rustle of Nature. To assist at the evolution of the whole life of the world is his craving, and intimately to feel it all:

> .   .   . "the glow, the thrill of life,
> Where, where do these abound?"

is what he asks: he resists being riveted and held stationary by any single impression, but would be borne on for ever down an enchanted stream. He goes into religion and out of religion, into society and out of society, not from the motives which impel men in general, but to feel what it is all like; he is thus hardly a moral agent, and, like the passive and ineffectual Uranus of Keats's poem, he may say:

> .   .   .   .   .   . "I am but a voice;
> My life is but the life of winds and tides;
> No more than winds and tides can I avail."

He hovers over the tumult of life, but does not really put his hand to it.

No one has expressed the aspirations of this temperament better than Guérin himself. In the last
year of his life he writes :—

"I return, as you see, to my old brooding over
the world of Nature, that line which my thoughts
irresistibly take; a sort of passion which gives me
enthusiasm, tears, bursts of joy, and an eternal food
for musing; and yet I am neither philosopher nor
naturalist, nor anything learned whatsoever. There
is one word which is the God of my imagination, the
tyrant, I ought rather to say, that fascinates it, lures
it onward, gives it work to do without ceasing, and
will finally carry it I know not where; the word
life."

And in one place in his journal he says :—

"My imagination welcomes every dream, every
impression, without attaching itself to any, and goes
on for ever seeking something new."

And again in another :—

"The longer I live, and the clearer I discern
between true and false in society, the more does the
inclination to live, not as a savage or a misanthrope,
but as a solitary man on the frontiers of society, on
the outskirts of the world, gain strength and grow in
me. The birds come and go and make nests around
our habitations, they are fellow-citizens of our farms
and hamlets with us ; but they take their flight in
a heaven which is boundless, but the hand of God
alone gives and measures to them their daily food,
but they build their nests in the heart of the thick
bushes, or hang them in the height of the trees

So would I, too, live, hovering round society, and having always at my back a field of liberty vast as the sky."

In the same spirit he longed for travel. "When one is a wanderer," he writes to his sister, "one feels that one fulfils the true condition of humanity." And the last entry in his journal is,—"The stream of travel is full of delight. Oh, who will set me adrift on this Nile!"

Assuredly it is not in this temperament that the active virtues have their rise. On the contrary, this temperament, considered in itself alone, indisposes for the discharge of them. Something morbid and excessive, as manifested in Guérin, it undoubtedly has. In him, as in Keats, and as in another youth of genius, whose name, but the other day unheard of, Lord Houghton has so gracefully written in the history of English poetry,—David Gray,—the temperament, the talent itself, is deeply influenced by their mysterious malady; the temperament is *devouring*; it uses vital power too hard and too fast, paying the penalty in long hours of unutterable exhaustion and in premature death. The intensity of Guérin's depression is described to us by Guérin himself with the same incomparable touch with which he describes happier feelings; far oftener than any pleasurable sense of his gift he has "the sense profound, near, immense, of my misery, of my inward poverty." And again: "My inward misery gains upon me; I no longer dare look within." And on another day of gloom he does look within, and here is the terrible analysis :—

"Craving, unquiet, seeing only by glimpses, my spirit is stricken by all those ills which are the sure fruit of a youth doomed never to ripen into manhood. I grow old and wear myself out in the most futile mental strainings, and make no progress. My head seems dying, and when the wind blows I fancy I feel it, as if I were a tree, blowing through a number of withered branches in my top. Study is intolerable to me, or rather it is quite out of my power. Mental work brings on, not drowsiness, but an irritable and nervous disgust which drives me out, I know not where, into the streets and public places. The Spring, whose delights used to come every year stealthily and mysteriously to charm me in my retreat, crushes me this year under a weight of sudden hotness. I should be glad of any event which delivered me from the situation in which I am. If I were free I would embark for some distant country where I could begin life anew."

Such is this temperament in the frequent hours when the sense of its own weakness and isolation crushes it to the ground. Certainly it was not for Guérin's happiness, or for Keats's, as men count happiness, to be as they were. Still the very excess and predominance of their temperament has given to the fruits of their genius a unique brilliancy and flavour. I have said that poetry interprets in two ways; it interprets by expressing with magical felicity the physiognomy and movement of the outward world, and it interprets by expressing, with inspired conviction, the ideas and laws of the inward world of man's móral and spiritual nature. In other words, poetry is interpretative both by having *natural magic* in it, and by having *moral profundity*. In both ways it illuminates man ; it gives him a satisfying sense of reality ; it reconciles him with himself and the universe. Thus Æschylus's " δράσαντι παθεῖν " and his " ἀνήριθμον γέλασμα " are alike interpretative. Shakspeare interprets both when he says,

> " Full many a glorious morning have I seen,
> Flatter the mountain-tops with sovran eye ; "

and when he says,

> " There's a divinity that shapes our ends,
> Rough-hew them as we will."

These great poets unite in themselves the faculty of both kinds of interpretation, the naturalistic and the moral. But it is observable that in the poets who unite both kinds, the latter (the moral) usually ends by making itself the master. In Shakspeare the two kinds seem wonderfully to balance one another; but even in him the balance leans; his expression tends to become too little sensuous and simple, too much intellectualised. The same thing may be yet more strongly affirmed of Lucretius and of Wordsworth. In Shelley there is not a balance of the two gifts, nor even a co-existence of them, but there is a passionate straining after them both, and this is what makes Shelley, as a man, so interesting : I will not now inquire how much Shelley achieves as a poet, but whatever he achieves, he in general fails to achieve natural magic in his expression ; in Mr. Palgrave's charming

Treasury may be seen a gallery of his failures.[1]   But in Keats and Guérin, in whom the faculty of natural-istic interpretation is overpoweringly predominant, the natural magic is perfect ; when they speak of the world they speak like Adam naming by divine in spiration the creatures ; their expression corresponds with the thing's essential reality.   Even between Keats and Guérin, however, there is a distinction to be drawn.   Keats has, above all, a sense of what is pleasurable and open in the life of nature ; for him she is the *Alma Parens :* his expression has, therefore, more than Guérin's, something genial, outward, and sensuous.   Guérin has, above all, a sense of what there is adorable and secret in the life of Nature ; for him she is the *Magna Parens ;* his expression has, there fore, more than Keats's, something mystic, inward, and profound.

So he lived like a man possessed ; with his eye not on his own career, not on the public, not on fame, but on the Isis whose veil he had uplifted. He published nothing : "There is more power and beauty," he writes, " in the well-kept secret of one's-self and one's thoughts, than in the display of a

---

[1] Compare, for example, his " Lines Written in the Euganean Hills," with Keats's " Ode to Autumn " (*Golden Treasury*, pp. 256, 284).   The latter piece *renders* Nature ; the former *tries to render* her.   I will not deny, however, that Shelley has natural magic in his rhythm ; what I deny is, that he has it in his language.   It always seems to me that the right sphere for Shelley's genius was the sphere of music, not of poetry ; the medium of sounds he can master, but to master the more diffi-cult medium of words he has neither intellectual force enough nor sanity enough

whole heaven that one may have inside one." "My
spirit," he answers the friends who urge him to write,
"is of the home-keeping order, and has no fancy for
adventure; literary adventure is above all distasteful
to it; for this, indeed (let me say so without the
least self-sufficiency), it has a contempt. The literary
career seems to me unreal, both in its own essence
and in the rewards which one seeks from it, and
therefore fatally marred by a secret absurdity." His
acquaintances, and among them distinguished men of
letters, full of admiration for the originality and delicacy of his talent, laughed at his self-depreciation,
warmly assured him of his powers. He received their
assurances with a mournful incredulity, which contrasts curiously with the self-assertion of poor David
Gray, whom I just now mentioned. "It seems to
me intolerable," he writes, "to appear to men other
than one appears to God. My worst torture at this
moment is the over-estimate which generous friends
form of me. We are told that at the last judgment
the secret of all consciences will be laid bare to the
universe; would that mine were so this day, and
that every passer-by could see me as I am!" "High
above my head," he says at another time, "far, far
away, I seem to hear the murmur of that world of
thought and feeling to which I aspire so often, but
where I can never attain. I think of those of my
own age who have wings strong enough to reach it,
but I think of them without jealousy, and as men on
earth contemplate the elect and their felicity." And,
criticising his own composition, "When I begin a

subject, my self-conceit" (says this exquisite artist) "imagines I am doing wonders; and when I have finished, I see nothing but a wretched made-up imita-tion, composed of odds and ends of colour stolen from other people's palettes, and tastelessly mixed together on mine." Such was his *passion for perfection*, his disdain for all poetical work not perfectly adequate and felicitous. The magic of expression, to which by the force of this passion he won his way, will make the name of Maurice de Guérin remembered in litera-ture.

I have already mentioned the *Centaur*, a sort of prose poem by Guérin, which Madame Sand published after his death. The idea of this composition came to him, M. Sainte-Beuve says, in the course of some visits which he made with his friend, M. Trebutien, a learned antiquarian, to the Museum of Antiquities in the Louvre. The free and wild life which the Greeks expressed by such creations as the Centaur had, as we might well expect, a strong charm for him; under the same inspiration he composed a *Bacchante*, which was meant by him to form part of a prose poem on the adventures of Bacchus in India. Real as was the affinity which Guérin's nature had for these subjects, I doubt whether, in treating them, he would have found the full and final employment of his talent. But the beauty of his *Centaur* is extraordinary; in its whole conception and expression this piece has in a wonderful degree that natural magic of which I have said so much, and the rhythm has a charm which bewitches even a foreigner. An old Centaur on his mountain is supposed to relate to Melampus, a human questioner, the life of his youth. Untranslatable as the piece is, I shall conclude with some extracts from it :—

" The Centaur.

" I had my birth in the caves of these mountains. Like the stream of this valley, whose first drops trickle from some weeping rock in a deep cavern, the first moment of my life fell in the darkness of a remote abode, and without breaking the silence. When our mothers draw near to the time of their delivery, they withdraw to the caverns, and in the depth of the loneliest of them, in the thickest of its gloom, bring forth, without uttering a plaint, a fruit silent as themselves. Their puissant milk makes us surmount, without weakness or dubious struggle, the first difficulties of life ; and yet we leave our caverns later than you your cradles. The reason is that we have a doctrine that the early days of existence should be kept apart and enshrouded, as days filled with the presence of the gods. Nearly the whole term of my growth was passed in the darkness where I was born. The recesses of my dwelling ran so far under the mountain that I should not have known on which side was the exit, had not the winds, when they sometimes made their way through the opening, sent fresh airs in, and a sudden trouble. Sometimes, too, my mother came back to me, having about her the odours of the valleys, or streaming from the waters which were her haunt. Her returning thus, without

a word said of the valleys or the rivers, but with the
emanations from them hanging about her, troubled
my spirit, and I moved up and down restlessly in my
darkness.   'What is it,' I cried, 'this outside world
whither my mother is borne, and what reigns there
in it so potent as to attract her so often?'   At these
moments my own force began to make me unquiet.   I
felt in it a power which could not remain idle; and
betaking myself either to toss my arms or to gallop
backwards and forwards in the spacious darkness of
the cavern, I tried to make out from the blows which
I dealt in the empty space, or from the transport of
my course through it, in what direction my arms
were meant to reach, or my feet to bear me.   Since
that day, I have wound my arms round the bust of
Centaurs, and round the body of heroes, and round
the trunk of oaks; my hands have assayed the rocks,
the waters, plants without number, and the subtlest
impressions of the air,—for I uplift them in the dark
and still nights to catch the breaths of wind, and to
draw signs whereby I may augur my road; my feet,
—look, O Melampus, how worn they are!   And yet,
all benumbed as I am in this extremity of age, there
are days when, in broad sunlight, on the mountain-tops,
I renew these gallopings of my youth in the cavern,
and with the same object, brandishing my arms and
employing all the fleetness which yet is left to me.

"O Melampus, thou who wouldst know the life of
the Centaurs, wherefore have the gods willed that
thy steps should lead thee to me, the oldest and most

forlorn of them all? It is long since I have ceased to practise any part of their life. I quit no more this mountain summit, to which age has confined me. The point of my arrows now serves me only to uproot some tough-fibred plant; the tranquil lakes know me still, but the rivers have forgotten me. I will tell thee a little of my youth; but these recollections, issuing from a worn memory, come like the drops of a niggardly libation poured from a damaged urn.

"The course of my youth was rapid and full of agitation. Movement was my life, and my steps knew no bound. One day when I was following the course of a valley seldom entered by the Centaurs, I discovered a man making his way up the stream-side on the opposite bank. He was the first whom my eyes had lighted on: I despised him. 'Behold,' I cried, 'at the utmost but the half of what I am! How short are his steps! and his movement how full of labour! Doubtless he is a Centaur overthrown by the gods, and reduced by them to drag himself along thus.'

.   .   .   .   .

"Wandering along at my own will like the rivers, feeling wherever I went the presence of Cybele, whether in the bed of the valleys, or on the height of the mountains, I bounded whither I would, like a blind and chainless life. But when Night, filled with the charm of the gods, overtook me on the slopes of the mountain, she guided me to the mouth of the caverns, and there tranquillised me as she tranquillises the billows of the sea. Stretched across the

threshold of my retreat, my flanks hidden within the
cave, and my head under the open sky, I watched
the spectacle of the dark.   The sea-gods, it is said,
quit during the hours of darkness their palaces under
the deep ; they seat themselves on the promontories,
and their eyes wander over the expanse of the waves
Even so I kept watch, having at my feet an expanse
of life like the hushed sea.   My regards had free
range, and travelled to the most distant points.   Like
sea-beaches which never lose their wetness, the line of
mountains to the west retained the imprint of gleams
not perfectly wiped out by the shadows.   In that
quarter still survived, in pale clearness, mountain-
summits naked and pure.   There I beheld at one
time the god Pan descend, ever solitary ; at another,
the choir of the mystic divinities ; or I saw pass some
mountain nymph charm-struck by the night.   Sometimes the eagles of Mount Olympus traversed the
upper sky, and were lost to view among the far-off
constellations, or in the shade of the dreaming forests.

"Thou pursuest after wisdom, O Melampus, which
is the science of the will of the gods ; and thou roam-
est from people to people like a mortal driven by the
destinies.   In the times when I kept my night-watches
before the caverns, I have sometimes believed that I
was about to surprise the thought of the sleeping
Cybele, and that the mother of the gods, betrayed by
her dreams, would let fall some of her secrets ; but I
have never made out more than sounds which faded
away in the murmur of night, or words inarticulate
as the bubbling of the rivers.

"'O Macareus,' one day said the great Chiron to me, whose old age I tended; 'we are, both of us, Centaurs of the mountain; but how different are our lives! Of my days all the study is (thou seest it) the search for plants; thou, thou art like those mortals who have picked up on the waters or in the woods, and carried to their lips, some pieces of the reed-pipe thrown away by the god Pan. From that hour these mortals, having caught from their relics of the god a passion for wild life, or perhaps smitten with some secret madness, enter into the wilderness, plunge among the forests, follow the course of the streams, bury themselves in the heart of the mountains, restless, and haunted by an unknown purpose. The mares beloved of the winds in the farthest Scythia are not wilder than thou, nor more cast down at nightfall, when the North Wind has departed. Seekest thou to know the gods, O Macareus, and from what source men, animals, and the elements of the universal fire have their origin? But the aged Ocean, the father of all things, keeps locked within his own breast these secrets; and the nymphs, who stand around, sing as they weave their eternal dance before him, to cover any sound which might escape from his lips half-opened by slumber. The mortals, dear to the gods for their virtue, have received from their hands lyres to give delight to man, or the seeds of new plants to make him rich; but from their inexorable lips, nothing!'

"Such were the lessons which the old Chiron gave

me. Waned to the very extremity of life, the Centaur
yet nourished in his spirit the most lofty discourse.

"For me, O Melampus, I decline into my last
days, calm as the setting of the constellations. I still
retain enterprise enough to climb to the top of the
rocks, and there I linger late, either gazing on the
wild and restless clouds, or to see come up from the
horizon the rainy Hyades, the Pleiades, or the great
Orion; but I feel myself perishing and passing quickly
away, like a snow-wreath floating on the stream; and
soon shall I be mingled with the waters which flow
in the vast bosom of Earth."

IV.

EUGÉNIE DE GUÉRIN.

WHO that had spoken of Maurice de Guérin could refrain from speaking of his sister Eugénie, the most devoted of sisters, one of the rarest and most beautiful of souls? "There is nothing fixed, no duration, no vitality in the sentiments of women towards one another; their attachments are mere pretty knots of ribbon, and no more. In all the friendships of women I observe this slightness of the tie. I know no instance to the contrary, even in history. Orestes and Pylades have no sisters." So she herself speaks of the friendships of her own sex. But Electra can attach herself to Orestes, if not to Chrysothemis. And to her brother Maurice, Eugénie de Guérin was Pylades and Electra in one.

The name of Maurice de Guérin,—that young man so gifted, so attractive, so careless of fame, and so early snatched away; who died at twenty-nine; who, says his sister, "let what he did be lost with a carelessness so unjust to himself, set no value on any of his own productions, and departed hence without

reaping the rich harvest which seemed his due;"
who, in spite of his immaturity, in spite of his fragility,
exercised such a charm, "furnished to others so much
of that which all live by," that some years after his
death his sister found in a country-house where he
used to stay, in the journal of a young girl who had
not known him, but who heard her family speak of
him, his name, the date of his death, and these words,
"*il était leur vie*" (he was their life); whose talent,
exquisite as that of Keats, with much less of sunlight,
abundance, inventiveness, and facility in it than that
of Keats, but with more of distinction and power, had
"that winning, delicate, and beautifully happy turn
of expression" which is the stamp of the master,—is
beginning to be well known to all lovers of literature.
This establishment of Maurice's name was an object
for which his sister Eugénie passionately laboured.
While he was alive, she placed her whole joy in the
flowering of this gifted nature; when he was dead,
she had no other thought than to make the world
know him as she knew him.   She outlived him nine
years, and her cherished task for those years was to
rescue the fragments of her brother's composition, to
collect them, to get them published.   In pursuing this
task she had at first cheering hopes of success; she
had at last baffling and bitter disappointment.   Her
earthly business was at an end; she died.   Ten years
afterwards, it was permitted to the love of a friend,
M. Trebutien, to effect for Maurice's memory what
the love of a sister had failed to accomplish.   But
those who read, with delight and admiration, the

journal and letters of Maurice de Guérin, could not
but be attracted and touched by this sister Eugénie,
who met them at every page. She seemed hardly
less gifted, hardly less interesting, than Maurice himself. And presently M. Trebutien did for the sister
what he had done for the brother. He published the
journal of Mdlle. Eugénie de Guérin, and a few (too
few, alas!) of her letters.[1] The book has made a profound impression in France; and the fame which she
sought only for her brother now crowns the sister also.

Parts of Mdlle. de Guérin's journal were several
years ago printed for private circulation, and a writer
in the *National Review* had the good fortune to fall in
with them. The bees of our English criticism do not
often roam so far afield for their honey, and this critic
deserves thanks for having flitted in his quest of
blossom to foreign parts, and for having settled upon
a beautiful flower found there. He had the discernment to see that Mdlle. de Guérin was well worth
speaking of, and he spoke of her with feeling and
appreciation. But that, as I have said, was several
years ago; even a true and feeling homage needs to
be from time to time renewed, if the memory of its
object is to endure; and criticism must not lose the
occasion offered by Mdlle. de Guérin's journal being
for the first time published to the world, of directing notice once more to this religious and beautiful
character.

[1] A volume of these, also, has just been brought out by M.
Trebutien. One good book, at least, in the literature of the year
1865!

Eugénie de Guérin was born in 1805, at the château
of Le Cayla, in Languedoc. Her family, though reduced in circumstances, was noble; and even when
one is a saint one cannot quite forget that one comes
of the stock of the Guarini of Italy, or that one counts
among one's ancestors a Bishop of Senlis, who had the
marshalling of the French order of battle on the day
of Bouvines. Le Cayla was a solitary place, with its
terrace looking down upon a stream-bed and valley;
" one may pass days there without seeing any living
thing but the sheep, without hearing any living thing
but the birds." M. de Guérin, Eugénie's father, lost
his wife when Eugénie was thirteen years old, and
Maurice seven; he was left with four children,—
Eugénie, Marie, Erembert, and Maurice,—of whom
Eugénie was the eldest, and Maurice was the youngest.
This youngest child, whose beauty and delicacy had
made him the object of his mother's most anxious
fondness, was commendéd by her in dying to the care
of his sister Eugénie. Maurice at eleven years old
went to school at Toulouse; then he went to the
Collège Stanislas at Paris; then he became a member
of the religious society which M. de Lamennais had
formed at La Chênaie in Brittany; afterwards he
lived chiefly at Paris, returning to Le Cayla, at the
age of twenty-nine, to die. Distance, in those days,
was a great obstacle to frequent meetings of the
separated members of a French family of narrow
means. Maurice de Guérin was seldom at Le Cayla
after he had once quitted it, though his few visits to
his home were long ones; but he passed five years,—

the period of his sojourn in Brittany, and of his first
settlement in Paris,—without coming home at all.
In spite of the check from these absences, in spite of
the more serious check from a temporary alteration in
Maurice's religious feelings, the union between the
brother and sister was wonderfully close and firm.
For they were knit together, not only by the tie of
blood and early attachment, but also by the tie of a
common genius. "We were," says Eugénie, "two
eyes looking out of one head." She, on her part,
brought to her love for her brother the devotedness
of a woman, the intensity of a recluse, almost the
solicitude of a mother. Her home duties prevented
her from following the wish, which often arose in her,
to join a religious sisterhood. There is a trace,—just
a trace,—of an early attachment to a cousin; but he
died when she was twenty-four. After that, she lived
for Maurice. It was for Maurice that, in addition to
her constant correspondence with him by letter, she
began in 1834 her journal, which was sent to him by
portions as it was finished. After his death she tried
to continue it, addressing it to "Maurice in heaven."
But the effort was beyond her strength; gradually
the entries become rarer and rarer; and on the last
day of December 1840 the pen dropped from her
hand: the journal ends.

Other sisters have loved their brothers, and it is
not her affection for Maurice, admirable as this was,
which alone could have made Eugénie de Guérin celebrated. I have said that both brother and sister had
genius: M. Sainte-Beuve goes so far as to say that

the sister's genius was equal, if not superior, to her brother's.   No one has a more profound respect for M. Sainte-Beuve's critical judgments than I have, but it seems to me that this particular judgment needs to be a little explained and guarded.   In Maurice's special talent, which was a talent for interpreting nature, for finding words which incomparably render the subtlest impressions which nature makes upon us, which bring the intimate life of nature wonderfully near to us, it seems to me that his sister was by no means his equal.   She never, indeed, expresses herself without grace and intelligence ; but her words, when she speaks of the life and appearances of nature, are in general but intellectual signs ; they are not like her brother's—symbols equivalent with the thing symbolised.   They bring the notion of the thing described to the mind, they do not bring the feeling of it to the imagination.   Writing from the Nivernais, that region of vast woodlands in the centre of France : " It does one good," says Eugénie, " to be going about in the midst of this enchanting nature, with flowers, birds, and verdure all round one, under this large and blue sky of the Nivernais.   How I love the gracious form of it, and those little white clouds here and there, like cushions of cotton, hung aloft to rest the eye in this immensity !"   It is pretty and graceful, but how different from the grave and pregnant strokes of Maurice's pencil !   " I have been along the Loire, and seen on its banks the plains where nature is puissant and gay ; I have seen royal and antique dwellings, all marked by memories which have their place in the

mournful legend of humanity,— Chambord, Blois,
Amboise, Chenonceaux ; then the towns on the two
banks of the river,—Orleans, Tours, Saumur, Nantes ;
and at the end of it all, the Ocean rumbling. From
these I passed back into the interior of the country,
as far as Bourges and Nevers, a region of vast woodlands, in which murmurs of an immense range and
fulness" (*ce beau torrent de rumeurs*, as, with an expression worthy of Wordsworth, he elsewhere calls
them) "prevail and never cease." Words whose
charm is like that of the sounds of the murmuring
forest itself, and whose reverberations, like theirs, die
away in the infinite distance of the soul.

Maurice's life was in the life of nature, and the
passion for it consumed him ; it would have been
strange if his accent had not caught more of the soul
of nature than Eugénie's accent, whose life was elsewhere. "You will find in him," Maurice says to
his sister of a friend whom he was recommending to
her, "you will find in him that which you love, and
which suits you better than anything else,—*l'onction,
l'effusion, la mysticité*." Unction, the pouring out of
the soul, the rapture of the mystic, were dear to
Maurice also ; but in him the bent of his genius gave
even to those a special direction of its own. In
Eugénie they took the direction most native and
familiar to them ; their object was the religious life.

And yet, if one analyses this beautiful and most
interesting character quite to the bottom, it is not
exactly as a saint that Eugénie de Guérin is remarkable. The ideal saint is a nature like Saint François

de Sales or Fénelon ; a nature of ineffable sweetness and serenity, a nature in which struggle and revolt is over, and the whole man (so far as is possible to human infirmity) swallowed up in love. Saint Theresa (it is Mdlle. de Guérin herself who reminds us of it) endured twenty years of unacceptance and of repulse in her prayers ; yes, but the Saint Theresa whom Christendom knows is Saint Theresa repulsed no longer ! it is Saint Theresa accepted, rejoicing in love, radiant with ecstasy. Mdlle. de Guérin is not one of these saints arrived at perfect sweetness and calm, steeped in ecstasy ; there is something primitive, indomitable in her, which she governs, indeed, but which chafes, which revolts. Somewhere in the depths of that strong nature there is a struggle, an impatience, an inquietude, an ennui, which endures to the end, and which leaves one, when one finally closes her journal, with an impression of profound melancholy. "There are days," she writes to her brother, "when one's nature rolls itself up, and becomes a hedgehog. If I had you here at this moment, here close by me, how I should prick you ! how sharp and hard !" "Poor soul, poor soul," she cries out to herself another day, "what is the matter, what would you have ? Where is that which will do you good ? Everything is green, everything is in bloom, all the air has a breath of flowers. How beautiful it is ! well, I will go out. No, I should be alone, and all this beauty, when one is alone, is worth nothing. What shall I do then ? Read, write, pray, take a basket of sand on my head like that hermit-saint, and walk with it? Yes, work, work! keep busy the body which does mischief to the soul! I have been too little occupied to-day, and that is bad for one, and it gives a certain ennui which I have in me time to ferment."

A certain ennui which I have in me: her wound is there. In vain she follows the counsel of Fénelon: "If God tires you, *tell him that he tires you.*" No doubt she obtained great and frequent solace and restoration from prayer: "This morning I was suffering; well, at present I am calm, and this I owe to faith, simply to faith, to an act of faith. I can think of death and eternity without trouble, without alarm. Over a deep of sorrow there floats a divine calm, a suavity which is the work of God only. In vain have I tried other things at a time like this: nothing human comforts the soul, nothing human upholds it :—

> ' A l'enfant il faut sa mère,
> A mon âme il faut mon Dieu.' "

Still the ennui reappears, bringing with it hours of unutterable forlornness, and making her cling to her one great earthly happiness,—her affection for her brother,—with an intenseness, an anxiety, a desperation in which there is something morbid, and by which she is occasionally carried into an irritability, a jealousy which she herself is the first, indeed, to censure, which she severely represses, but which nevertheless leaves a sense of pain.

Mdlle. de Guérin's admirers have compared her to Pascal, and in some respects the comparison is just. But she cannot exactly be classed with Pascal, any more than with Saint François de Sales. Pascal is a man, and the inexhaustible power and activity of his mind leave him no leisure for ennui. He has not the sweetness and serenity of the perfect saint; he is, perhaps, "der strenge, kranke Pascal — *the severe, morbid Pascal*," — as Goethe (and, strange to say, Goethe at twenty-three, an age which usually feels Pascal's charm most profoundly) calls him. But the stress and movement of the lifelong conflict waged in him between his soul and his reason keep him full of fire, full of agitation, and keep his reader, who witnesses this conflict, animated and excited; the sense of forlornness and dejected weariness which clings to Eugénie de Guérin does not belong to Pascal. Eugénie de Guérin is a woman, and longs for a state of firm happiness, for an affection in which she may repose. The inward bliss of Saint Theresa or Fénelon would have satisfied her; denied this, she cannot rest satisfied with the triumphs of self-abasement, with the sombre joy of trampling the pride of life and of reason underfoot, of reducing all human hope and joy to insignificance; she repeats the magnificent words of Bossuet, words which both Catholicism and Protestantism have uttered with indefatigable iteration : "On trouve au fond de tout le vide et le néant—*at the bottom of everything one finds emptiness and nothingness,*" but she feels, as every one but the true mystic must ever feel, their incurable sterility.

She resembles Pascal, however, by the clearness and firmness of her intelligence, going straight and instinctively to the bottom of any matter she is dealing with, and expressing herself about it with incomparable precision ; never fumbling with what she has to say, never imperfectly seizing or imperfectly presenting her thought. And to this admirable precision she joins a lightness of touch, a feminine ease and grace, a flowing facility which are her own. " I do not say," writes her brother Maurice, an excellent judge, " that I find in myself a dearth of expression ; but I have not this abundance of yours, this productiveness of soul which streams forth, which courses along without ever failing, and always with an infinite charm." And writing to her of some composition of hers, produced after her religious scruples had for a long time kept her from the exercise of her talent : " You see, my dear Tortoise," he writes, " that your talent is no illusion, since after a period, I know not how long, of poetical inaction,—a trial to which any half-talent would have succumbed,—it rears its head again more vigorous than ever. It is really heartbreaking to see you repress and bind down, with I know not what scruples, your spirit, which tends with all the force of its nature to develop itself in this direction. Others have made it a case of conscience for you to resist this impulse, and I make it one for you to follow it." And she says of herself, on one of her freer days : " It is the instinct of my life to write, as it is the instinct of the fountain to flow." The charm of her expression is not a sensuous and imaginative charm like that of Maurice, but rather an intellectual charm ; it comes from the texture of the style rather than from its elements ; it is not so

much in the words as in the turn of the phrase, in
the happy cast and flow of the sentence. Recluse as
she was, she had a great correspondence : every one
wished to have letters from her ; and no wonder.

To this strength of intelligence and talent of expression she joined a great force of character. Religion
had early possessed itself of this force of character,
and reinforced it : in the shadow of the Cevennes, in
the sharp and tonic nature of this region of Southern
France, which has seen the Albigensians, which has
seen the Camisards, Catholicism too is fervent and
intense. Eugénie de Guérin was brought up amidst
strong religious influences, and they found in her a
nature on which they could lay firm hold. I have
said that she was not a saint of the order of Saint
François de Sales or Fénelon ; perhaps she had too
keen an intelligence to suffer her to be this, too forcible and impetuous a character. But I did not mean
to imply the least doubt of the reality, the profoundness, of her religious life. She was penetrated by the
power of religion ; religion was the master-influence
of her life ; she derived immense consolations from
religion, she earnestly strove to conform her whole
nature to it ; if there was an element in her which
religion could not perfectly reach, perfectly transmute,
she groaned over this element in her, she chid it, she
made it bow. Almost every thought in her was
brought into harmony with religion ; and what few
thoughts were not thus brought into harmony were
brought into subjection.

Then she had her affection for her brother ; and

this, too, though perhaps there might be in it something a little over-eager, a little too absolute, a little
too susceptible, was a pure, a devoted affection. It
was not only passionate, it was tender. It was tender,
pliant, and self-sacrificing to a degree that not in one
nature out of a thousand,—of natures with a mind
and will like hers,—is found attainable. She thus
united extraordinary power of intelligence, extraordinary force of character, and extraordinary strength
of affection; and all these under the control of a deep
religious feeling.

This is what makes her so remarkable, so interesting. I shall try and make her speak for herself, that
she may show us the characteristic sides of her rare
nature with her own inimitable touch.

It must be remembered that her journal is written
for Maurice only; in her lifetime no eye but his ever
saw it. "*Ceci n'est pas pour le public,*" she writes;
"*c'est de l'intime, c'est de l'âme, c'est pour un.*" "This
is not for the public; it contains my inmost thoughts,
my very soul; it is for *one.*" And Maurice, this *one,*
was a kind of second self to her. "We see things
with the same eyes; what you find beautiful, I find
beautiful; God has made our souls of one piece."
And this genuine confidence in her brother's sympathy
gives to the entries in her journal a naturalness and
simple freedom rare in such compositions. She felt
that he would understand her, and be interested in
all that she wrote.

One of the first pages of her journal relates an incident of the home-life of Le Cayla, the smallest detail

of which Maurice liked to hear; and in relating it she
brings this simple life before us.   She is writing in
November, 1834 :—

"I am furious with the gray cat.   The mischievous
beast has made away with a little half-frozen pigeon,
which I was trying to thaw by the side of the fire.
The poor little thing was just beginning to come
round; I meant to tame him; he would have grown
fond of me; and there is my whole scheme eaten up
by a cat!   This event, and all the rest of to-day's
history, has passed in the kitchen.   Here I take up
my abode all the morning and a part of the evening,
ever since I am without Mimi.[1]   I have to superin-
tend the cook; sometimes papa comes down, and I
read to him by the oven, or by the fireside, some bits
out of the *Antiquities of the Anglo-Saxon Church.*
This book struck Pierril[2] with astonishment.   '*Que
de mouts aqui dédins!*   What a lot of words there are
inside it!'   This boy is a real original.   One evening
he asked me if the soul was immortal; then afterwards, what a philosopher was?   We had got upon
great questions, as you see.   When I told him that a
philosopher was a person who was wise and learned:
'Then, mademoiselle, you are a philosopher.'   This
was said with an air of simplicity and sincerity which
might have made even Socrates take it as a compli-
ment; but it made me laugh so much that my gravity
as catechist was gone for that evening.   A day or two
ago Pierril left us, to his great sorrow: his time with

---

[1] The familiar name of her sister Marie.
[2] A servant-boy at Le Cayla.

us was up on Saint Brice's day. Now he goes about with his little dog, truffle-hunting. If he comes this way I shall go and ask him if he still thinks I look like a philosopher."

Her good sense and spirit made her discharge with alacrity her household tasks in this patriarchal life of Le Cayla, and treat them as the most natural thing in the world. She sometimes complains, to be sure, of burning her fingers at the kitchen-fire. But when a literary friend of her brother expresses enthusiasm about her and her poetical nature: "The poetess," she says, "whom this gentleman believes me to be, is an ideal being, infinitely removed from the life which is actually mine—a life of occupations, a life of household-business, which takes up all my time. How could I make it otherwise? I am sure I do not know; and, besides, my duty is in this sort of life, and I have no wish to escape from it."

Among these occupations of the patriarchal life of the châtelaine of Le Cayla intercourse with the poor fills a prominent place :—

"To-day," she writes on the 9th of December 1834, " I have been warming myself at every fireside in the village. It is a round which Mimi and I often make, and in which I take pleasure. To-day we have been seeing sick people, and holding forth on doses and sick-room drinks. 'Take this, do that;' and they attend to us just as if we were the doctor. We prescribed shoes for a little thing who was amiss from having gone barefoot; to the brother, who, with a bad headache, was lying quite flat, we prescribed a pillow; the pillow did him good, but I am afraid it will hardly cure him. He is at the beginning of a bad feverish cold: and these poor people live in the filth of their hovels like animals in their stable; the bad air poisons them. When I come home to Le Cayla I seem to be in a palace."

She had books, too; not in abundance, not for the fancying them; the list of her library is small, and it is enlarged slowly and with difficulty. The *Letters of Saint Theresa*, which she had long wished to get, she sees in the hands of a poor servant girl, before she can procure them for herself. "What then?" is her comment: "very likely she makes a better use of them than I could." But she has the *Imitation*, the *Spiritual Works* of Bossuet and Fénelon, the *Lives of the Saints*, Corneille, Racine, André Chénier, and Lamartine; Madame de Staël's book on Germany, and French translations of Shakspeare's plays, Ossian, the *Vicar of Wakefield*, Scott's *Old Mortality* and *Redgauntlet*, and the *Promessi Sposi* of Manzoni. Above all, she has her own mind; her meditations in the lonely fields, on the oak-grown hill-side of "The Seven Springs;" her meditations and writing in her own room, her *chambrette*, her *délicieux chez moi*, where every night, before she goes to bed, she opens the window to look out upon the sky,—the balmy moonlit sky of Languedoc. This life of reading, thinking, and writing was the life she liked best, the life that most truly suited her. "I find writing has become almost a necessity to me. Whence does it arise, this impulse to give utterance to the voice of one's spirit to pour out my thoughts before God and one human being? I say one human being, because I always imagine that you are present, that you see what I write. In the stillness of a life like this my spirit is happy, and, as it were, dead to all that goes on up-stairs or downstairs, in the house or out of the house. But this does not last long. 'Come, my poor spirit,' I then say to myself, 'we must go back to the things of this world.' And I take my spinning, or a book, or a saucepan, or I play with Wolf or Trilby. Such a life as this I call heaven upon earth."

Tastes like these, joined with a talent like Mdlle. de Guérin's, naturally inspire thoughts of literary composition. Such thoughts she had, and perhaps she would have been happier if she had followed them; but she never could satisfy herself that to follow them was quite consistent with the religious life, and her projects of composition were gradually relinquished :—

"Would to God that my thoughts, my spirit, had never taken their flight beyond the narrow round in which it is my lot to live! In spite of all that people say to the contrary, I feel that I cannot go beyond my needlework and my spinning without going too far : I feel it, I believe it : well, then, I will keep in my proper sphere; however much I am tempted, my spirit shall not be allowed to occupy itself with great matters until it occupies itself with them in Heaven."

And again :—

"My journal has been untouched for a long while. Do you want to know why? It is because the time

seems to me misspent which I spend in writing it.
We owe God an account of every minute; and is it
not a wrong use of our minutes to employ them in
writing a history of our transitory days?"

She overcomes her scruples, and goes on writing
the journal; but again and again they return to her.
Her brother tells her of the pleasure and comfort
something she has written gives to a friend of his in
affliction.   She answers :—

"It is from the Cross that those thoughts come,
which your friend finds so soothing, so unspeakably
tender. None of them come from me. I feel my
own aridity; but I feel, too, that God, when he will,
can make an ocean flow upon this bed of sand. It is
the same with so many simple souls, from which proceed the most admirable things; because they are in
direct relation with God, without false science and
without pride. And thus I am gradually losing my
taste for books; I say to myself : 'What can they
teach me which I shall not one day know in Heaven?
let God be my master and my study here!' I try to
make him so, and I find myself the better for it. I
read little; I go out little; I plunge myself in the
inward life. How infinite are the sayings, doings,
feelings, events of that life! Oh, if you could but
see them! But what avails it to make them known?
God alone should be admitted to the sanctuary of the
soul."

Beautifully as she says all this, one cannot, I think,
read it without a sense of disquietude, without a presentiment that this ardent spirit is forcing itself from

its natural bent, that the beatitude of the true mystic
will never be its earthly portion.   And yet how simple
and charming is her picture of the life of religion
which she chose as her ark of refuge, and in which
she desired to place all her happiness :—

"Cloaks, clogs, umbrellas, all the apparatus of
winter, went with us this morning to Andillac, where
we have passed the whole day; some of it at the
curé's house, the rest in church.   How I like this life
of a country Sunday, with its activity, its journeys to
church, its liveliness !   You find all your neighbours
on the road ; you have a curtsey from every woman
you meet, and then, as you go along, such a talk
about the poultry, the sheep and cows, the good man
and the children !   My great delight is to give a kiss
to these children, and see them run away and hide
their blushing faces in their mother's gown.   They
are alarmed at *las doumaïsélos*,[1] as at a being of
another world.   One of these little things said the
other day to its grandmother, who was talking of
coming to see us : '*Minino*, you mustn't go to that
castle ; there is a black hole there.'   What is the
reason that in all ages the noble's château has been
an object of terror ?   Is it because of the horrors
that were committed there in old times ?   I suppose so."

This vague horror of the château, still lingering in
the mind of the French peasant fifty years after he
has stormed it, is indeed curious, and is one of the
thousand indications how unlike aristocracy on the

[1] The young lady.

Continent has been to aristocracy in England. But this is one of the great matters with which Mdlle. de Guérin would not have us occupied; let us pass to the subject of Christmas in Languedoc :—

"Christmas is come; the beautiful festival, the one I love most, and which gives me the same joy as it gave the shepherds of Bethlehem. In real truth, one's whole soul sings with joy at this beautiful coming of God upon earth,—a coming which here is announced on all sides of us by music and by our charming *nadalet*.[1] Nothing at Paris can give you a notion of what Christmas is with us. You have not even the midnight-mass. We all of us went to it, papa at our head, on the most perfect night possible. Never was there a finer sky than ours was that midnight;—so fine that papa kept perpetually throwing back the hood of his cloak, that he might look up at the sky. The ground was white with hoar-frost, but we were not cold; besides, the air, as we met it, was warmed by the bundles of blazing torchwood which our servants carried in front of us to light us on our way. It was delightful, I do assure you; and I should like you to have seen us there on our road to church, in those lanes with the bushes along their banks as white as if they were in flower. The hoar-frost makes the most lovely flowers. We saw a long spray so beautiful that we wanted to take it with us as a garland for the communion-table, but it melted in our hands: all flowers fade so soon! I was very sorry about my

---

[1] A peculiar peal rung at Christmas-time by the church bells of Languedoc.

garland; it was mournful to see it drip away, and get smaller and smaller every minute."

The religious life is at bottom everywhere alike; but it is curious to note the variousness of its setting and outward circumstance. Catholicism has these so different from Protestantism! and in Catholicism these accessories have, it cannot be denied, a nobleness and amplitude which in Protestantism is often wanting to them. In Catholicism they have, from the antiquity of this form of religion, from its pretensions to universality, from its really widespread prevalence, from its sensuousness, something European, august, and imaginative: in Protestantism they often have, from its inferiority in all these respects, something provincial, mean, and prosaic. In revenge, Protestantism has a future before it, a prospect of growth in alliance with the vital movement of modern society; while Catholicism appears to be bent on widening the breach between itself and the modern spirit, to be fatally losing itself in the multiplication of dogmas, Mariolatry, and miracle-mongering. But the style and circumstance of actual Catholicism is grander than its present tendency, and the style and circumstance of Protestantism is meaner than its tendency. While I was reading the journal of Mdlle. de Guérin there came into my hands the memoir and poems of a young Englishwoman, Miss Emma Tatham; and one could not but be struck with the singular contrast which the two lives,—in their setting rather than in their inherent quality,—present. Miss Tatham had not, certainly, Mdlle. de Guérin's talent, but she had a sincere vein of poetic feeling, a genuine aptitude for composition. Both were fervent Christians, and, so far, the two lives have a real resemblance; but, in the setting of them, what a difference! The French-woman is a Catholic in Languedoc; the Englishwoman is a Protestant at Margate; Margate, that brick-and-mortar image of English Protestantism, representing it in all its prose, all its uncomeliness,—let me add, all its salubrity. Between the external form and fashion of these two lives, between the Catholic Mdlle. de Guérin's *nadalet* at the Languedoc Christmas, her chapel of moss at Easter-time, her daily reading of the life of a saint, carrying her to the most diverse times, places, and peoples,—her quoting, when she wants to fix her mind upon the staunchness which the religious aspirant needs, the words of Saint Macedonius to a hunter whom he met in the mountains, "I pursue after God, as you pursue after game," —her quoting, when she wants to break a village girl of disobedience to her mother, the story of the ten disobedient children whom at Hippo Saint Augustine saw palsied;—between all this and the bare, blank, narrowly English setting of Miss Tatham's Protes-tantism, her "union in church-fellowship with the worshippers at Hawley Square Chapel, Margate;" her "singing with soft, sweet voice, the animating lines—

> 'My Jesus to know, and feel His blood flow,
> 'Tis life everlasting, 'tis heaven below;'"

her "young female teachers belonging to the Sunday-school," and her "Mr. Thomas Rowe, a venerable class-leader,"—what a dissimilarity! In the ground of the two lives, a likeness; in all their circumstance, what unlikeness! An unlikeness, it will be said, in that which is non-essential and indifferent. Non-essential,—yes; indifferent,—no. The signal want of grace and charm in English Protestantism's setting of its religious life is not an indifferent matter; it is a real weakness. *This ought ye to have done, and not to have left the other undone.*

I have said that the present tendency of Catholicism,—the Catholicism of the main body of the Catholic clergy and laity,—seems likely to exaggerate rather than to remove all that in this form of religion is most repugnant to reason; but this Catholicism was not that of Mdlle. de Guérin. The insufficiency of her Catholicism comes from a doctrine which Protestantism, too, has adopted, although Protestantism, from its inherent element of freedom, may find it easier to escape from it; a doctrine with a certain attraction for all noble natures, but, in the modern world at any rate, incurably sterile,—the doctrine of the emptiness and nothingness of human life, of the superiority of renouncement to activity, of quietism to energy; the doctrine which makes effort for things on this side of the grave a folly, and joy in things on this side of the grave a sin. But her Catholicism is remarkably free from the faults which Protestants commonly think inseparable from Catholicism; the relation to the priest, the practice of confession, assume, when she speaks of them, an aspect which is not that under which Exeter Hall knows them, but which, —unless one is of the number of those who prefer

regarding that by which men and nations die to re
garding that by which they live,—one is glad to study.
" *La confession*," she says twice in her journal, "*n'est
qu'une expansion du repentir dans l'amour ;*" and her
weekly journey to the confessional in the little church
of Cahuzac is her "*cher pélerinage ;*" the little church
is the place where she has "*laissé tant de misères.*"

"This morning," she writes one 28th of November
"I was up before daylight, dressed quickly, said my
prayers, and started with Marie for Cahuzac. When
we got there, the chapel was occupied, which I was
not sorry for. I like not to be hurried, and to have
time, before I go in, to lay bare my soul before God.
This often takes me a long time, because my thoughts
are apt to be flying about like these autumn leaves.
At ten o'clock I was on my knees, listening to words
the most salutary that were ever spoken ; and I went
away, feeling myself a better being. Every burden
thrown off leaves us with a sense of brightness ; and
when the soul has laid down the load of its sins at
God's feet, it feels as if it had wings. What an
admirable thing is confession ! What comfort, what
light, what strength is given me every time after I
have said, *I have sinned.*"

This blessing of confession is the greater, she says,
"the more the heart of the priest to whom we con-
fide our repentance is like that divine heart which
'has so loved us.' This is what attaches me to M.
Bories." M. Bories was the curé of her parish, a
man no longer young, and of whose loss, when he
was about to leave them, she thus speaks :—

" What a grief for me! how much I lose in losing this faithful guide of my conscience, heart, and mind, of my whole self, which God has appointed to be in his charge, and which let itself be in his charge so gladly! He knew the resolves which God had put in my heart, and I had need of his help to follow them. Our new curé cannot supply his place: he is so young! and then he seems so inexperienced, so undecided! It needs firmness to pluck a soul out of the midst of the world, and to uphold it against the assaults of flesh and blood. It is Saturday, my day for going to Cahuzac; I am just going there, perhaps I shall come back more tranquil. God has always given me some good thing there, in that chapel where I have left behind me so many miseries."

Such is confession for her when the priest is worthy; and, when he is not worthy, she knows how to separate the man from the office :—

" To-day I am going to do something which I dislike; but I will do it, with God's help. Do not think I am on my way to the stake; it is only that I am going to confess to a priest in whom I have not confidence, but who is the only one here. In this act of religion the man must always be separated from the priest, and sometimes the man must be annihilated."

The same clear sense, the same freedom from superstition, shows itself in all her religious life. She tells us, to be sure, how once, when she was a little girl, she stained a new frock, and on praying, in her alarm, to an image of the Virgin which hung in her room,

saw the stains vanish : even the austerest Protestant
will not judge such Mariolatry as this very harshly.
But, in general, the Virgin Mary fills in the religious
parts of her journal no prominent place ; it is Jesus,
not Mary. "Oh, how well has Jesus said : 'Come
unto me, all ye that labour and are heavy laden.' It
is only there, only in the bosom of God, that we can
rightly weep, rightly rid ourselves of our burden."
And again : "The mystery of suffering makes one
grasp the belief of something to be expiated, something to be won. I see it in Jesus Christ, the Man of
Sorrow. *It was necessary that the Son of Man should
suffer.* That is all we know in the troubles and cala-
mities of life."

And who has ever spoken of justification more
impressively and piously than Mdlle. de Guérin speaks
of it, when, after reckoning the number of minutes
she has lived, she exclaims :—

"My God, what have we done with all these
minutes of ours, which thou, too, wilt one day reckon?
Will there be any of them to count for eternal life?
will there be many of them? will there be one of
them? 'If thou, O Lord, wilt be extreme to mark
what is done amiss, O Lord, who may abide it!'
This close scrutiny of our time may well make us
tremble, all of us who have advanced more than a
few steps in life; for God will judge us otherwise
than as he judges the lilies of the field. I have never
been able to understand the security of those who
placed their whole reliance, in presenting themselves
before God, upon a good conduct in the ordinary

relations of human life. As if all our duties were
confined within the narrow sphere of this world! To
be a good parent, a good child, a good citizen, a good
brother or sister, is not enough to procure entrance
into the kingdom of heaven. God demands other
things besides these kindly social virtues of him whom
he means to crown with an eternity of glory."

And, with this zeal for the spirit and power of
religion, what prudence in her counsels of religious
practice; what discernment, what measure! She has
been speaking of the charm of the *Lives of the Saints*,
and she goes on:—

"Notwithstanding this, the *Lives of the Saints* seem
to me, for a great many people, dangerous reading.
I would not recommend them to a young girl, or even
to some women who are no longer young. What one
reads has such power over one's feelings; and these,
even in seeking God, sometimes go astray. Alas, we
have seen it in poor C.'s case. What care one ought
to take with a young person; with what she reads,
what she writes, her society, her prayers,—all of them
matters which demand a mother's tender watchful-
ness! I remember many things I did at fourteen,
which my mother, had she lived, would not have let
me do. I would have done anything for God's sake;
I would have cast myself into an oven, and assuredly
things like that are not God's will; He is not pleased
by the hurt one does to one's health through that
ardent but ill-regulated piety which, while it impairs
the body, often leaves many a fault flourishing. And,
therefore, Saint François de Sales used to say to the

nuns who asked his leave to go bare-foot: Change
your brains and keep your shoes.'"

Meanwhile Maurice, in a five years' absence, and
amid the distractions of Paris, lost, or seemed to his
sister to lose, something of his fondness for his home
and its inmates: he certainly lost his early religious
habits and feelings. It is on this latter loss that
Mdlle. de Guérin's journal oftenest touches,—with
infinite delicacy, but with infinite anguish :—

"Oh, the agony of being in fear for a soul's salvation, who can describe it ! That which caused our
Saviour the keenest suffering, in the agony of his
Passion, was not so much the thought of the torments
he was to endure, as the thought that these torments
would be of no avail for a multitude of sinners ; for
all those who set themselves against their redemption,
or who do not care for it. The mere anticipation of
this obstinacy and this heedlessness had power to
make sorrowful, even unto death, the divine Son of
Man. And this feeling all Christian souls, according
to the measure of faith and love granted them, more
or less share."

Maurice returned to Le Cayla in the summer of
1837, and passed six months there. This meeting
entirely restored the union between him and his
family. "These six months with us," writes his
sister, "he ill, and finding himself so loved by us all,
had entirely reattached him to us. Five years without seeing us, had perhaps made him a little lose
sight of our affection for him ; having found it again,
he met it with all the strength of his own. He had

so firmly renewed, before he left us, all family-ties, that nothing but death could have broken them." The separation in religious matters between the brother and sister gradually diminished, and before Maurice died it had ceased. I have elsewhere spoken of Maurice's religious feeling and his character. It is probable that his divergence from his sister in this sphere of religion was never so wide as she feared, and that his reunion with her was never so complete as she hoped. "His errors were passed," she says, "his illusions were cleared away; by the call of his nature, by original disposition, he had come back to sentiments of order. I knew all, I followed each of his steps; out of the fiery sphere of the passions (which held him but a little moment) I saw him pass into the sphere of the Christian life. It was a beautiful soul, the soul of Maurice." But the illness which had caused his return to Le Cayla reappeared after he got back to Paris in the winter of 1837-8. Again he seemed to recover; and his marriage with a young Creole lady, Mdlle. Caroline de Gervain, took place in the autumn of 1838. At the end of September in that year Mdlle. de Guérin had joined her brother in Paris; she was present at his marriage, and stayed with him and his wife for some months afterwards. Her journal recommences in April 1839. Zealously as she had promoted her brother's marriage, cordial as were her relations with her sister-in-law, it is evident that a sense of loss, of loneliness, invades her, and sometimes weighs her down. She writes in her journal on the 4th of May :—

"God knows when we shall see one another again !
My own Maurice, must it be our lot to live apart, to
find that this marriage which I had so much share in
bringing about, which I hoped would keep us so much
together, leaves us more asunder than ever ? For the
present and for the future, this troubles me more than
I can say.   My sympathies, my inclinations, carry me
more towards you than towards any other member of
our family.   I have the misfortune to be fonder of
you than of anything else in the world, and my heart
had from of old built in you its happiness.   Youth
gone and life declining, I looked forward to quitting
the scene with Maurice.   At any time of life a great
affection is a great happiness ; the spirit comes to take
refuge in it entirely.   O delight and joy which will
never be your sister's portion !   Only in the direction
of God shall I find an issue for my heart to love as
it has the notion of loving, as it has the power of
loving."

From such complainings, in which there is undoubtedly something morbid,—complainings which
she herself blamed, to which she seldom gave way,
but which, in presenting her character, it is not just
to put wholly out of sight,—she was called by the
news of an alarming return of her brother's illness.
For some days the entries in the journal show her
agony of apprehension.   "He coughs, he coughs still !
Those words keep echoing for ever in my ears, and
pursue me wherever I go ; I cannot look at the leaves
on the trees without thinking that the winter will
come, and then the consumptive die."   She went to

him, and brought him back by slow stages to Le Cayla, dying. He died on the 19th of July 1839.

Thenceforward the energy of life ebbed in her; but the main chords of her being, the chord of affection, the chord of religious longing, the chord of intelligence, the chord of sorrow, gave, so long as they answered to the touch at all, a deeper and finer sound than ever. Always she saw before her, "that beloved pale face;" "that beautiful head, with all its different expressions, smiling, speaking, suffering, dying," regarded her always :—

"I have seen his coffin in the same room, in the same spot where I remember seeing, when I was a very little girl, his cradle, when I was brought home from Gaillac, where I was then staying, for his christening. This christening was a grand one, full of rejoicing, more than that of any of the rest of us; specially marked. I enjoyed myself greatly, and went back to Gaillac next day, charmed with my new little brother. Two years afterwards I came home, and brought with me a frock for him of my own making. I dressed him in the frock, and took him out with me along by the warren at the north of the house, and there he walked a few steps alone,—his first walking alone,—and I ran with delight to tell my mother the news: 'Maurice, Maurice has begun to walk by himself!'—Recollections which, coming back to-day, break one's heart."

The shortness and suffering of her brother's life filled her with an agony of pity. "Poor beloved soul, you have had hardly any happiness here below;

your life has been so short, your repose so rare. O
God, uphold me, establish my heart in thy faith!
Alas, I have too little of this supporting me! How
we have gazed at him and loved him, and kissed him,
—his wife, and we, his sisters; he lying lifeless in his
bed, his head on the pillow as if he were asleep! Then
we followed him to the churchyard, to the grave, to
his last resting-place, and prayed over him, and wept
over him; and we are here again, and I am writing
to him again, as if he were staying away from home,
as if he were in Paris. My beloved one, can it be,
shall we never see one another again on earth?"

But in heaven?—and here, though love and hope
finally prevailed, the very passion of the sister's longing sometimes inspired torturing inquietudes:—

"I am broken down with misery. I want to see
him. Every moment I pray to God to grant me this
grace. Heaven, the world of spirits, is it so far from
us? O depth, O mystery of the other life which
separates us! I, who was so eagerly anxious about
him, who wanted so to know all that happened to
him,—wherever he may be now, it is over! I follow
him into the three abodes; I stop wistfully before the
place of bliss, I pass on to the place of suffering,—to
the gulf of fire. My God, my God, no! Not there
let my brother be! not there! And he is not: his
soul, the soul of Maurice, among the lost . . . horrible
fear, no! But in purgatory, where the soul is cleansed
by suffering, where the failings of the heart are ex
piated, the doubtings of the spirit, the half-yieldings
to evil? Perhaps my brother is there and suffers, and

calls to us amidst his anguish of repentance, as he used
to call to us amidst his bodily suffering: 'Help me,
you who love me.' Yes, beloved one, by prayer. I
will go and pray; prayer has been such a power to
me, and I will pray to the end. Prayer! Oh! and
prayer for the dead; it is the dew of purgatory."

Often, alas, the gracious dew would not fall; the
air of her soul was parched; the arid wind, which
was somewhere in the depths of her being, blew.
She marks in her journal the 1st of May, "this return
of the loveliest month in the year," only to keep up
the old habit; even the month of May can no longer
give her any pleasure: "*Tout est changé*—all is changed."
She is crushed by "the misery which has nothing good
in it, the tearless, dry misery, which bruises the heart
like a hammer."

"I am dying to everything. I am dying of a slow
moral agony, a condition of unutterable suffering.
Lie there, my poor journal! be forgotten with all this
world which is fading away from me. I will write
here no more until I come to life again, until God
re-awakens me out of this tomb in which my soul lies
buried. Maurice, my beloved! it was not thus with
me when I had *you!* The thought of Maurice could
revive me from the most profound depression: to
have him in the world was enough for me. With
Maurice, to be buried alive would have not seemed
dull to me."

And, as a burden to this funereal strain, the old
vide et néant of Bossuet, profound, solemn, sterile:—

"So beautiful in the morning, and in the evening,

that ! how the thought disenchants one, and turns one from the world ! I can understand that Spanish grandee who, after lifting up the winding-sheet of a beautiful queen, threw himself into the cloister and became a great saint. I would have all my friends at La Trappe, in the interest of their eternal welfare. Not that in the world one cannot be saved, not that there are not in the world duties to be discharged as sacred and as beautiful as there are in the cloister, but . . . ."

And there she stops, and a day or two afterwards her journal comes to an end. A few fragments, a few letters carry us on a little later, but after the 22d of August 1845 there is nothing. To make known her brother's genius to the world was the one task she set herself after his death ; in 1840 came Madame Sand's noble tribute to him in the *Revue des Deux Mondes ;* then followed projects of raising a yet more enduring monument to his fame, by collecting and publishing his scattered compositions ; these projects I have already said, were baffled ;—Mdlle. de Guérin's letter of the 22d of August 1845 relates to this disappointment. In silence, during nearly three years more, she faded away at Le Cayla. She died on the 31st of May 1848.

M. Trebutien has accomplished the pious task in which Mdlle. de Guérin was baffled, and has established Maurice's fame ; by publishing this journal he has established Eugénie's also. She was very different from her brother ; but she too, like him, had that in her which preserves a reputation. Her soul had the same characteristic quality as his talent,—*distinction*. Of this quality the world is impatient; it chafes against it, rails at it, insults it, hates it;—it ends by receiving its influence, and by undergoing its law. This quality at last inexorably corrects the world's blunders, and fixes the world's ideals. It procures that the popular poet shall not finally pass for a Pindar, nor the popular historian for a Tacitus, nor the popular preacher for a Bossuet. To the circle of spirits marked by this rare quality, Maurice and Eugénie de Guérin belong; they will take their place in the sky which these inhabit, and shine close to one another, *lucida sidera*.

V.

HEINRICH HEINE.

"I know not if I deserve that a laurel-wreath should one day be laid on my coffin. Poetry, dearly as I have loved it, has always been to me but a divine plaything. I have never attached any great value to poetical fame; and I trouble myself very little whether people praise my verses or blame them. But lay on my coffin a *sword;* for I was a brave soldier in the Liberation War of humanity."

Heine had his full share of love of fame, and cared quite as much as his brethren of the *genus irritabile* whether people praised his verses or blamed them. And he was very little of a hero. Posterity will certainly decorate his tomb with the emblem of the laurel rather than with the emblem of the sword. Still, for his contemporaries, for us, for the Europe of the present century, he is significant chiefly for the reason which he himself in the words just quoted assigns. He is significant because he was, if not pre-eminently a brave, yet a brilliant, a most effective soldier in the Liberation War of humanity.

To ascertain the master-current in the literature of an epoch, and to distinguish this from all minor currents, is one of the critic's highest functions; in discharging it he shows how far he possesses the most indispensable quality of his office, — justness of spirit. The living writer who has done most to make England acquainted with German authors, a man of genius, but to whom precisely this one quality of justness of spirit is perhaps wanting,—I mean Mr. Carlyle,—seems to me in the result of his labours on German literature to afford a proof how very necessary to the critic this quality is. Mr. Carlyle has spoken admirably of Goethe; but then Goethe stands before all men's eyes, the manifest centre of German literature; and from this central source many rivers flow. Which of these rivers is the main stream? which of the courses of spirit which we see active in Goethe is the course which will most influence the future, and attract and be continued by the most powerful of Goethe's successors?—that is the question. Mr. Carlyle attaches, it seems to me, far too much importance to the romantic school of Germany,— Tieck, Novalis, Jean Paul Richter,—and gives to these writers, really gifted as two, at any rate, of them are, an undue prominence. These writers, and others with aims and a general tendency the same as theirs, are not the real inheritors and continuators of Goethe's power; the current of their activity is not the main current of German literature after Goethe. Far more in Heine's works flows this main current; Heine, far more than Tieck or Jean Paul Richter, is the continuator of that which, in Goethe's varied activity, is the most powerful and vital; on Heine, of all German authors who survived Goethe, incomparably the largest portion of Goethe's mantle fell. I do not forget that when Mr. Carlyle was dealing with German literature, Heine, though he was clearly risen above the horizon, had not shone forth with all his strength; I do not forget, too, that after ten or twenty years many things may come out plain before the critic which before were hard to be discerned by him; and assuredly no one would dream of imputing it as a fault to Mr. Carlyle that twenty years ago he mistook the central current in German literature, overlooked the rising Heine, and attached undue importance to that romantic school which Heine was to destroy; one may rather note it as a misfortune, sent perhaps as a delicate chastisement to a critic, who,— man of genius as he is, and no one recognises his genius more admirably than I do,—has, for the functions of the critic, a little too much of the self-will and eccentricity of a genuine son of Great Britain.

Heine is noteworthy, because he is the most important German successor and continuator of Goethe in Goethe's most important line of activity. And which of Goethe's lines of activity is this?—His line of activity as "a soldier in the war of liberation of humanity."

Heine himself would hardly have admitted this affiliation, though he was far too powerful-minded a man to decry, with some of the vulgar German liberals, Goethe's genius. "The wind of the Paris

Revolution," he writes after the three days of 1830, "blew about the candles a little in the dark night of Germany, so that the red curtains of a German throne or two caught fire; but the old watchmen, who do the police of the German kingdoms, are already bringing out the fire engines, and will keep the candles closer snuffed for the future. Poor, fast-bound German people, lose not all heart in thy bonds! The fashionable coating of ice melts off from my heart, my soul quivers and my eyes burn, and that is a disadvantageous state of things for a writer, who should control his subject-matter and keep himself beautifully objective, as the artistic school would have us, and as Goethe has done; he has come to be eighty years old doing this, and minister, and in good condition:—poor German people! that is thy greatest man!"

But hear Goethe himself: "If I were to say what I had really been to the Germans in general, and to the young German poets in particular, I should say I had been their *liberator*."

Modern times find themselves with an immense system of institutions, established facts, accredited dogmas, customs, rules, which have come to them from times not modern. In this system their life has to be carried forward; yet they have a sense that this system is not of their own creation, that it by no means corresponds exactly with the wants of their actual life, that, for them, it is customary, not rational. The awakening of this sense is the awakening of the modern spirit. The modern spirit is now awake

almost everywhere; the sense of want of correspondence between the forms of modern Europe and its
spirit, between the new wine of the eighteenth and
nineteenth centuries, and the old bottles of the
eleventh and twelfth centuries, or even of the sixteenth and seventeenth, almost every one now per-
ceives; it is no longer dangerous to affirm that this
want of correspondence exists; people are even beginning to be shy of denying it. To remove this
want of correspondence is beginning to be the settled
endeavour of most persons of good sense. Dissolvents
of the old European system of dominant ideas and
facts we must all be, all of us who have any power
of working; what we have to study is that we may
not be acrid dissolvents of it.

And how did Goethe, that grand dissolvent in an
age when there were fewer of them than at present,
proceed in his task of dissolution, of liberation of the
modern European from the old routine? He shall
tell us himself. "Through me the German poets
have become aware that, as man must live from
within outwards, so the artist must work from within
outwards, seeing that, make what contortions he will,
he can only bring to light his own individuality. I
can clearly mark where this influence of mine has
made itself felt; there arises out of it a kind of poetry
of nature, and only in this way is it possible to be
original."

My voice shall never be joined to those which
decry Goethe, and if it is said that the foregoing is a
lame and impotent conclusion to Goethe's declaration

that he had been the liberator of the Germans in general, and of the young German poets in particular, I say it is not. Goethe's profound, imperturbable naturalism is absolutely fatal to all routine thinking; he puts the standard, once for all, inside every man instead of outside him; when he is told, such a thing must be so, there is immense authority and custom in favour of its being so, it has been held to be so for a thousand years, he answers with Olympian politeness, "But *is* it so? is it so to *me?*" Nothing could be more really subversive of the foundations on which the old European order rested; and it may be remarked that no persons are so radically detached from this order, no persons so thoroughly modern, as those who have felt Goethe's influence most deeply. If it is said that Goethe professes to have in this way deeply influenced but a few persons, and those persons poets, one may answer that he could have taken no better way to secure, in the end, the ear of the world; for poetry is simply the most beautiful, impressive, and widely effective mode of saying things, and hence its importance. Nevertheless the process of liberation, as Goethe worked it, though sure, is undoubtedly slow; he came, as Heine says, to be eighty years old in thus working it, and at the end of that time the old Middle-Age machine was still creaking on, the thirty German courts and their chamberlains subsisted in all their glory; Goethe himself was a minister, and the visible triumph of the modern spirit over prescription and routine seemed as far off as ever. It was the year 1830; the German sovereigns had passed the preceding fifteen years in breaking the promises of freedom they had made to their subjects when they wanted their help in the final struggle with Napoleon.   Great events were happening in France ; the revolution, defeated in 1815, had arisen from its defeat, and was wresting from its adversaries the power. Heinrich Heine, a young man of genius, born at Hamburg,[1] and with all the culture of Germany, but by race a Jew ; with warm sympathies for France, whose revolution had given to his race the rights of citizenship, and whose rule had been, as is well known, popular in the Rhine provinces, where he passed his youth ; with a passionate admiration for the great French Emperor, with a passionate contempt for the sovereigns who had overthrown him, for their agents, and for their policy,—Heinrich Heine was in 1830 in no humour for any such gradual process of liberation from the old order of things as that which Goethe had followed. His counsel was for open war. Taking that terrible modern weapon, the pen, in his hand, he passed the remainder of his life in one fierce battle. What was that battle ? the reader will ask. It was a life and death battle with Philistinism.

Philistinism !—we have not the expression in English. Perhaps we have not the word because we have so much of the thing. At Soli, I imagine, they did not talk of solecisms ; and here, at the very headquarters of Goliath, nobody talks of Philistinism. The French have adopted the term *épicier* (grocer), to designate the sort of being whom the Germans desig-

1 Heine's birthplace was not Hamburg, but Düs eldorf.—ED

nate by the term Philistine ; but the French term,—
besides that it casts a slur upon a respectable class,
composed of living and susceptible members, while
the original Philistines are dead and buried long ago,
—is really, I think, in itself much less apt and expressive than the German term. Efforts have been
made to obtain in English some term equivalent to
Philister or *épicier;* Mr. Carlyle has made several such
efforts : " respectability with its thousand gigs," he
says ;—well, the occupant of every one of these gigs
is, Mr Carlyle means, a Philistine. However, the
word *respectable* is far too valuable a word to be thus
perverted from its proper meaning; if the English are
ever to have a word for the thing we are speaking of,
—and so prodigious are the changes which the modern
spirit is introducing, that even we English shall perhaps one day come to want such a word,—I think we
had much better take the term *Philistine* itself.

Philistine must have originally meant, in the mind
of those who invented the nickname, a strong, dogged,
unenlightened opponent of the chosen people, of the
children of the light. The party of change, the would-
be remodellers of the old traditional European order,
the invokers of reason against custom, the representatives of the modern spirit in every sphere where it is
applicable, regarded themselves, with the robust self-
confidence natural to reformers as a chosen people, as
children of the light. They regarded their adversaries
as humdrum people, slaves to routine, enemies to
light ; stupid and oppressive, but at the same time
very strong. This explains the love which Heine,

that Paladin of the modern spirit, has for France; it
explains the preference which he gives to France over
Germany: "the French," he says, "are the chosen
people of the new religion, its first gospels and dogmas
have been drawn up in their language; Paris is
the new Jerusalem, and the Rhine is the Jordan
which divides the consecrated land of freedom from
the land of the Philistines." He means that the
French, as a people, have shown more accessibility to
ideas than any other people; that prescription and
routine have had less hold upon them than upon any
other people; that they have shown most readiness
to move and to alter at the bidding (real or supposed)
of reason. This explains, too, the detestation which
Heine had for the English: "I might settle in England," he says, in his exile, "if it were not that I
should find there two things, coal-smoke and Englishmen; I cannot abide either." What he hated in the
English was the "ächtbrittische Beschränktheit," as he
calls it,—the *genuine British narrowness.* In truth, the
English, profoundly as they have modified the old
Middle-Age order, great as is the liberty which they
have secured for themselves, have in all their changes
proceeded, to use a familiar expression, by the rule of
thumb; what was intolerably inconvenient to them they
have suppressed, and as they have suppressed it, not
because it was irrational, but because it was practically
inconvenient, they have seldom in suppressing it ap-
pealed to reason, but always, if possible, to some pre-
cedent, or form, or letter, which served as a convenient
instrument for their purpose, and which saved them

from the necessity of recurring to general principles.
They have thus become, in a certain sense, of all
people the most inaccessible to ideas and the most im-
patient of them; inaccessible to them, because of their
want of familiarity with them; and impatient of them
because they have got on so well without them, that
they despise those who, not having got on as well as
themselves, still make a fuss for what they themselves
have done so well without. But there has certainly
followed from hence, in this country, somewhat of a
general depression of pure intelligence: Philistia has
come to be thought by us the true Land of Promise,
and it is anything but that; the born lover of ideas.
the born hater of commonplaces, must feel in this
country, that the sky over his head is of brass and
iron. The enthusiast for the idea, for reason, values
reason, the idea, in and for themselves; he values
them, irrespectively of the practical conveniences
which their triumph may obtain for him; and the
man who regards the possession of these practical
conveniences as something sufficient in itself, something which compensates for the absence or surrender
of the idea, of reason, is, in his eyes, a Philistine.
This is why Heine so often and so mercilessly attacks
the liberals; much as he hates conservatism he hates
Philistinism even more, and whoever attacks conservatism itself ignobly, not as a child of light, not in the
name of the idea, is a Philistine. Our Cobbett is thus
for him, much as he disliked our clergy and aristocracy whom Cobbett attacked, a Philistine with six
fingers on every hand and on every foot six toes, four

and-twenty in number: a Philistine, the staff of whose
spear is like a weaver's beam. Thus he speaks of him:—

"While I translate Cobbett's words, the man himself comes bodily before my mind's eye, as I saw him
at that uproarious dinner at the Crown and Anchor
Tavern, with his scolding red face and his radical
laugh, in which venomous hate mingles with a mocking exultation at his enemies' surely approaching
downfall. He is a chained cur, who falls with equal
fury on every one whom he does not know, often
bites the best friend of the house in his calves, barks
incessantly, and just because of this incessantness of
his barking cannot get listened to, even when he barks
at a real thief. Therefore the distinguished thieves
who plunder England do not think it necessary to
throw the growling Cobbett a bone to stop his mouth.
This makes the dog furiously savage, and he shows
all his hungry teeth. Poor old Cobbett! England's
dog! I have no love for thee, for every vulgar nature
my soul abhors; but thou touchest me to the inmost
soul with pity, as I see how thou strainest in vain to
break loose and to get at those thieves, who make off
with their booty before thy very eyes, and mock at
thy fruitless springs and thine impotent howling."

There is balm in Philistia as well as in Gilead. A
chosen circle of children of the modern spirit, perfectly emancipated from prejudice and commonplace,
regarding the ideal side of things in all its efforts for
change, passionately despising half-measures and con-
descension to human folly and obstinacy,—with a
bewildered, timid, torpid multitude behind,—conducts

a country to the government of Herr von Bismarck.
A nation regarding the practical side of things in its
efforts for change, attacking not what is irrational,
but what is pressingly inconvenient, and attacking
this as one body, "moving altogether if it move at
all," and treating children of light like the very
harshest of stepmothers, comes to the prosperity and
liberty of modern England. For all that, however,
Philistia (let me say it again) is not the true promised
land, as we English commonly imagine it to be; and
our excessive neglect of the idea, and consequent in-
aptitude for it, threatens us, at a moment when the
idea is beginning to exercise a real power in human
society, with serious future inconvenience, and, in the
meanwhile, cuts us off from the sympathy of other
nations, which feel its power more than we do.

But, in 1830, Heine very soon found that the fire-
engines of the German governments were too much
for his direct efforts at incendiarism. "What demon
drove me," he cries, "to write my *Reisebilder*, to edit
a newspaper, to plague myself with our time and its
interests, to try and shake the poor German Hodge
out of his thousand years' sleep in his hole? What
good did I get by it? Hodge opened his eyes, only
to shut them again immediately; he yawned, only to
begin snoring again the next minute louder than ever;
he stretched his stiff ungainly limbs, only to sink
down again directly afterwards, and lie like a dead
man in the old bed of his accustomed habits. I must
have rest; but where am I to find a resting-place?
In Germany I can no longer stay."

This is Heine's jesting account of his own efforts to rouse Germany : now for his pathetic account of them ; it is because he unites so much wit with so much pathos that he is so effective a writer :—

"The Emperor Charles the Fifth sate in sore straits, in the Tyrol, encompassed by his enemies. All his knights and courtiers had forsaken him ; not one came to his help. I know not if he had at that time the cheese face with which Holbein has painted him for us. But I am sure that under lip of his, with its contempt for mankind, stuck out even more than it does in his portraits. How could he but contemn the tribe which in the sunshine of his prosperity had fawned on him so devotedly, and now, in his dark distress, left him all alone ? Then suddenly his door opened, and there came in a man in disguise, and, as he threw back his cloak, the Kaiser recognised in him his faithful Conrad von der Rosen, the court jester, This man brought him comfort and counsel, and he was the court jester !

"O German fatherland ! dear German people ! I am thy Conrad von der Rosen. The man whose proper business was to amuse thee, and who in good times should have catered only for thy mirth, makes his way into thy prison in time of need ; here, under my cloak, I bring thee thy sceptre and crown ; dost thou not recognise me, my Kaiser ? If I cannot free thee, I will at least comfort thee, and thou shalt at least have one with thee who will prattle with thee about thy sorest affliction, and whisper courage to thee, and love thee, and whose best joke and best

blood shall be at thy service. For thou, my people,
art the true Kaiser, the true lord of the land ; thy
will is sovereign, and more legitimate far than that
purple *Tel est notre plaisir*, which invokes a divine
right with no better warrant than the anointings of
shaven and shorn jugglers ; thy will, my people, is
the sole rightful source of power. Though now thou
liest down in thy bonds, yet in the end will thy rightful cause prevail; the day of deliverance is at hand,
a new time is beginning. My Kaiser, the night is
over, and out there glows the ruddy dawn.

" 'Conrad von der Rosen, my fool, thou art mis-
taken ; perhaps thou takest a headsman's gleaming
axe for the sun, and the red of dawn is only blood.'

" 'No, my Kaiser, it is the sun, though it is rising
in the west; these six thousand years it has always
risen in the east ; it is high time there should come a
change.'

" 'Conrad von der Rosen, my fool, thou hast lost
the bells out of thy red cap, and it has now such an
odd look, that red cap of thine !'

" 'Ah, my Kaiser, thy distress has made me shake
my head so hard and fierce, that the fool's bells have
dropped off my cap; the cap is none the worse for that.'

" 'Conrad von der Rosen, my fool, what is that
noise of breaking and cracking outside there ?'

" 'Hush ! that is the saw and the carpenter's axe,
and soon the doors of thy prison will be burst open,
and thou wilt be free, my Kaiser !'

" 'Am I then really Kaiser ? Ah, I forgot, it is
the fool who tells me so !'

"'Oh, sigh not, my dear master, the air of thy prison makes thee so desponding! when once thou hast got thy rights again, thou wilt feel once more the bold imperial blood in thy veins, and thou wilt be proud like a Kaiser, and violent, and gracious, and unjust, and smiling, and ungrateful, as princes are.'

"'Conrad von der Rosen, my fool, when I am free, what wilt thou do then?'

"'I will then sew new bells on to my cap.'

"'And how shall I recompense thy fidelity?'

"'Ah, dear master, by not leaving me to die in a ditch!'"

I wish to mark Heine's place in modern European literature, the scope of his activity, and his value. I cannot attempt to give here a detailed account of his life, or a description of his separate works. In May 1831 he went over his Jordan, the Rhine, and fixed himself in his new Jerusalem, Paris. There, henceforward, he lived, going in general to some French watering-place in the summer, but making only one or two short visits to Germany during the rest of his life. His works, in verse and prose, succeeded each other without stopping; a collected edition of them, filling seven closely-printed octavo volumes, has been published in America;[1] in the collected editions of few people's works is there so little to skip. Those who wish for a single good specimen of him should read his first important work, the work which made his reputation, the *Reisebilder*, or "Travelling Sketches:" prose and

---

[1] A complete edition has at last appeared in Germany.

verse, wit and seriousness, are mingled in it, and the mingling of these is characteristic of Heine, and is nowhere to be seen practised more naturally and happily than in his *Reisebilder*. In 1847 his health, which till then had always been perfectly good, gave way. He had a kind of paralytic stroke. His malady proved to be a softening of the spinal marrow : it was incurable ; it made rapid progress. In May 1848, not a year after his first attack, he went out of doors for the last time ; but his disease took more than eight years to kill him. For nearly eight years he lay helpless on a couch, with the use of his limbs gone, wasted almost to the proportions of a child, wasted so that a woman could carry him about ; the sight of one eye lost, that of the other greatly dimmed, and requiring, that it might be exercised, to have the palsied eyelid lifted and held up by the finger ; all this, and, besides this, suffering at short intervals paroxysms of nervous agony. I have said he was not pre-eminently brave ; but in the astonishing force of spirit with which he retained his activity of mind, even his gaiety, amid all his suffering, and went on composing with undiminished fire to the last, he was truly brave. Nothing could clog that aërial lightness. "Pouvez-vous siffler ?" his doctor asked him one day, when he was almost at his last gasp ;—"siffler," as every one knows, has the double meaning of *to whistle* and *to hiss :*—"Hélas ! non," was his whispered answer ; "pas même une comédie de M. Scribe !" M. Scribe is, or was, the favourite dramatist of the French Philistine. "My nerves," he said to some one who asked him about them in 1855, the year of the great Exhibition in Paris, "my nerves are of that quite singularly remarkable miserableness of nature, that I am convinced they would get at the Exhibition the grand medal for pain and misery." He read all the medical books which treated of his complaint. "But," said he to some one who found him thus engaged, "what good this reading is to do me I don't know, except that it will qualify me to give lectures in heaven on the ignorance of doctors on earth about diseases of the spinal marrow." What a matter of grim seriousness are our own ailments to most of us! yet with this gaiety Heine treated his to the end. That end, so long in coming, came at last. Heine died on the 17th of February 1856, at the age of fifty-eight. By his will he forbade that his remains should be transported to Germany. He lies buried in the cemetery of Montmartre, at Paris.

His direct political action was null, and this is neither to be wondered at nor regretted; direct political action is not the true function of literature, and Heine was a born man of letters. Even in his favourite France the turn taken by public affairs was not at all what he wished, though he read French politics by no means as we in England, most of us, read them. He thought things were tending there to the triumph of communism; and to a champion of the idea like Heine, what there is gross and narrow in communism was very repulsive. "It is all of no use," he cried on his death-bed, " the future belongs to our enemies, the Communists, and Louis Napoleon is their John the Baptist." "And yet," —he added with all his old love for that remarkable entity, so full of attraction for him, so profoundly unknown in England, the French people,—"do not believe that God lets all this go forward merely as a grand comedy. Even though the Communists deny him to-day, he knows better than they do, that a time will come when they will learn to believe in him." After 1831, his hopes of soon upsetting the German Governments had died away, and his propagandism took another, a more truly literary, character. It took the character of an intrepid application of the modern spirit to literature. To the ideas with which the burning questions of modern life filled him, he made all his subject-matter minister. He touched all the great points in the career of the human race, and here he but followed the tendency of the wide culture of Germany; but he touched them with a wand which brought them all under a light where the modern eye cares most to see them. and here he gave a lesson to the culture of Germany, —so wide, so impartial, that it is apt to become slack and powerless, and to lose itself in its materials for want of a strong central idea round which to group all its other ideas. So the mystic and romantic school of Germany lost itself in the Middle Ages, was overpowered by their influence, came to ruin by its vain dreams of renewing them. Heine, with a far profounder sense of the mystic and romantic charm of the Middle Age than Goerres, or Brentano, or Arnim, Heine the chief romantic poet of Germany, is yet also much more than a romantic poet; he is a great modern poet, he is not conquered by the Middle Age, he has a talisman by which he can feel,—along with but above the power of the fascinating Middle Age itself,—the power of modern ideas.

A French critic of Heine thinks he has said enough in saying that Heine proclaimed in German countries, with beat of drum, the ideas of 1789, and that at the cheerful noise of his drum the ghosts of the Middle Age took to flight. But this is rather too French an account of the matter. Germany, that vast mine of ideas, had no need to import ideas, as such, from any foreign country; and if Heine had carried ideas, as such, from France into Germany, he would but have been carrying coals to Newcastle. But that for which France, far less meditative than Germany, is eminent, is the prompt, ardent, and practical application of an idea, when she seizes it, in all departments of human activity which admit it. And that in which Germany most fails, and by failing in which she appears so helpless and impotent, is just the practical application of her innumerable ideas. "When Candide," says Heine himself, "came to Eldorado, he saw in the streets a number of boys who were playing with gold-nuggets instead of marbles. This degree of luxury made him imagine that they must be the king's children, and he was not a little astonished when he found that in Eldorado gold-nuggets are of no more value than marbles are with us, and that the schoolboys play with them. A similar thing happened

to a friend of mine, a foreigner, when he came to
Germany and first read German books. He was
perfectly astounded at the wealth of ideas which he
found in them; but he soon remarked that ideas in
Germany are as plentiful as gold-nuggets in Eldorado,
and that those writers whom he had taken for intellectual princes, were in reality only common schoolboys." Heine was, as he calls himself, a "Child of
the French Revolution," an "Initiator," because he
vigorously assured the Germans that ideas were not
counters or marbles, to be played with for their own
sake; because he exhibited in literature modern ideas
applied with the utmost freedom, clearness, and originality. And therefore he declared that the great task
of his life had been the endeavour to establish a
cordial relation between France and Germany. It
is because he thus operates a junction between the
French spirit, and German ideas and German culture,
that he founds something new, opens a fresh period,
and deserves the attention of criticism far more than
the German poets his contemporaries, who merely
continue an old period till it expires. It may be
predicted that in the literature of other countries,
too, the French spirit is destined to make its influence
felt,—as an element, in alliance with the native spirit,
of novelty and movement,—as it has made its influence felt in German literature; fifty years hence a
critic will be demonstrating to our grandchildren how
this phenomenon has come to pass.

We in England, in our great burst of literature
during the first thirty years of the present century,

had no manifestation of the modern spirit, as this spirit manifests itself in Goethe's works or Heine's. And the reason is not far to seek. We had neither the German wealth of ideas, nor the French enthusiasm for applying ideas. There reigned in the mass of the nation that inveterate inaccessibility to ideas, that Philistinism,—to use the German nickname,—which reacts even on the individual genius that is exempt from it. In our greatest literary epoch, that of the Elizabethan age, English society at large was accessible to ideas, was permeated by them, was vivified by them, to a degree which has never been reached in England since. Hence the unique greatness in English literature of Shakspeare and his contemporaries. They were powerfully upheld by the intellectual life of their nation; they applied freely in literature the then modern ideas,—the ideas of the Renascence and the Reformation. A few years afterwards the great English middle class, the kernel of the nation, the class whose intelligent sympathy had upheld a Shakspeare, entered the prison of Puritanism, and had the key turned on its spirit there for two hundred years. *He enlargeth a nation*, says Job, *and straiteneth it again.*

In the literary movement of the beginning of the nineteenth century the signal attempt to apply freely the modern spirit was made in England by two members of the aristocratic class, Byron and Shelley. Aristocracies are, as such, naturally impenetrable by ideas; but their individual members have a high courage and a turn for breaking bounds; and a man

of genius, who is the born child of the idea, happening
to be born in the aristocratic ranks, chafes against the
obstacles which prevent him from freely developing
it. But Byron and Shelley did not succeed in their
attempt freely to apply the modern spirit in English
literature; they could not succeed in it; the resistance
to baffle them, the want of intelligent sympathy to
guide and uphold them, were too great. Their literary creation, compared with the literary creation of
Shakspeare and Spenser, compared with the literary
creation of Goethe and Heine, is a failure. The
best literary creation of that time in England proceeded from men who did not make the same bold
attempt as Byron and Shelley. What, in fact, was
the career of the chief English men of letters, their
contemporaries? The gravest of them, Wordsworth,
retired (in Middle-Age phrase) into a monastery. I
mean, he plunged himself in the inward life, he
voluntarily cut himself off from the modern spirit.
Coleridge took to opium. Scott became the historio-
grapher-royal of feudalism. Keats passionately gave
himself up to a sensuous genius, to his faculty for
interpreting nature; and he died of consumption at
twenty-five. Wordsworth, Scott, and Keats have
left admirable works; far more solid and complete
works than those which Byron and Shelley have left.
But their works have this defect,—they do not belong
to that which is the main current of the literature of
modern epochs, they do not apply modern ideas to
life; they constitute, therefore, *minor currents*, and all
other literary work of our day, however popular,

which has the same defect, also constitutes but a
minor current.   Byron and Shelley will long be remembered, long after the inadequacy of their actual
work is clearly recognised for their passionate, their
Titanic effort to flow in the main stream of modern
literature ; their names will be greater than their
writings ; *stat magni nominis umbra.*

Heine's literary good fortune was superior to that
of Byron and Shelley.   His theatre of operations was
Germany, whose Philistinism does not consist in her
want of ideas, or in her inaccessibility to ideas, for she
teems with them and loves them, but, as I have said,
in her feeble and hesitating application of modern
ideas to life.   Heine's intense modernism, his absolute
freedom, his utter rejection of stock classicism and
stock romanticism, his bringing all things under the
point of view of the nineteenth century, were understood and laid to heart by Germany, through virtue
of her immense, tolerant intellectualism, much as
there was in all Heine said to affront and wound
Germany.   The wit and ardent modern spirit of
France Heine joined to the culture, the sentiment,
the thought of Germany.   This is what makes him so
remarkable ; his wonderful clearness, lightness, and
freedom, united with such power of feeling, and
width of range.   Is there anywhere keener wit than
in his story of the French abbé who was his tutor,
and who wanted to get from him that *la religion* is
French for *der Glaube :* " Six times did he ask me the
question : ' Henry, what is *der Glaube* in French ?'
and six times, and each time with a greater burst of

tears, did I answer him—'It is *le crédit.*' And at
the seventh time, his face purple with rage, the in-
furiated questioner screamed out: 'It is *la religion ;*'
and a rain of cuffs descended upon me, and all the
other boys burst out laughing. Since that day I have
never been able to hear *la religion* mentioned, without
feeling a tremor run through my back, and my cheeks
grow red with shame." Or in that comment on the
fate of Professor Saalfeld, who had been addicted to
writing furious pamphlets against Napoleon, and who
was a professor at Göttingen, a great seat, according
to Heine, of pedantry and Philistinism : "It is
curious," says Heine, "the three greatest adversaries
of Napoleon have all of them ended miserably.
Castlereagh cut his own throat ; Louis the Eighteenth
rotted upon his throne ; and Professor Saalfeld is
still a professor at Göttingen." It is impossible to go
beyond that.

What wit, again, in that saying which every one
has heard : "The Englishman loves liberty like his
lawful wife, the Frenchman loves her like his mistress,
the German loves her like his old grandmother."
But the turn Heine gives to this incomparable saying
is not so well known ; and it is by that turn he shows
himself the born poet he is,—full of delicacy and
tenderness, of inexhaustible resource, infinitely new
and striking :—

"And yet, after all, no one can ever tell how
things may turn out. The grumpy Englishman, in
an ill-temper with his wife, is capable of some day
putting a rope round her neck, and taking her to

be sold at Smithfield. The inconstant Frenchman
may become unfaithful to his adored mistress, and be
seen fluttering about the Palais Royal after another.
*But the German will never quite abandon his old grand-
mother ;* he will always keep for her a nook by the
chimney-corner, where she can tell her fairy stories
to the listening children."

Is it possible to touch more delicately and happily
both the weakness and the strength of Germany ;—
pedantic, simple, enslaved, free, ridiculous, admirable
Germany ?

And Heine's verse,—his *Lieder ?* Oh, the comfort,
after dealing with French people of genius, irresistibly
impelled to try and express themselves in verse,
launching out into a deep which destiny has sown
with so many rocks for them,—the comfort of coming
to a man of genius, who finds in verse his freest and
most perfect expression, whose voyage over the deep
of poetry destiny makes smooth ! After the rhythm,
to us, at any rate, with the German paste in our
composition, so deeply unsatisfying, of—

> " Ah ! que me dites-vous, et que vous dit mon âme ?
> Que dit le ciel à l'aube et la flamme à la flamme ?"

what a blessing to arrive at rhythms like—

> " Take, oh, take those lips away,
> That so sweetly were forsworn—"

or—

> "Siehst sehr sterbeblässlich aus,
> Doch getrost ! du bist zu Haus—"

in which one's soul can take pleasure ! The magic
of Heine's poetical form is incomparable ; he chiefly

uses a form of old German popular poetry, a ballad-
form which has more rapidity and grace than any
ballad-form of ours; he employs this form with the
most exquisite lightness and ease, and yet it has at
the same time the inborn fulness, pathos, and old-
world charm of all true forms of popular poetry.
Thus in Heine's poetry, too, one perpetually blends
the impression of French modernism and clearness,
with that of German sentiment and fulness; and to
give this blended impression is, as I have said, Heine's
great characteristic. To feel it, one must read him;
he gives it in his form as well as in his contents, and
by translation I can only reproduce it so far as his
contents give it. But even the contents of many of
his poems are capable of giving a certain sense of it.
Here, for instance, is a poem in which he makes his
profession of faith to an innocent beautiful soul, a
sort of Gretchen, the child of some simple mining
people having their hut among the pines at the foot
of the Hartz Mountains, who reproaches him with not
holding the old articles of the Christian creed :—

"Ah, my child, while I was yet a little boy, while
I yet sate upon my mother's knee, I believed in God
the Father, who rules up there in Heaven, good and
great ;

"Who created the beautiful earth, and the beautiful men and women thereon ; who ordained for sun,
moon, and stars their courses.

"When I got bigger, my child, I comprehended
yet a great deal more than this, and comprehended,
and grew intelligent ; and I believe on the Son also ;

"On the beloved Son, who loved us, and revealed love to us; and, for his reward, as always happens, was crucified by the people.

"Now, when I am grown up, have read much, have travelled much, my heart swells within me, and with my whole heart I believe on the Holy Ghost.

"The greatest miracles were of his working, and still greater miracles doth he even now work; he burst in sunder the oppressor's stronghold, and he burst in sunder the bondsman's yoke.

"He heals old death-wounds, and renews the old right; all mankind are one race of noble equals before him.

"He chases away the evil clouds and the dark cobwebs of the brain, which have spoilt love and joy for us, which day and night have loured on us.

"A thousand knights, well harnessed, has the Holy Ghost chosen out to fulfil his will, and he has put courage into their souls.

"Their good swords flash, their bright banners wave; what, thou wouldst give much, my child, to look upon such gallant knights?

"Well, on me, my child, look! kiss me, and look boldly upon me! one of those knights of the Holy Ghost am I."

One has only to turn over the pages of his *Romancero*,—a collection of poems written in the first years of his illness, with his whole power and charm still in them, and not, like his latest poems of all, painfully touched by the air of his *Matrazzen-gruft*, his "mattress-grave"—to see Heine's width of range

the most varied figures succeed one another,—Rhamp-
sinitus, Edith with the Swan Neck, Charles the First,
Marie Antoinette, King David, a heroine of *Mabille*,
Melisanda of Tripoli, Richard Cœur de Lion, Pedro
the Cruel, Firdusi, Cortes, Dr. Döllinger;—but never
does Heine attempt to be *hübsch objectiv*, "beautifully
objective," to become in spirit an old Egyptian, or an
old Hebrew, or a Middle-Age knight, or a Spanish
adventurer, or an English royalist; he always remains
Heinrich Heine, a son of the nineteenth century.   To
give a notion of his tone, I will quote a few stanzas at
the end of the *Spanish Atridœ*, in which he describes,
in the character of a visitor at the court of Henry of
Transtamare at Segovia, Henry's treatment of the
children of his brother, Pedro the Cruel.   Don Diego
Albuquerque, his neighbour, strolls after dinner
through the castle with him :

"In the cloister-passage, which leads to the kennels
where are kept the king's hounds, that with their
growling and yelping let you know a long way off
where they are,

"There I saw, built into the wall, and with a strong
iron grating for its outer face, a cell like a cage.

"Two human figures sate therein, two young boys;
chained by the leg, they crouched in the dirty straw.

"Hardly twelve years old seemed the one, the
other not much older ; their faces fair and noble, but
pale and wan with sickness.

"They were all in rags, almost naked ; and their
lean bodies showed wounds, the marks of ill-usage ;
both of them shivered with fever

"They looked up at me out of the depth of their misery ; 'who,' I cried in horror to Don Diego, 'are these pictures of wretchedness ?'

"Don Diego seemed embarrassed; he looked round to see that no one was listening; then he gave a deep sigh ; and at last, putting on the easy tone of a man of the world, he said :

"'These are a pair of king's sons, who were early left orphans ; the name of their father was King Pedro, the name of their mother, Maria de Padilla.

"'After the great battle of Navarette, when Henry of Transtamare had relieved his brother, King Pedro, of the troublesome burden of the crown,

"'And likewise of that still more troublesome burden, which is called life, then Don Henry's victorious magnanimity had to deal with his brother's children.

"'He has adopted them, as an uncle should ; and he has given them free quarters in his own castle.

"'The room which he has assigned to them is certainly rather small, but then it is cool in summer, and not intolerably cold in winter.

"'Their fare is rye-bread, which tastes as sweet as if the goddess Ceres had baked it express for her beloved Proserpine.

"'Not unfrequently, too, he sends a scullion to them with garbanzos, and then the young gentlemen know that it is Sunday in Spain.

"'But it is not Sunday every day, and garbanzos do not come every day ; and the master of the hounds gives them the treat of his whip.

" 'For the master of the hounds, who has under his superintendence the kennels and the pack, and the nephews' cage also,

" 'Is the unfortunate husband of that lemon-faced woman with the white ruff, whom we remarked to-day at dinner.

" 'And she scolds so sharp, that often her husband snatches his whip, and rushes down here, and gives it to the dogs and to the poor little boys.

" 'But his majesty has expressed his disapproval of such proceedings, and has given orders that for the future his nephews are to be treated differently from the dogs.

" 'He has determined no longer to entrust the disciplining of his nephews to a mercenary stranger, but to carry it out with his own hands.'

"Don Diego stopped abruptly; for the seneschal of the castle joined us, and politely expressed his hope that we had dined to our satisfaction."

Observe how the irony of the whole of that, finishing with the grim innuendo of the last stanza but one, is at once truly masterly and truly modern.

No account of Heine is complete which does not notice the Jewish element in him. His race he treated with the same freedom with which he treated everything else, but he derived a great force from it, and no one knew this better than he himself. He has excellently pointed out how in the sixteenth century there was a double renascence,—a Hellenic renascence and a Hebrew renascence,—and how both have been great powers ever since. He himself had in him both the spirit of Greece and the spirit of Judæa; both these spirits reach the infinite, which is the true goal of all poetry and all art,—the Greek spirit by beauty, the Hebrew spirit by sublimity. By his perfection of literary form, by his love of clearness, by his love of beauty, Heine is Greek; by his intensity, by his untamableness, by his "longing which cannot be uttered," he is Hebrew. Yet what Hebrew ever treated the things of the Hebrews like this ?—

"There lives at Hamburg, in a one-roomed lodging in the Baker's Broad Walk, a man whose name is Moses Lump; all the week he goes about in wind and rain, with his pack on his back, to earn his few shillings; but when on Friday evening he comes home, he finds the candlestick with seven candles lighted, and the table covered with a fair white cloth, and he puts away from him his pack and his cares, and he sits down to table with his squinting wife and yet more squinting daughter, and eats fish with them, fish which has been dressed in beautiful white garlic sauce, sings therewith the grandest psalms of King David, rejoices with his whole heart over the deliverance of the children of Israel out of Egypt, rejoices, too, that all the wicked ones who have done the children of Israel hurt, have ended by taking themselves off; that King Pharaoh, Nebuchadnezzar, Haman, Antiochus, Titus, and all such people, are well dead, while he, Moses Lump, is yet alive, and eating fish with wife and daughter; and I can tell you, Doctor, the fish is delicate and the man is happy he has no call to torment himself about culture, he sits contented in his religion and in his green bed-gown, like Diogenes in his tub, he contemplates with satisfaction his candles, which he on no account will snuff for himself ; and I can tell you, if the candles burn a little dim, and the snuffers-woman, whose business it is to snuff them, is not at hand, and Rothschild the Great were at that moment to come in, with all his brokers, bill discounters, agents, and chief clerks, with whom he conquers the world, and Rothschild were to say : 'Moses Lump, ask of me what favour you will, and it shall be granted you ;'— Doctor, I am convinced, Moses Lump would quietly answer : 'Snuff me those candles !' and Rothschild the Great would exclaim with admiration : 'If I were not Rothschild, I would be Moses Lump.' "

There Heine shows us his own people by its comic side ; in the poem of the *Princess Sabbath* he shows it to us by a more serious side. The Princess Sabbath, "the *tranquil Princess*, pearl and flower of all beauty, fair as the Queen of Sheba, Solomon's bosom friend, that blue stocking from Ethiopia, who wanted to shine by her *esprit*, and with her wise riddles made herself in the long run a bore" (with Heine the sarcastic turn is never far off), this princess has for her betrothed a prince whom sorcery has transformed into an animal of lower race, the Prince Israel.

"A dog with the desires of a dog, he wallows all the week long in the filth and refuse of life, amidst the jeers of the boys in the street.

"But every Friday evening, at the twilight hour.

suddenly the magic passes off, and the dog becomes once more a human being.

"A man with the feelings of a man, with head and heart raised aloft, in festal garb, in almost clean garb, he enters the halls of his Father.

"Hail, beloved halls of my royal Father! Ye tents of Jacob, I kiss with my lips your holy door-posts!"

Still more he shows us this serious side in his beautiful poem on Jehuda ben Halevy, a poet belonging to "the great golden age of the Arabian, Old-Spanish, Jewish school of poets," a contemporary of the troubadours :—

"He, too,—the hero whom we sing,—Jehuda ben Halevy, too, had his lady-love; but she was of a special sort.

"She was no Laura, whose eyes, mortal stars, in the cathedral on Good Friday kindled that world-renowned flame.

"She was no châtelaine, who in the blooming glory of her youth presided at tourneys, and awarded the victor's crown.

"No casuistess in the Gay Science was she, no lady *doctrinaire*, who delivered her oracles in the judgment-chamber of a Court of Love.

"She, whom the Rabbi loved, was a woe-begone poor darling, a mourning picture of desolation . . and her name was Jerusalem."

Jehuda ben Halevy, like the Crusaders, makes his pilgrimage to Jerusalem; and there, amid the ruins, sings a song of Sion which has become famous among his people :—

"That lay of pearled tears is the wide-famed Lament, which is sung in all the scattered tents of Jacob throughout the world.

"On the ninth day of the month which is called Ab, on the anniversary of Jerusalem's destruction by Titus Vespasianus.

"Yes, that is the song of Sion, which Jehuda ben Halevy sang with his dying breath amid the holy ruins of Jerusalem.

"Barefoot, and in penitential weeds, he sate there upon the fragment of a fallen column; down to his breast fell,

"Like a gray forest, his hair; and cast a weird shadow on the face which looked out through it,—his troubled pale face, with the spiritual eyes.

"So he sate and sang, like unto a seer out of the foretime to look upon; Jeremiah, the Ancient, seemed to have risen out of his grave.

"But a bold Saracen came riding that way, aloft on his barb, lolling in his saddle, and brandishing a naked javelin;

"Into the breast of the poor singer he plunged his deadly shaft, and shot away like a winged shadow.

"Quietly flowed the Rabbi's life-blood, quietly he sang his song to an end; and his last dying sigh was Jerusalem!"

But, most of all, Heine shows us this side in a strange poem describing a public dispute, before King Pedro and his Court, between a Jewish and a Christian champion, on the merits of their respective faiths. In the strain of the Jew all the fierceness of the old

Hebrew genius, all its rigid defiant Monotheism, appear :—

"Our God has not died like a poor innocent lamb for mankind ; he is no gushing philanthropist, no declaimer.

"Our God is not love, caressing is not his line ; but he is a God of thunder, and he is a God of revenge.

"The lightnings of his wrath strike inexorably every sinner, and the sins of the fathers are often visited upon their remote posterity.

"Our God, he is alive, and in his hall of heaven he goes on existing away, throughout all the eternities.

"Our God, too, is a God in robust health, no myth, pale and thin as sacrificial wafers, or as shadows by Cocytus.

"Our God is strong. In his hand he upholds sun, moon, and stars ; thrones break, nations reel to and fro, when he knits his forehead.

"Our God loves music, the voice of the harp and the song of feasting ; but the sound of church-bells he hates, as he hates the grunting of pigs."

Nor must Heine's sweetest note be unheard,—his plaintive note, his note of melancholy. Here is a strain which came from him as he lay, in the winter night, on his "mattress-grave" at Paris, and let his thoughts wander home to Germany, "the great child, entertaining herself with her Christmas-tree." "Thou tookest,"—he cries to the German exile,—

"Thou tookest thy flight towards sunshine and

happiness; naked and poor returnest thou back. German truth, German shirts,—one gets them worn to tatters in foreign parts.

"Deadly pale are thy looks, but take comfort, thou art at home! one lies warm in German earth, warm as by the old pleasant fireside.

"Many a one, alas, became crippled, and could get home no more! longingly he stretches out his arms; God have mercy upon him!"

God have mercy upon him! for what remain of the days of the years of his life are few and evil. "Can it be that I still actually exist? My body is so shrunk that there is hardly anything of me left but my voice, and my bed makes me think of the melodious grave of the enchanter Merlin, which is in the forest of Broceliand in Brittany, under high oaks whose tops shine like green flames to heaven. Ah, I envy thee those trees, brother Merlin, and their fresh waving! for over my mattress-grave here in Paris no green leaves rustle; and early and late I hear nothing but the rattle of carriages, hammering, scolding, and the jingle of the piano. A grave without rest, death without the privileges of the departed, who have no longer any need to spend money, or to write letters, or to compose books. What a melancholy situation!"

He died, and has left a blemished name; with his crying faults,—his intemperate susceptibility, his unscrupulousness in passion, his inconceivable attacks on his enemies, his still more inconceivable attacks on his friends, his want of generosity, his sensuality his incessant mocking,—how could it be otherwise? Not only was he not one of Mr. Carlyle's "respectable" people, he was profoundly *dis*respectable; and not even the merit of not being a Philistine can make up for a man's being that. To his intellectual deliverance there was an addition of something else wanting, and that something else was something immense; the old-fashioned, laborious, eternally needful moral deliverance. Goethe says that he was deficient in *love*; to me his weakness seems to be not so much a deficiency in love as a deficiency in self-respect, in true dignity of character. But on this negative side of one's criticism of a man of great genius, I for my part, when I have once clearly marked that this negative side is and must be there, have no pleasure in dwelling. I prefer to say of Heine something positive. He is not an adequate interpreter of the modern world. He is only a brilliant soldier in the Liberation War of humanity. But, such as he is, he is (and posterity too, I am quite sure, will say this), in the European poetry of that quarter of a century which follows the death of Goethe, incomparably the most important figure.

What a spendthrift, one is tempted to cry, is Nature! With what prodigality, in the march of generations, she employs human power, content to gather almost always little result from it, sometimes none! Look at Byron, that Byron whom the present generation of Englishmen are forgetting; Byron, the greatest natural force, the greatest elementary power, I cannot but think which has appeared in our literature since Shakspeare. And what became of this

wonderful production of nature? He shattered himself, he inevitably shattered himself to pieces against
the huge, black, cloud-topped, interminable precipice
of British Philistinism. But Byron, it may be said,
was eminent only by his genius, only by his inborn
force and fire; he had not the intellectual equip-
ment of a supreme modern poet; except for his genius
he was an ordinary nineteenth-century English gentleman, with little culture and with no ideas. Well,
then, look at Heine. Heine had all the culture of
Germany; in his head fermented all the ideas of
modern Europe. And what have we got from Heine?
A half-result, for want of moral balance, and of nobleness of soul and character. That is what I say;
there is so much power, so many seem able to run
well, so many give promise of running well;—so few
reach the goal, so few are chosen. *Many are called,
few chosen.*

VI.

PAGAN AND MEDIÆVAL RELIGIOUS SENTIMENT.

I READ the other day in the *Dublin Review* :—"We Catholics are apt to be cowed and scared by the lordly oppression of public opinion, and not to bear our selves as men in the face of the anti-Catholic society of England. It is good to have an habitual conscious-ness that the public opinion of Catholic Europe looks upon Protestant England with a mixture of impatience and compassion, which more than balances the arro-gance of the English people towards the Catholic Church in these countries."

The Holy Catholic Church, Apostolic and Roman, can take very good care of herself, and I am not going to defend her against the scorns of Exeter Hall. Catholicism is not a great visible force in this country, and the mass of mankind will always treat lightly even things the most venerable, if they do not pre-sent themselves as visible forces before its eyes. In Catholic countries, as the *Dublin Review* itself says with triumph, they make very little account of the great

ness of Exeter Hall. The majority has eyes only for
the things of the majority, and in England the immense majority is Protestant. And yet, in spite of
all the shocks which the feeling of a good Catholic,
like the writer in the *Dublin Review*, has in this Protestant country inevitably to undergo, in spite of the
contemptuous insensibility to the grandeur of Rome
which he finds so general and so hard to bear, how
much has he to console him, how many acts of homage
to the greatness of his religion may he see if he has
his eyes open! I will tell him of one of them. Let him
go in London to that delightful spot, that Happy
Island in Bloomsbury, the reading-room of the British Museum. Let him visit its sacred quarter, the
region where its theological books are placed. I am
almost afraid to say what he will find there, for fear
Mr. Spurgeon, like a second Caliph Omar, should give
the library to the flames. He will find an immense
Catholic work, the collection of the Abbé Migne,
lording it over that whole region, reducing to insignificance the feeble Protestant forces which hang upon
its skirts. Protestantism is duly represented, indeed;
the librarian knows his business too well to suffer it
to be otherwise; all the varieties of Protestantism are
there; there is the Library of Anglo-Catholic Theology, learned, decorous, exemplary, but a little unin-
teresting; there are the works of Calvin, rigid, militant, menacing; there are the works of Dr. Chalmers,
the Scotch thistle valiantly doing duty as the rose of
Sharon, but keeping something very Scotch about it
all the time; there are the works of Dr. Channing,

the last word of religious philosophy in a land where
every one has some culture, and where superiorities
are discountenanced,—the flower of moral and intelligent mediocrity. But how are all these divided against
one another, and how, though they were all united,
are they dwarfed by the Catholic Leviathan, their
neighbour! Majestic in its blue and gold unity, this
fills shelf after shelf and compartment after compartment, its right mounting up into heaven among the
white folios of the *Acta Sanctorum*, its left plunging
down into hell among the yellow octavos of the *Law
Digest*. Everything is there, in that immense *Patro-
logiæ Cursus Completus*, in that *Encyclopédie Théologique*,
that *Nouvelle Encyclopédie Théologique*, that *Troisième
Encyclopédie Théologique;* religion, philosophy, history,
biography, arts, sciences, bibliography, gossip.   The
work embraces the whole range of human interests;
like one of the great Middle-Age Cathedrals, it is in
itself a study for a life. Like the net in Scripture,
it drags everything to land, bad and good, lay and
ecclesiastical, sacred and profane, so that it be but
matter of human concern.   Wide-embracing as the
power whose product it is! a power, for history at
any rate, eminently *the Church;* not, perhaps, the
Church of the future, but indisputably the Church of
the past and, in the past, the Church of the multitude.

This is why the man of imagination—nay, and the
philosopher too, in spite of her propensity to burn
him—will always have a weakness for the Catholic
Church; because of the rich treasures of human life

which have been stored within her pale. The mention of other religious bodies, or of their leaders, at once calls up in our mind the thought of men of a definite type as their adherents; the mention of Catholicism suggests no such special following. Anglicanism suggests the English episcopate; Calvin's name suggests Dr Candlish; Chalmers's, the Duke of Argyll; Channing's, Boston society; but Catholicism suggests,— what shall I say?—all the pell-mell of the men and women of Shakspeare's plays. This abundance the Abbé Migne's collection faithfully reflects. People talk of this or that work which they would choose, if they were to pass their life with only one; for my part I think I would choose the Abbé Migne's collection. *Quicquid agunt homines,*—everything, as I have said, is there. Do not seek in it splendour of form, perfection of editing; its paper is common, its type ugly, its editing indifferent, its printing careless. The greatest and most baffling crowd of misprints I ever met with in my life occurs in a very important page of the introduction to the *Dictionnaire des Apocryphes.* But this is just what you have in the world,—quantity rather than quality. Do not seek in it impartiality, the critical spirit; in reading it you must do the criticism for yourself; it loves criticism as little as the world loves it. Like the world, it chooses to have things all its own way, to abuse its adversary, to back its own notion through thick and thin, to put forward all the *pros* for its own notion, to suppress all the *contras;* it does just all that the world does, and all that the critical shrinks from. Open the *Diction-*

naire des Erreurs Sociales : "The religious persecutions
of Henry the Eighth's and Edward the Sixth's time
abated a little in the reign of Mary, to break out
again with new fury in the reign of Elizabeth."
There is a summary of the history of religious persecution under the Tudors ! But how unreasonable
to reproach the Abbé Migne's work with wanting a
criticism, which, by the very nature of things, it cannot have, and not rather to be grateful to it for its
abundance, its variety, its infinite suggestiveness, its
happy adoption, in many a delicate circumstance, of
the urbane tone and temper of the man of the world,
instead of the acrid tone and temper of the fanatic !

Still, in spite of their fascinations, the contents of
this collection sometimes rouse the critical spirit within
one.   It happened that lately, after I had been thinking much of Marcus Aurelius and his times, I took
down the *Dictionnaire des Origines du Christianisme,* to
see what it had to say about paganism and pagans.
I found much what I expected.   I read the article,
Révélation Évangélique, sa Nécessité.   There I found
what a sink of iniquity was the whole pagan world ;
how one Roman fed his oysters on his slaves, how
another put a slave to death that a curious friend
might see what dying was like ; how Galen's mother
tore and bit her waiting-women when she was in a
passion with them.   I found this account of the religion of paganism : "Paganism invented a mob of
divinities with the most hateful character, and attributed to them the most monstrous and abominable
crimes.   It personified in them drunkenness, incest,

kidnapping, adultery, sensuality, knavery, cruelty, and rage." And I found that from this religion there followed such practice as was to be expected: "What must naturally have been the state of morals under the influence of such a religion, which penetrated with its own spirit the public life, the family life, and the individual life of antiquity?"

The colours in this picture are laid on very thick, and I for my part cannot believe that any human societies, with a religion and practice such as those just described, could ever have endured as the societies of Greece and Rome endured, still less have done what the societies of Greece and Rome did. We are not brought far by descriptions of the vices of great cities, or even of individuals driven mad by unbounded means of self-indulgence. Feudal and aristocratic life in Christendom has produced horrors of selfishness and cruelty not surpassed by the grandee of pagan Rome; and then, again, in antiquity there is Marcus Aurelius's mother to set against Galen's. Eminent examples of vice and virtue in individuals prove little as to the state of societies. What, under the first emperors, was the condition of the Roman poor upon the Aventine compared with that of our poor in Spital-fields and Bethnal Green? What, in comfort, morals, and happiness, were the rural population of the Sabine country under Augustus's rule, compared with the rural population of Hertfordshire and Buckingham-shire under the rule of Queen Victoria?

But these great questions are not now for me. Without trying to answer them, I ask myself, when I read such declamation as the foregoing, if I can find anything that will give me a near, distinct sense of the real difference in spirit and sentiment between paganism and Christianity, and of the natural effect of this difference upon people in general. I take a representative religious poem of paganism,—of the paganism which all the world has in its mind when it speaks of paganism. To be a representative poem, it must be one for popular use, one that the multitude listens to. Such a religious poem may be found at the end of one of the best and happiest of Theocritus's idylls, the fifteenth. In order that the reader may the better go along with me in the line of thought I am following, I will translate it; and, that he may see the medium in which religious poetry of this sort is found existing, the society out of which it grows, the people who form it and are formed by it, I will translate the whole, or nearly the whole, of the idyll (it is not long) in which the poem occurs.

The idyll is dramatic. Somewhere about two hundred and eighty years before the Christian era, a couple of Syracusan women, staying at Alexandria, agreed on the occasion of a great religious solemnity, —the feast of Adonis,—to go together to the palace of King Ptolemy Philadelphus, to see the image of Adonis, which the queen Arsinoe, Ptolemy's wife, had had decorated with peculiar magnificence. A hymn, by a celebrated performer, was to be recited over the image. The names of the two women are Gorgo and Praxinoe; their maids, who are mentioned in the poem, are called Eunoe and Eutychis. Gorgo comes

by appointment to Praxinoe's house to fetch her, and
there the dialogue begins :—

Gorgo.—Is Praxinoe at home?

Praxinoe.—My dear Gorgo, at last! Yes, here I
am. Eunoe, find a chair,—get a cushion for it.

Gorgo.—It will do beautifully as it is.

Praxinoe.—Do sit down.

Gorgo.—Oh, this gad-about spirit! I could hardly
get to you, Praxinoe, through all the crowd and all
the carriages. Nothing but heavy boots, nothing but
men in uniform. And what a journey it is! My
dear child, you really live *too* far off.

Praxinoe.—It is all that insane husband of mine.
He has chosen to come out here to the end of the
world, and take a hole of a place,—for a house it is
not,—on purpose that you and I might not be neighbours. He is always just the same;—anything to
quarrel with one! anything for spite!

Gorgo.—My dear, don't talk so of your husband
before the little fellow. Just see how astonished he
looks at you. Never mind, Zopyrio, my pet, she is
not talking about papa.

Praxinoe.—Good heavens! the child does really
understand.

Gorgo.—Pretty papa!

Praxinoe.—That pretty papa of his the other day
(though I told him beforehand to mind what he was
about), when I sent him to a shop to buy soap and
rouge, brought me home salt instead ;—stupid, great,
big, interminable animal!

Gorgo.—Mine is just the fellow to him. . . . But

never mind now, get on your things and let us be off to the palace to see the Adonis. I hear the Queen's decorations are something splendid.

Praxinoe.—In grand people's houses everything is grand. What things you have seen in Alexandria! What a deal you will have to tell to anybody who has never been here!

Gorgo.—Come, we ought to be going.

Praxinoe.—Every day is holiday to people who have nothing to do. Eunoe, pick up your work; and take care, lazy girl, how you leave it lying about again; the cats find it just the bed they like. Come, stir yourself, fetch me some water, quick! I wanted the water first, and the girl brings me the soap. Never mind; give it me. Not all that, extravagant. Now pour out the water;—stupid! why don't you take care of my dress? That will do. I have got my hands washed as it pleased God. Where is the key of the large wardrobe? Bring it here;—quick!

Gorgo.—Praxinoe, you can't think how well that dress, made full, as you have got it, suits you. Tell me, how much did it cost?—the dress by itself, I mean.

Praxinoe.—Don't talk of it, Gorgo: more than eight guineas of good hard money. And about the work on it I have almost worn my life out.

Gorgo.—Well, you couldn't have done better.

Praxinoe.—Thank you. Bring me my shawl, and put my hat properly on my head;—properly. No, child (*to her little boy*), I am not going to take you; there's a bogy on horseback, who bites. Cry as much

as you like; I'm not going to have you lamed for
life. Now we'll start. Nurse, take the little one and
amuse him; call the dog in, and shut the street-door.
(*They go out.*) Good heavens! what a crowd of
people! How on earth are we ever to get through
all this? They are like ants: you can't count them.
My dearest Gorgo, what will become of us? here are
the royal Horse Guards. My good man, don't ride
over me! Look at that bay horse rearing bolt up-
right; what a vicious one! Eunoe, you mad girl, do
take care!—that horse will certainly be the death of
the man on his back. How glad I am now, that I
left the child safe at home!

Gorgo.—All right, Praxinoe, we are safe behind
them; and they have gone on to where they are
stationed.

Praxinoe.—Well, yes, I begin to revive again.
From the time I was a little girl I have had more
horror of horses and snakes than of anything in the
world. Let us get on; here's a great crowd coming
this way upon us.

Gorgo (*to an old woman*).—Mother, are you from the
palace?

Old Woman.—Yes, my dears.

Gorgo.—Has one a tolerable chance of getting there?

Old Woman.—My pretty young lady, the Greeks
got to Troy by dint of trying hard; trying will do
anything in this world.

Gorgo.—The old creature has delivered herself of
an oracle and departed.

Praxinoe.—Women can tell you everything about

everything, Jupiter's marriage with Juno not excepted.

Gorgo.—Look, Praxinoe, what a squeeze at the palace gates!

Praxinoe.—Tremendous! Take hold of me, Gorgo, and you, Eunoe, take hold of Eutychis!—tight hold, or you'll be lost. Here we go in all together. Hold tight to us, Eunoe! Oh, dear! oh, dear! Gorgo, there's my scarf torn right in two. For heaven's sake, my good man, as you hope to be saved, take care of my dress!

Stranger.—I'll do what I can, but it doesn't depend upon me.

Praxinoe.—What heaps of people! They push like a drove of pigs.

Stranger.—Don't be frightened, ma'am, we are all right.

Praxinoe.—May you be all right, my dear sir, to the last day you live, for the care you have taken of us! What a kind, considerate man! There is Eunoe jammed in a squeeze. Push, you goose, push! Capital! We are all of us the right side of the door, as the bridegroom said when he had locked himself in with the bride.

Gorgo.—Praxinoe, come this way. Do but look at that work, how delicate it is!—how exquisite! Why, they might wear it in heaven.

Praxinoe.—Heavenly patroness of needlewomen, what hands were hired to do that work? Who designed those beautiful patterns? They seem to stand up and move about, as if they were real;—as if they were living things, and not needlework. Well, man is a wonderful creature! And look, look, how charming he lies there on his silver couch, with just a soft down on his cheeks, that beloved Adonis,—Adonis, whom one loves even though he is dead!

Another Stranger.—You wretched women, do stop your incessant chatter! Like turtles, you go on for ever. They are enough to kill one with their broad lingo,—nothing but *a, a, a*.

Gorgo.—Lord, where does the man come from? What is it to you if we *are* chatterboxes? Order about your own servants! Do you give orders to Syracusan women? If you want to know, we came originally from Corinth, as Bellerophon did; we speak Peloponnesian. I suppose Dorian women may be allowed to have a Dorian accent.

Praxinoe.—Oh, honey-sweet Proserpine, let us have no more masters than the one we've got! We don't the least care for *you;* pray don't trouble yourself for nothing.

Gorgo.—Be quiet, Praxinoe! That first-rate singer, the Argive woman's daughter, is going to sing the *Adonis* hymn. She is the same who was chosen to sing the dirge last year. We are sure to have something first-rate from *her*. She is going through her airs and graces ready to begin.—

So far the dialogue; and, as it stands in the original, it can hardly be praised too highly. It is a page torn fresh out of the book of human life. What freedom! What animation! What gaiety! What naturalness! It is said that Theocritus, in composing

this poem, borrowed from a work of Sophron, a poet
of an earlier and better time ; but, even if this is so,
the form is still Theocritus's own, and how excellent
is that form, how masterly ! And this in a Greek
poem of the decadence !—for Theocritus's poetry, after
all, is poetry of the decadence.　When such is Greek
poetry of the decadence, what must be Greek poetry
of the prime ?

Then the singer begins her hymn :—

" Mistress, who loveth the haunts of Golgi, and
Idalium, and high-peaked Eryx, Aphrodite that play-
est with gold ! how have the delicate-footed Hours,
after twelve months, brought thy Adonis back to thee
from the ever-flowing Acheron !　Tardiest of the
immortals are the boon Hours, but all mankind wait
their approach with longing, for they ever bring something with them.　O Cypris, Dione's child ! thou
didst change—so is the story among men—Berenice
from mortal to immortal, by dropping ambrosia into
her fair bosom ; and in gratitude to thee for this, O
thou of many names and many temples !　Berenice's
daughter, Arsinoe, lovely Helen's living counterpart,
makes much of Adonis with all manner of braveries.

" All fruits that the tree bears are laid before him,
all treasures of the garden in silver baskets, and ala-
baster boxes, gold-inlaid, of Syrian ointment ; and all
confectionery that cunning women make on their
kneading-tray, kneading up every sort of flowers with
white meal, and all that they make of sweet honey
and delicate oil, and all winged and creeping things
are here set before him.　And there are built for him

green bowers with wealth of tender anise, and little boy-loves flutter about over them, like young nightingales trying their new wings on the tree, from bough to bough. Oh, the ebony, the gold, the eagle of white ivory that bears aloft his cup-bearer to Cronos-born Zeus! And up there, see! a second couch strewn for lovely Adonis, scarlet coverlets softer than sleep itself (so Miletus and the Samian wool-grower will say); Cypris has hers, and the rosy-armed Adonis has his, that eighteen or nineteen-year-old bridegroom. His kisses will not wound, the hair on his lip is yet light.

"Now, Cypris, good-night, we leave thee with thy bridegroom; but to-morrow morning, with the earliest dew, we will one and all bear him forth to where the waves splash upon the sea-strand, and letting loose our locks, and letting fall our robes, with bosoms bare, we will set up this, our melodious strain:

"'Beloved Adonis, alone of the demigods (so men say) thou art permitted to visit both us and Acheron! This lot had neither Agamemnon, nor the mighty moon-struck hero Ajax, nor Hector the first-born of Hecuba's twenty children, nor Patroclus, nor Pyrrhus who came home from Troy, nor those yet earlier Lapithæ and the sons of Deucalion, nor the Pelasgians, the root of Argos and of Pelop's isle. Be gracious to us now, loved Adonis, and be favourable to us for the year to come! Dear to us hast thou been at this coming, dear to us shalt thou be when thou comest again.'"

The poem concludes with a characteristic speech from Gorgo:—

"Praxinoe, certainly women are wonderful things

That lucky woman to know all that ! and luckier still
to have such a splendid voice ! And now we must
see about getting home. My husband has not had
his dinner. That man is all vinegar, and nothing
else ; and if you keep him waiting for his dinner, he's
dangerous to go near. Adieu, precious Adonis, and
may you find us all well when you come next year ! "

So, with the hymn still in her ears, says the incor-
rigible Gorgo.

But what a hymn that is ! Of religious emotion,
in our acceptation of the words, and of the comfort
springing from religious emotion, not a particle. And
yet many elements of religious emotion are contained
in the beautiful story of Adonis. Symbolically treated,
as the thoughtful man might treat it, as the Greek
mysteries undoubtedly treated it, this story was capable of a noble and touching application, and could
lead the soul to elevating and consoling thoughts.
Adonis was the sun in his summer and in his winter
course, in his time of triumph and his time of defeat ;
but in his time of triumph still moving towards his
defeat, in his time of defeat still returning towards
his triumph. Thus he became an emblem of the
power of life and the bloom of beauty, the power of
human life and the bloom of human beauty, hasten-
ing inevitably to diminution and decay, yet in that
very decay finding

> "Hope, and a renovation without end."

But nothing of this appears in the story as prepared
for popular religious use, as presented to the multitude

in a popular religious ceremony. Its treatment is
not devoid of a certain grace and beauty, but it
has nothing whatever that is elevating, nothing
that is consoling, nothing that is in our sense of the
word religious. The religious ceremonies of Christendom, even on occasion of the most joyful and
mundane matters, present the multitude with strains
of profoundly religious character, such as the *Kyrie
eleison* and the *Te Deum.* But this Greek hymn to
Adonis adapts itself exactly to the tone and temper of
a gay and pleasure-loving multitude,—of light-hearted
people, like Gorgo and Praxinoe, whose moral nature
is much of the same calibre as that of Phillina in
Goethe's *Wilhelm Meister,* people who seem never
made to be serious, never made to be sick or sorry.
And, if they happen to be sick or sorry, what will
they do then? But that we have no right to ask.
Phillina, within the enchanted bounds of Goethe's
novel, Gorgo and Praxinoe, within the enchanted
bounds of Theocritus's poem, never will be sick and
sorry, never can be sick and sorry. The ideal, cheerful, sensuous, pagan life is not sick or sorry. No;
yet its natural end is in the sort of life which Pompeii
and Herculaneum bring so vividly before us,—a life
which by no means in itself suggests the thought of
horror and misery, which even, in many ways, grati-
fies the senses and the understanding; but by the
very intensity and unremittingness of its appeal to
the senses and the understanding, by its stimulating
a single side of us too absolutely, ends by fatiguing
and revolting us; ends by leaving us with a sense

of confinement, of oppression, — with a desire for an utter change, for clouds, storms, effusion, and relief.

In the beginning of the thirteenth century, when the clouds and storms had come, when the gay sensuous pagan life was gone, when men were not living by the senses and understanding, when they were looking for the speedy coming of Antichrist, there appeared in Italy, to the north of Rome, in the beautiful Umbrian country at the foot of the Apennines, a figure of the most magical power and charm, St Francis. His century is, I think, the most interesting in the history of Christianity after its primitive age, more interesting than even the century of the Reformation; and one of the chief figures, perhaps the very chief, to which this interest attaches itself, is St. Francis. And why? Because of the profound popular instinct which enabled him, more than any man since the primitive age, to fit religion for popular use. He brought religion to the people. He founded the most popular body of ministers of religion that has ever existed in the Church. He transformed monachism by uprooting the stationary monk, delivering him from the bondage of property, and sending him, as a mendicant friar, to be a stranger and sojourner, not in the wilderness, but in the most crowded haunts of men, to console them and to do them good. This popular instinct of his is at the bottom of his famous marriage with poverty. Poverty and suffering are the condition of the people, the multitude, the immense majority of mankind; and it was towards this *people* that his soul yearned. "He listens," it was said of him, " to those to whom God himself will not listen."

So in return, as no other man he was listened to. When an Umbrian town or village heard of his approach, the whole population went out in joyful procession to meet him, with green boughs, flags, music, and songs of gladness. The master, who began with two disciples, could in his own lifetime (and he died at forty-four) collect to keep Whitsuntide with him, in presence of an immense multitude, five thousand of his Minorites. And thus he found fulfilment to his prophetic cry : "I hear in my ears the sound of the tongues of all the nations who shall come unto us; Frenchmen, Spaniards, Germans, Englishmen. The Lord will make of us a great people, even unto the ends of the earth."

Prose could not satisfy this ardent soul, and he made poetry. Latin was too learned for this simple, popular nature, and he composed in his mother tongue, in Italian. The beginnings of the mundane poetry of the Italians are in Sicily, at the court of kings ; the beginnings of their religious poetry are in Umbria, with St. Francis. His are the humble upper waters of a mighty stream ; at the beginning of the thirteenth century it is St. Francis, at the end, Dante. Now it happens that St. Francis, too, like the Alexandrian songstress, has his hymn for the sun, for Adonis. *Canticle of the Sun, Canticle of the Creatures*,—the poem goes by both names. Like the Alexandrian hymn, it is designed for popular use, but not for use by King Ptolemy's people ; artless in language,

irregular in rhythm, it matches with the childlike
genius that produced it, and the simple natures that
loved and repeated it :—

"O most high, almighty, good Lord God, to thee
belong praise, glory, honour, and all blessing !

"Praised be my Lord God with all his creatures ;
and specially our brother the sun, who brings us the
day, and who brings us the light ; fair is he, and
shining with a very great splendour : O Lord, he
signifies to us thee !

"Praised be my Lord for our sister the moon, and
for the stars, the which he has set clear and lovely in
heaven.

"Praised be my Lord for our brother the wind,
and for air and cloud, calms and all weather, by the
which thou upholdest in life all creatures.

"Praised be my Lord for our sister water, who is
very serviceable unto us, and humble, and precious,
and clean.

"Praised be my Lord for our brother fire, through
whom thou givest us light in the darkness ; and he is
bright, and pleasant, and very mighty, and strong.

"Praised be my Lord for our mother the earth,
the which doth sustain us and keep us, and bringeth
forth divers fruits, and flowers of many colours, and
grass.

"Praised be my Lord for all those who pardon
one another for his love's sake, and who endure weakness and tribulation ; blessed are they who peaceably
shall endure, for thou, O most Highest, shalt give
them a crown !

"Praised be my Lord for our sister, the death of the body, from whom no man escapeth. Woe to him who dieth in mortal sin! Blessed are they who are found walking by thy most holy will, for the second death shall have no power to do them harm.

"Praise ye, and bless ye the Lord, and give thanks unto him, and serve him with great humility."

It is natural that man should take pleasure in his senses. But it is natural, also, that he should take refuge in his heart and imagination from his misery. And when one thinks what human life is for the vast majority of mankind, how little of a feast for their senses it can possibly be, one understands the charm for them of a refuge offered in the heart and imagination. Above all, when one thinks what human life was in the Middle Ages, one understands the charm of such a refuge.

Now, the poetry of Theocritus's hymn is poetry treating the world according to the demand of the senses; the poetry of St. Francis's hymn is poetry treating the world according to the demand of the heart and imagination. The first takes the world by its outward, sensible side; the second by its inward, symbolical side. The first admits as much of the world as is pleasure-giving; the second admits the whole world, rough and smooth, painful and pleasure-giving, all alike, but all transfigured by the power of a spiritual emotion, all brought under a law of super-sensual love, having its seat in the soul. It can thus even say: "Praised be my Lord for *our sister, the death of the body.*"

But these very words are, perhaps, an indication that we are touching upon an extreme. When we see Pompeii, we can put our finger upon the pagan sentiment in its extreme. And when we read of Monte Alverno and the *stigmata;* when we read of the repulsive, because self-caused, sufferings of the end of St. Francis's life; when we find him even saying, "I have sinned against my brother the ass," meaning by these words that he had been too hard upon his own body; when we find him assailed, even himself, by the doubt "whether he who had destroyed himself by the severity of his penances could find mercy in eternity," we can put our finger on the mediæval Christian sentiment in its extreme. Human nature is neither all senses and understanding, nor all heart and imagination. Pompeii was a sign that for humanity at large the measure of sensualism had been overpassed; St. Francis's doubt was a sign that for humanity at large the measure of spiritualism had been overpassed. Humanity, in its violent rebound from one extreme, had swung from Pompeii to Monte Alverno; but it was sure not to stay there.

The Renascence is, in part, a return towards the pagan spirit, in the special sense in which I have been using the word pagan; a return towards the life of the senses and the understanding. The Reformation, on the other hand, is the very opposite to this; in Luther there is nothing Greek or pagan; vehemently as he attacked the adoration of St. Francis, Luther had himself something of St. Francis in him; he was a thousand times more akin to St. Francis than to Theocritus or to Voltaire. The Reformation—I do not mean the inferior piece given under that name, by Henry the Eighth and a second-rate company, in this island, but the real Reformation, the German Reformation, Luther's Reformation—was a reaction of the moral and spiritual sense against the carnal and pagan sense ; it was a religious revival like St. Francis's, but this time against the Church of Rome, not within her ; for the carnal and pagan sense had now, in the government of the Church of Rome herself, its prime representative. But the grand reaction against the rule of the heart and imagination, the strong return towards the rule of the senses and understanding, is in the eighteenth century. And this reaction has had no more brilliant champion than a man of the nineteenth, of whom I have already spoken ; a man who could feel not only the pleasurableness but the poetry of the life of the senses (and the life of the senses has its deep poetry) ; a man who, in his very last poem, divided the whole world into " barbarians and Greeks,"—Heinrich Heine. No man has reproached the Monte Alverno extreme in sentiment, the Christian extreme, the heart and imagination subjugating the senses and understanding, more bitterly than Heine ; no man has extolled the Pompeii extreme, the pagan extreme, more rapturously.

" All through the Middle Age these sufferings, this fever, this over-tension lasted ; and we moderns still feel in all our limbs the pain and weakness from them.

Even those of us who are cured have still to live with
a hospital-atmosphere all around us, and find ourselves
as wretched in it as a strong man among the sick.
Some day or other, when humanity shall have got
quite well again, when the body and soul shall have
made their peace together, the fictitious quarrel which
Christianity has cooked up between them will appear
something hardly comprehensible.   The fairer and
happier generations, offspring of unfettered unions,
that will rise up and bloom in the atmosphere of a
religion of pleasure, will smile sadly when they think
of their poor ancestors, whose life was passed in
melancholy abstinence from the joys of this beautiful
earth, and who faded away into spectres, from the
mortal compression which they put upon the warm
and glowing emotions of sense.   Yes, with assurance
I say it, our descendants will be fairer and happier
than we are; for I am a believer in progress, and I
hold God to be a kind being who has intended man
to be happy."

That is Heine's sentiment, in the prime of life, in
the glow of activity, amid the brilliant whirl of Paris.
I will no more blame it than I blamed the sentiment
of the Greek hymn to Adonis. I wish to decide
nothing as of my own authority; the great art of
criticism is to get oneself out of the way and to let
humanity decide. Well, the sentiment of the "religion of pleasure" has much that is natural in it;
humanity will gladly accept it if it can live by it; to
live by it one must never be sick or sorry, and the
old, ideal, limited, pagan world never, I have said.

was sick or sorry, never at least shows itself to us sick
or sorry :—

"What pipes and timbrels! what wild ecstasy!"

For our imagination, Gorgo and Praxinoe cross the
human stage chattering in their blithe Doric,—*like
turtles*, as the cross stranger said,—and keep gaily
chattering on till they disappear. But in the new,
real, immense, post-pagan world,—in the barbarian
world, — the shock of accident is unceasing, the
serenity of existence is perpetually troubled, not even
a Greek like Heine can get across the mortal stage
without bitter calamity. How does the sentiment of
the "religion of pleasure" serve then? does it help,
does it console? Can a man live by it? Heine again
shall answer; Heine just twenty years older, stricken
with incurable disease, waiting for death :—

"The great pot stands smoking before me, but I
have no spoon to help myself. What does it profit
me that my health is drunk at banquets out of gold
cups and in most exquisite wines, if I myself, while
these ovations are going on, lonely and cut off from
the pleasures of the world, can only just wet my lips
with barley-water? What good does it do me that
all the roses of Shiraz open their leaves and burn for
me with passionate tenderness? Alas! Shiraz is some
two thousand leagues from the Rue d'Amsterdam,
where in the solitude of my sick chamber all the
perfume I smell is that of hot towels. Alas! the
mockery of God is heavy upon me! The great
author of the universe, the Aristophanes of Heaven,
has determined to make the petty earthly author, the

so-called Aristophanes of Germany, feel to his heart's core what pitiful needle-pricks his cleverest sarcasms have been, compared with the thunderbolts which his divine humour can launch against feeble mortals ! . . .

"In the year 1340, says the Chronicle of Limburg, all over Germany everybody was strumming and humming certain songs more lovely and delightful than any which had ever yet been known in German countries ; and all people, old and young, the women particularly, were perfectly mad about them, so that from morning till night you heard nothing else. Only, the Chronicle adds, the author of these songs happened to be a young clerk, afflicted with leprosy, and living apart from all the world in a desolate place. The excellent reader does not require to be told how horrible a complaint was leprosy in the Middle Ages, and how the poor wretches who had this incurable plague were banished from society, and had to keep at a distance from every human being. Like living corpses, in a gray gown reaching down to the feet, and with the hood brought over their face, they went about, carrying in their hands an enormous rattle, called Saint Lazarus's rattle. With this rattle they gave notice of their approach, that every one might have time to get out of their way. This poor clerk, then, whose poetical gift the Limburg Chronicle extols, was a leper, and he sate moping in the dismal deserts of his misery, whilst all Germany, gay and tuneful, was praising his songs.

"Sometimes, in my sombre visions of the night, I imagine that I see before me the poor leprosy-stricken

clerk of the Limburg Chronicle, and then from under
his gray hood his distressed eyes look out upon me
in a fixed and strange fashion; but the next instant
he disappears, and I hear dying away in the distance,
like the echo of a dream, the dull creak of Saint
Lazarus's rattle."

We have come a long way from Theocritus there;
the expression of that has nothing of the clear, positive, happy, pagan character; it has much more the
character of one of the indeterminate grotesques of
the suffering Middle Age. Profoundness and power
it has, though at the same time it is not truly poetical;
it is not natural enough for that, there is too much
waywardness in it, too much bravado. But as a condition of sentiment to be popular,—to be a comfort
for the mass of mankind, under the pressure of calamity, to live by,—what a manifest failure is this last
word of the religion of pleasure! One man in many
millions, a Heine, may console himself, and keep himself erect in suffering, by a colossal irony of this sort,
by covering himself and the universe with the red
fire of this sinister mockery; but the many millions
cannot,—cannot if they would. That is where the
sentiment of a religion of sorrow has such a vast
advantage over the sentiment of a religion of pleasure;
in its power to be a general, popular, religious sentiment, a stay for the mass of mankind, whose lives are
full of hardship. It really succeeds in conveying far
more joy, far more of what the mass of mankind are
so much without, than its rival. I do not mean joy
in prospect only, but joy in possession, actual enjoy-

ment of the world.   Mediæval Christianity is reproached with its gloom and austerities ; it assigns
the material world, says Heine, to the devil.   But
yet what a fulness of delight does St. Francis manage
to draw from this material world itself, and from its
commonest and most universally enjoyed elements,—
sun, air, earth, water, plants !   His hymn expresses a
far more cordial sense of happiness, even in the material world, than the hymn of Theocritus.   It is this
which made the fortune of Christianity,—its gladness,
not its sorrow ; not its assigning the spiritual world
to Christ, and the material world to the devil, but
its drawing from the spiritual world a source of joy
so abundant that it ran over upon the material world
and transfigured it.

I have said a great deal of harm of paganism ; and,
taking paganism to mean a state of things which it is
commonly taken to mean, and which did really exist,
no more harm than it well deserved.   Yet I must not
end without reminding the reader, that before this
state of things appeared, there was an epoch in Greek
life,—in pagan life,—of the highest possible beauty
and value.   That epoch by itself goes far towards
making Greece the Greece we mean when we speak
of Greece,—a country hardly less important to mankind than Judæa.   The poetry of later paganism
lived by the senses and understanding ; the poetry
of mediæval Christianity lived by the heart and
imagination.   But the main element of the modern
spirit's life is neither the senses and understanding,
nor the heart and imagination ; it is the imaginative

reason. And there is a century in Greek life,—the century preceding the Peloponnesian war, from about the year 530 to the year 430 B.C.,—in which poetry made, it seems to me, the noblest, the most successful effort she has ever made as the priestess of the imaginative reason, of the element by which the modern spirit, if it would live right, has chiefly to live. Of this effort, of which the four great names are Simonides, Pindar, Æschylus, Sophocles, I must not now attempt more than the bare mention; but it is right, it is necessary, after all I have said, to indicate it. No doubt that effort was imperfect. Perhaps everything, take it at what point in its existence you will, carries within itself the fatal law of its own ulterior development. Perhaps, even of the life of Pindar's time, Pompeii was the inevitable bourne. Perhaps the life of their beautiful Greece could not afford to its poets all that fulness of varied experience, all that power of emotion, which

> '. . . the heavy and the weary weight
> Of all this unintelligible world'

affords the poet of after-times. Perhaps in Sophocles the thinking-power a little overbalances the religious sense, as in Dante the religious sense overbalances the thinking-power. The present has to make its own poetry, and not even Sophocles and his compeers, any more than Dante and Shakspeare, are enough for it. That I will not dispute; nor will I set up the Greek poets, from Pindar to Sophocles, as objects of blind worship. But no other poets so well show to the

poetry of the present the way it must take ; no other
poets have lived so much by the imaginative reason ;
no other poets have made their work so well balanced ;
no other poets, who have so well satisfied the thinking-
power, have so well satisfied the religious sense :—

"Oh ! that my lot may lead me in the path of holy
innocence of word and deed, the path which august
laws ordain, laws that in the highest empyrean had
their birth, of which Heaven is the father alone,
neither did the race of mortal men beget them, nor
shall oblivion ever put them to sleep. The power of
God is mighty in them, and groweth not old."

Let St. Francis,—nay, or Luther either,—beat
that !

VII.

A PERSIAN PASSION PLAY.

EVERYBODY has this last autumn[1] been either seeing the Ammergau Passion Play or hearing about it ; and to find any one who has seen it and not been deeply interested and moved by it, is very rare. The peasants of the neighbouring country, the great and fashionable world, the ordinary tourist, were all at Ammergau, and were all delighted ; but what is said to have been especially remarkable was the affluence there of ministers of religion of all kinds. That Catholic peasants, whose religion has accustomed them to show and spectacle, should be attracted by an admirable scenic representation of the great moments in the history of their religion, was natural ; that tourists and the fashionable world should be attracted by what was at once the fashion and a new sensation of a powerful sort, was natural ; that many of the ecclesiastics present should be attracted there, was natural too. Roman Catholic priests mustered strong, of course. The Protestantism of a great number of

[1] 1871.

the Anglican clergy is supposed to be but languid,
and Anglican ministers at Ammergau were sympa-
thisers to be expected. But Protestant ministers of
the most unimpeachable sort, Protestant Dissenting
ministers, were there, too, and showing favour and
sympathy ; and this, to any one who remembers the
almost universal feeling of Protestant Dissenters in
this country, not many years ago, towards Rome and
her religion,—the sheer abhorrence of Papists and
all their practices,—could not but be striking. It
agrees with what is seen also in literature, in the
writings of Dissenters of the younger and more pro
gressive sort, who show a disposition for regarding
the Church of Rome historically rather than polemic-
ally, a wish to do justice to the undoubted grandeur
of certain institutions and men produced by that
Church, quite novel, and quite alien to the simple
belief of earlier times, that between Protestants and
Rome there was a measureless gulf fixed. Something
of this may, no doubt, be due to that keen eye for
Nonconformist business in which our great bodies of
Protestant Dissenters, to do them justice, are never
wanting ; to a perception that the case against the
Church of England may be yet further improved by
contrasting her with the genuine article in her own
ecclesiastical line, by pointing out that she is neither
one thing nor the other to much purpose, by dilating
on the magnitude, reach, and impressiveness, on the
great place in history, of her rival, as compared with
anything she can herself pretend to. Something of
this there is, no doubt, in some of the modern Pro-

testant sympathy for things Catholic. But in general that sympathy springs, in Churchmen and Dissenters alike, from another and a better cause,—from the spread of larger conceptions of religion, of man, and of history, than were current formerly. We have seen lately in the newspapers, that a clergyman, who in a popular lecture gave an account of the Passion Play at Ammergau, and enlarged on its impressiveness, was admonished by certain remonstrants, who told him it was his business, instead of occupying himself with these sensuous shows, to learn to walk by faith, not by sight, and to teach his fellow-men to do the same. But this severity seems to have excited wonder rather than praise; so far had those wider notions about religion and about the range of our interest in religion, of which I have just spoken, conducted us. To this interest I propose to appeal in what I am going to relate. The Passion Play at Ammergau, with its immense audiences, the seriousness of its actors, the passionate emotion of its spectators, brought to my mind something of which I had read an account lately; something produced, not in Bavaria nor in Christendom at all, but far away in that wonderful East, from which, whatever airs of superiority Europe may justly give itself, all our religion has come, and where religion, of some sort or other, has still an empire over men's feelings such as it has nowhere else. This product of the remote East I wish to exhibit while the remembrance of what has been seen at Ammergau is still fresh; and we will see whether that bringing together of strangers and enemies who once seemed to be as far as the poles asunder, which Ammergau in such a remarkable way effected, does not hold good and find a parallel even in Persia.

Count Gobineau, formerly Minister of France at Teheran and at Athens, published, a few years ago, an interesting book on the present state of religion and philosophy in Central Asia. He is favourably known also by his studies in ethnology. His accomplishments and intelligence deserve all respect, and in his book on religion and philosophy in Central Asia he has the great advantage of writing about things which he has followed with his own observation and inquiry in the countries where they happened. , The chief purpose of his book is to give a history of the career of Mirza Ali Mahommed, a Persian religious reformer, the original *Bâb*, and the founder of *Bâbism*, of which most people in England have at least heard the name. Bâb means *gate*, the door or gate of life ; and in the ferment which now works in the Mahometan East, Mirza Ali Mahommed,—who seems to have been made acquainted by Protestant missionaries with our Scriptures and by the Jews of Shiraz with Jewish traditions, to have studied, besides, the religion of the Ghebers, the old national religion of Persia, and to have made a sort of amalgam of the whole with Mahometanism,—presented himself, about five-and-twenty years ago, as *the door*, *the gate* of life ; found disciples, sent forth writings, and finally became the cause of disturbances which led to his being executed on the 19th of July 1849, in the

citadel of Tabriz. The Bâb and his doctrines are a
theme on which much might be said; but I pass
them by, except for one incident in the Bâb's life,
which I will notice. Like all religious Mahometans,
he made the pilgrimage to Mecca; and his meditations at that centre of his religion first suggested his
mission to him. But soon after his return to Bagdad
he made another pilgrimage; and it was in this pilgrimage that his mission became clear to him, and
that his life was fixed. "He desired"—I will give
an abridgment of Count Gobineau's own words—" to
complete his impressions by going to Kufa, that he
might visit the ruined mosque where Ali was assassinated, and where the place of his murder is still
shown. He passed several days there in meditation.
The place appears to have made a great impression
on him; he was entering on a course which might
and must lead to some such catastrophe as had happened on the very spot where he stood, and where
his mind's eye showed him the Imam Ali lying at his
feet, with his body pierced and bleeding. His followers say that he then passed through a sort of
moral agony which put an end to all the hesitations of
the natural man within him. It is certain that when
he arrived at Shiraz, on his return, he was a changed
man. No doubts troubled him any more: he was
penetrated and persuaded; his part was taken."

This Ali also, at whose tomb the Bâb went through
the spiritual crisis here recorded, is a familiar name
to most of us. In general our knowledge of the East
goes but a very little way; yet almost every one has

at least heard the name of Ali, the Lion of God,
Mahomet's young cousin, the first person, after his
wife, who believed in him, and who was declared by
Mahomet in his gratitude his brother, delegate, and
vicar. Ali was one of Mahomet's best and most
successful captains. He married Fatima, the daughter
of the Prophet; his sons, Hassan and Hussein, were,
as children, favourites with Mahomet, who had no
son of his own to succeed him, and was expected to
name Ali as his successor. He named no successor.
At his death (the year 632 of our era) Ali was passed
over, and the first caliph, or *vicar* and *lieutenant* of
Mahomet in the government of the state, was Abu
Bekr; only the spiritual inheritance of Mahomet, the
dignity of Imam, or *Primate*, devolved by right on
Ali and his children. Ali, lion of God as in war he
was, held aloof from politics and political intrigue,
loved retirement and prayer, was the most pious and
disinterested of men. At Abu-Bekr's death he was
again passed over in favour of Omar. Omar was
succeeded by Othman, and still Ali remained tranquil. Othman was assassinated, and then Ali, chiefly
to prevent disturbance and bloodshed, accepted (A.D.
655) the caliphate. Meanwhile, the Mahometan
armies had conquered Persia, Syria, and Egypt; the
Governor of Syria, Moawiyah, an able and ambitious
man, set himself up as caliph, his title was recognised
by Amrou, the Governor of Egypt, and a bloody and
indecisive battle was fought in Mesopotamia between
Ali's army and Moawiyah's. Gibbon shall tell the
rest :—"In the temple of Mecca three Charegites or

enthusiasts discoursed of the disorders of the church and state; they soon agreed that the deaths of Ali, of Moawiyah, and of his friend Amrou, the Viceroy of Egypt, would restore the peace and unity of religion. Each of the assassins chose his victim, poisoned his dagger, devoted his life, and secretly repaired to the scene of action. Their resolution was equally desperate; but the first mistook the person of Amrou, and stabbed the deputy who occupied his seat; the prince of Damascus was dangerously hurt by the second; Ali, the lawful caliph, in the mosque of Kufa, received a mortal wound from the hand of the third."

The events through which we have thus rapidly run ought to be kept in mind, for they are the elements of Mahometan history: any right understanding of the state of the Mahometan world is impossible without them. For that world is divided into the two great sects of Shiahs and Sunis. The Shiahs are those who reject the first three caliphs as usurpers, and begin with Ali as the first lawful successor of Mahomet; the Sunis recognise Abu-Bekr, Omar, and Othman, as well as Ali, and regard the Shiahs as impious heretics. The Persians are Shiahs, and the Arabs and Turks are Sunis. Hussein, one of Ali's two sons, married a Persian princess, the daughter of Yezdejerd the last of the Sassanian kings, the king whom the Mahometan conquest of Persia expelled; and Persia, through this marriage, became specially connected with the house of Ali. "In the fourth age of the Hegira," says Gibbon, "a tomb, a

temple, a city, arose near the ruins of Kufa. Many
thousands of the Shiahs repose in holy ground at the
feet of the vicar of God ; and the desert is vivified by
the numerous and annual visits of the Persians, who
esteem their devotion not less meritorious than the
pilgrimage of Mecca."

But, to comprehend what I am going to relate
from Count Gobineau, we must push our researches
into Mahometan history a little further than the
assassination of Ali. Moawiyah died in the year
680 of our era, nearly fifty years after the death of
Mahomet. His son Yezid succeeded him on the
throne of the caliphs at Damascus. During the
reign of Moawiyah Ali's two sons, the Imams,
Hassan and Hussein, lived with their families in
religious retirement at Medina, where their grand-
father Mahomet was buried. In them the character
of abstention and renouncement, which we have
noticed in Ali himself, was marked yet more
strongly ; but, when Moawiyah died, the people of
Kufa, the city on the lower Euphrates where Ali
had been assassinated, sent offers to make Hussein
caliph if he would come among them, and to support
him against the Syrian troops of Yezid. Hussein
seems to have thought himself bound to accept the
proposal. He left Medina, and, with his family and
relations, to the number of about eighty persons, set
out on his way to Kufa. Then ensued the tragedy
so familiar to every Mahometan, and to us so little
known, the tragedy of Kerbela. "O death," cries
the bandit-minstrel of Persia, Kurroglou, in his last

song before his execution, " O death, whom didst thou spare? Were even Hassan and Hussein, those footstools of the throne of God on the seventh heaven, spared by thee. *No! thou madest them martyrs at Kerbela.*"

We cannot do better than again have recourse to Gibbon's history for an account of this famous tragedy " Hussein traversed the desert of Arabia with a timorous retinue of women and children; but, as he approached the confines of Irak, he was alarmed by the solitary or hostile face of the country, and suspected either the defection or the ruin of his party. His fears were just; Obeidallah, the governor of Kufa, had extinguished the first sparks of an insurrection; and Hussein, in the plain of Kerbela, was encompassed by a body of 5000 horse, who intercepted his communication with the city and the river. In a conference with the chief of the enemy he proposed the option of three conditions :—that he should be allowed to return to Medina, or be stationed in a frontier garrison against the Turks, or safely conducted to the presence of Yezid. But the commands of the caliph or his lieutenant were stern and absolute, and Hussein was informed that he must either submit as a captive and a criminal to the Commander of the Faithful, or expect the consequences of his rebellion. " Do you think," replied he, " to terrify me with death?" And during the short respite of a night he prepared, with calm and solemn resignation, to encounter his fate. He checked the lamentations of his sister Fatima, who deplored the impending ruin of his house. "Our trust," said Hussein, "is in God alone. All things, both in heaven and earth, must perish and return to their Creator. My brother, my father, my mother, were better than I, and every Mussulman has an example in the Prophet." He pressed his friends to consult their safety by a timely flight; they unanimously refused to desert or survive their beloved master, and their courage was fortified by a fervent prayer and the assurance of paradise. On the morning of the fatal day he mounted on horseback, with his sword in one hand and the Koran in the other; the flanks and rear of his party were secured by the tent-ropes and by a deep trench, which they had filled with lighted fagots, according to the practice of the Arabs. The enemy advanced with reluctance; and one of their chiefs deserted, with thirty followers, to claim the partnership of inevitable death. In every close onset or single combat the despair of the Fatimites was invincible; but the surrounding multitudes galled them from a distance with a cloud of arrows, and the horses and men were successively slain. A truce was allowed on both sides for the hour of prayer; and the battle at length expired by the death of the last of the companions of Hussein."

The details of Hussein's own death will come better presently; suffice it at this moment to say he was slain, and that the women and children of his family were taken in chains to the Caliph Yezid at Damascus. Gibbon concludes the story thus: "In a distant age and climate, the tragic scene of the death of Hussein will awaken the sympathy of the coldest reader. On the annual festival of his martyrdom, in the devout pilgrimage to his sepulchre, his Persian votaries abandon their souls to the religious phrenzy of sorrow and indignation."

Thus the tombs of Ali and of his son, the Meshed Ali and the Meshed Hussein, standing some thirty miles apart from one another in the plain of the Euphrates, had, when Gibbon wrote, their yearly pilgrims and their tribute of enthusiastic mourning. But Count Gobineau relates, in his book of which I have spoken, a development of these solemnities which was unknown to Gibbon. Within the present century there has arisen, on the basis of this story of the martyrs of Kerbela, a drama, a Persian national drama, which Count Gobineau, who has seen and heard it, is bold enough to rank with the Greek drama as a great and serious affair, engaging the heart and life of the people who have given birth to it; while the Latin, English, French, and German drama is, he says, in comparison a mere pastime or amusement, more or less intellectual and elegant. To me it seems that the Persian *tazyas*—for so these pieces are called—find a better parallel in the Ammergau Passion Play than in the Greek drama. They turn entirely on one subject—the sufferings of the *Family of the Tent*, as the Imam Hussein and the company of persons gathered around him at Kerbela are called. The subject is sometimes introduced by a prologue, which may perhaps one day, as the need of variety is more felt, become a piece by itself; but at present the prologue leads invariably to the martyrs. For instance : the Emperor Tamerlane, in his conquering progress through the world, arrives at Damascus. The keys of the city are brought to him by the governor ; but the governor is a descendant of one of the murderers of the Imam Hussein ; Tamerlane is informed of it, loads him with reproaches, and drives him from his presence. The emperor presently sees the governor's daughter splendidly dressed, thinks of the sufferings of the holy women of the Family of the Tent, and upbraids and drives her away as he did her father. But after this he is haunted by the great tragedy which has been thus brought to his mind, and he cannot sleep and cannot be comforted. He calls his vizier, and his vizier tells him that the only way to soothe his troubled spirit is to see a *tazya*. And so the *tazya* commences. Or, again (and this will show how strangely, in the religious world which is now occupying us, what is most familiar to us is blended with that of which we know nothing) : Joseph and his brethren appear on the stage, and the old Bible story is transacted. Joseph is thrown into the pit and sold to the merchants, and his blood-stained coat is carried by his brothers to Jacob ; Jacob is then left alone, weeping and bewailing himself ; the angel Gabriel enters, and reproves him for his want of faith and constancy, telling him that what he suffers is not a hundredth part of what Ali, Hussein, and the children of Hussein will one day suffer. Jacob seems to doubt it ; Gabriel, to convince him, orders the angels to per-

form a *tazya* of what will one day happen at Kerbela.
And so the *tazya* commences.

These pieces are given in the first ten days of the
month of Moharrem, the anniversary of the martyrdom at Kerbela. They are so popular that they now
invade other seasons of the year also ; but this is the
season when the world is given up to them. King
and people, every one is in mourning ; and at night
and while the *tazyas* are not going on, processions
keep passing, the air resounds with the beating of
breasts and with litanies of " O Hassan ! Hussein ! "
while the Seyids,—a kind of popular friars claiming
to be descendants of Mahomet, and in whose incessant
popularising and amplifying of the legend of Kerbela
in their homilies during pilgrimages and at the tombs
of the martyrs, the *tazyas*, no doubt, had their origin,
—keep up by their sermons and hymns the enthusiasm which the drama of the day has excited. It
seems as if no one went to bed ; and certainly no one
who went to bed could sleep. Confraternities go in
procession with a black flag and torches, every man
with his shirt torn open, and beating himself with
the right hand on the left shoulder in a kind of
measured cadence to accompany a canticle in honour
of the martyrs. These processions come and take
post in the theatres where the Seyids are preaching.
Still more noisy are the companies of dancers, striking a kind of wooden castanets together, at one time
in front of their breasts, at another time behind their
heads, and marking time with music and dance to a
dirge set up by the bystanders. in which the names

of the Imams perpetually recur as a burden.   Noisiest
of all are the Berbers, men of a darker skin and
another race, their feet and the upper part of their
body naked, who carry, some of them tambourines
and cymbals, others iron chains and long needles.
One of their race is said to have formerly derided the
Imams in their affliction, and the Berbers now appear
in expiation of that crime.   At first their music and
their march proceed slowly together, but presently
the music quickens, the chain and needle-bearing
Berbers move violently round, and begin to beat
themselves with their chains and to prick their arms
and cheeks with the needles—first gently, then with
more vehemence ; till suddenly the music ceases, and
all stops.   So we are carried back, on this old
Asiatic soil, where beliefs and usages are heaped
layer upon layer and ruin upon ruin, far past the
martyred Imams, past Mahometanism, past Christianity, to the priests of Baal gashing themselves
with knives and to the worship of Adonis.

The *tekyas*, or theatres for the drama which calls
forth these celebrations, are constantly multiplying.
The king, the great functionaries, the towns, wealthy
citizens like the king's goldsmith, or any private
person who has the means and the desire, provide
them.   Every one sends contributions; it is a religious act to furnish a box or to give decorations for a
tekya ; and as religious offerings, all gifts down to the
smallest are accepted.   There are tekyas for not more
than three or four hundred spectators, and there are
tekyas for three or four thousand.   At Ispahan there

are representations which bring together more than
twenty thousand people. At Teheran, the Persian
capital, each quarter of the town has its tekyas,
every square and open place is turned to account for
establishing them, and spaces have been expressly
cleared, besides, for fresh tekyas. Count Gobineau
describes particularly one of these theatres,—a tekya
of the best class, to hold an audience of about four
thousand,—at Teheran. The arrangements are very
simple. The tekya is a walled parallelogram, with a
brick platform, *sakou*, in the centre of it; this *sakou*
is surrounded with black poles at some distance from
each other, the poles are joined at the top by hori-
zontal rods of the same colour, and from these rods
hang coloured lamps, which are lighted for the praying and preaching at night when the representation
is over. The *sakou*, or central platform, makes the
stage; in connection with it, at one of the opposite
extremities of the parallelogram lengthwise, is a
reserved box, *tâgnumâ*, higher than the *sakou*. This
box is splendidly decorated, and is used for peculiarly
interesting and magnificent tableaux,—the court of
the Caliph, for example—which occur in the course
of the piece. A passage of a few feet wide is left
free between the stage and this box; all the rest of
the space is for the spectators, of whom the foremost
rows are sitting on their heels close up to this passage,
so that they help the actors to mount and descend
the high steps of the *tâgnumâ* when they have to pass
between that and the *sakou*. On each side of the
tâgnumâ are boxes, and along one wall of the en-

closure are other boxes with fronts of elaborate woodwork, which are left to stand as a permanent part of
the construction ; facing these, with the floor and
stage between, rise tiers of seats as in an amphi-
theatre.   All places are free ; the great people have
generally provided and furnished the boxes, and take
care to fill them ; but if a box is not occupied when
the performance begins, any ragged street-urchin or
beggar may walk in and seat himself there.   A row
of gigantic masts runs across the middle of the space,
one or two of them being fixed in the *sakou* itself ;
and from these masts is stretched an immense awning
which protects the whole audience.   Up to a certain
height these masts are hung with tiger and panther
skins, to indicate the violent character of the scenes
to be represented.   Shields of steel and of hippo-
potamus skin, flags, and naked swords, are also attached to these masts.   A sea of colour and splendour
meets the eye all round.   Woodwork and brickwork
disappear under cushions, rich carpets, silk hangings,
India muslin embroidered with silver and gold,
shawls from Kerman and from Cashmere.   There are
lamps, lustres of coloured crystal, mirrors, Bohemian
and Venetian glass, porcelain vases of all degrees of
magnitude from China and from Europe, paintings
and engravings, displayed in profusion everywhere.
The taste may not always be soberly correct, but the
whole spectacle has just the effect of prodigality,
colour, and sumptuousness which we are accustomed
to associate with the splendours of the Arabian
Nights.

In marked contrast with this display is the poverty
of scenic contrivance and stage illusion. The subject
is far too interesting and too solemn to need them.
The actors are visible on all sides, and the exits, en-
trances, and stage-play of our theatres are impossible ;
the imagination of the spectator fills up all gaps and
meets all requirements. On the Ammergau arrangements one feels that the archæologists and artists of
Munich have laid their correct finger ; at Teheran
there has been no schooling of this sort. A copper
basin of water represents the Euphrates ; a heap of
chopped straw in a corner is the sand of the desert of
Kerbela, and the actor goes and takes up a handful
of it, when his part requires him to throw, in Oriental
fashion, dust upon his head. There is no attempt at
proper costume ; all that is sought is to do honour
to the personages of chief interest by dresses and
jewels which would pass for rich and handsome things
to wear in modern Persian life. The power of the
actors is in their genuine sense of the seriousness of
the business they are engaged in. They are, like the
public around them, penetrated with this, and so the
actor throws his whole soul into what he is about, the
public meets the actor halfway, and effects of extraordinary impressiveness are the result. "The actor
is under a charm," says Count Gobineau ; "he is
under it so strongly and completely that almost
always one sees Yezid himself (the usurping caliph),
the wretched Ibn-Said (Yezid's general), the infamous
Shemer (Ibn-Said's lieutenant), at the moment they
vent the cruellest insults against the Imams whom

they are going to massacre, or against the women of
the Imam's family whom they are ill-using, burst into
tears and repeat their part with sobs. The public is
neither surprised nor displeased at this; on the contrary, it beats its breast at the sight, throws up its
arms towards heaven with invocations of God, and
redoubles its groans. So it often happens that the
actor identifies himself with the personage he represents to such a degree that, when the situation carries
him away, he cannot be said to act, he *is* with such
truth, such complete enthusiasm, such utter self-for-
getfulness, what he represents, that he reaches a
reality at one time sublime, at another terrible, and
produces impressions on his audience which it would
be simply absurd to look for from our more artificial
performances. There is nothing stilted, nothing false,
nothing conventional; nature, and the facts represented, themselves speak."

The actors are men and boys, the parts of angels
and women being filled by boys. The children who
appear in the piece are often the children of the principal families of Teheran; their appearance in this
religious solemnity (for such it is thought) being
supposed to bring a blessing upon them and their
parents. "Nothing is more touching," says Count
Gobineau, "than to see these little things of three or
four years old, dressed in black gauze frocks with
large sleeves, and having on their heads small round
black caps embroidered with silver and gold, kneeling
beside the body of the actor who represents the
martyr of the day, embracing him, and with their

little hands covering themselves with chopped straw
for sand in sign of grief. These children evidently,"
he continues, " do not consider themselves to be
acting ; they are full of the feeling that what they
are about is something of deep seriousness and importance ; and though they are too young to comprehend fully the story, they know, in general, that it is
a matter sad and solemn. They are not distracted
by the audience, and they are not shy, but go through
their prescribed part with the utmost attention and
seriousness, always crossing their arms respectfully
to receive the blessing of the Imam Hussein ; the
public beholds them with emotions of the liveliest
satisfaction and sympathy."

The dramatic pieces themselves are without any
author's name. They are in popular language, such
as the commonest and most ignorant of the Persian
people can understand, free from learned Arabic
words,—free, comparatively speaking, from Oriental
fantasticality and hyperbole. The Seyids, or popular
friars, already spoken of, have probably had a hand
in the composition of many of them. The Moollahs,
or regular ecclesiastical authorities, condemn the whole
thing. It is an innovation which they disapprove and
think dangerous ; it is addressed to the eye, and their
religion forbids to represent religious things to the
eye ; it departs from the limits of what is revealed
and appointed to be taught as the truth, and brings
in novelties and heresies ;—for these dramas keep
growing under the pressure of the actor's imagination
and emotion, and of the imagination and emotion of

the public, and receive new developments every day. The learned, again, say that these pieces are a heap of lies, the production of ignorant people, and have no words strong enough to express their contempt for them. Still, so irresistible is the vogue of these sacred dramas that, from the king on the throne to the beggar in the street, every one, except perhaps the Moollahs, attends them, and is carried away by them. The Imams and their families speak always in a kind of lyrical chant, said to have rhythmical effects, often of great pathos and beauty; their persecutors, the villains of the piece, speak always in prose.

The stage is under the direction of a choragus, called *oostad*, or "master," who is a sacred personage by reason of the functions which he performs. Sometimes he addresses to the audience a commentary on what is passing before them, and asks their compassion and tears for the martyrs; sometimes in default of a Seyid, he prays and preaches. He is always listened to with veneration, for it is he who arranges the whole sacred spectacle which so deeply moves everybody. With no attempt at concealment, with the book of the piece in his hand, he remains constantly on the stage, gives the actors their cue, puts the children and any inexperienced actor in their right places, dresses the martyr in his winding-sheet when he is going to his death, holds the stirrup for him to mount his horse, and inserts a supply of chopped straw into the hands of those who are about to want it. Let us now see him at work.

The theatre is filled, and the heat is great ; young men of rank, the king's pages, officers of the army, smart functionaries of State, move through the crowd with water-skins slung on their backs, dealing out water all round, in memory of the thirst which on these solemn days the Imams suffered in the sands of Kerbela. Wild chants and litanies, such as we have already described, are from time to time set up by a dervish, a soldier, a workman in the crowd. These chants are taken up, more or less, by the audience ; sometimes they flag and die away for want of support, sometimes they are continued till they reach a paroxysm, and then abruptly stop. Presently a strange, insignificant figure in a green cotton garment, looking like a petty tradesman of one of the Teheran bazaars, mounts upon the *sakou.* He beckons with his hand to the audience, who are silent directly, and addresses them in a tone of lecture and expostulation, thus :—

"Well, you seem happy enough, Mussulmans, sitting there at your ease under the awning; and you imagine Paradise already wide open to you. Do you know what Paradise is ? It is a garden, doubtless, but such a garden as you have no idea of. You will say to me : 'Friend, tell us what it is like.' I have never been there, certainly ; but plenty of prophets have described it, and angels have brought news of it However, all I will tell you is, that there is room for all good people there, for it is 330,000 cubits long. If you do not believe, inquire. As for getting to be one of the good people, let me tell you it is not enough to read the Koran of the Prophet (the salvation and blessing of God be upon him !); it is not enough to do everything which this divine book enjoins; it is not enough to come and weep at the *tazyas*, as you do every day, you sons of dogs you, who know nothing which is of any use; it behoves, besides, that your good works (if you ever do any, which I greatly doubt) should be done in the name and for the love of Hussein.   It is Hussein, Mussulmans, who is the door to Paradise; it is Hussein, Mussulmans, who upholds the world; it is Hussein, Mussulmans, by whom comes salvation !   Cry, Hassan, Hussein !"

And all the multitude cry : "O Hassan ! O Hussein !"

"That is well; and now cry again."   And again all cry : "O Hassan ! O Hussein !"   "And now," the strange speaker goes on, "pray to God to keep you continually in the love of Hussein. Come, make your cry to God."   Then the multitude, as one man, throw up their arms into the air, and with a deep and long-drawn cry exclaim : " *Ya Allah !* O God !"

Fifes, drums, and trumpets break out ; the *kernas*, great copper trumpets five or six feet long, give notice that the actors are ready and that the *tazya* is to commence.   The preacher descends from the *sakou*, and the actors occupy it.

To give a clear notion of the cycle which these dramas fill, we should begin, as on the first day of the Moharrem the actors begin, with some piece relating to the childhood of the Imams, such as, for instance, the piece called *The Children Digging*. Ali and Fatima are living at Medina with their little sons

Hassan and Hussein. The simple home and occupations of the pious family are exhibited; it is morning, Fatima is seated with the little Hussein on her lap, dressing him. She combs his hair, talking caressingly to him all the while. A hair comes out with the comb; the child starts. Fatima is in distress at having given the child even this momentary uneasiness, and stops to gaze upon him tenderly. She falls into an anxious reverie, thinking of her fondness for the child, and of the unknown future in store for him. While she muses, the angel Gabriel stands before her. He reproves her weakness: "A hair falls from the child's head," he says, "and you weep; what would you do if you knew the destiny that awaits him, the countless wounds with which that body shall one day be pierced, the agony that shall rend your own soul!" Fatima, in despair, is comforted by her husband Ali, and they go together into the town to hear Mahomet preach. The boys and some of their little friends begin to play; every one makes a great deal of Hussein; he is at once the most spirited and the most amiable child of them all. The party amuse themselves with digging, with making holes in the ground and building mounds. Ali returns from the sermon and asks what they are about; and Hussein is made to reply in ambiguous and prophetic answers, which convey that by these holes and mounds in the earth are prefigured interments and tombs. Ali departs again; there rush in a number of big and fierce boys, and begin to pelt the little Imams with stones. A companion shields Hussein with his own body, but he

is struck down with a stone, and with another stone
Hussein, too, is stretched on the ground senseless.
Who are those boy-tyrants and persecutors? They
are Ibn-Said, and Shemer, and others, the future
murderers at Kerbela. The audience perceive it with
a shudder; the hateful assailants go off in triumph;
Ali re-enters, picks up the stunned and wounded
children, brings them round, and takes Hussein back
to his mother Fatima.

But let us now come at once to the days of martyrdom and to Kerbela. One of the most famous pieces
of the cycle is a piece called the *Marriage of Kassem*,
which brings us into the very middle of these crowning days. Count Gobineau has given a translation of
it, and from this translation we will take a few extracts. Kassem is the son of Hussein's elder brother,
the Imam Hassan, who had been poisoned by Yezid's
instigation at Medina. Kassem and his mother are
with the Imam Hussein at Kerbela; there, too, are
the women and children of the holy family, Omm-
Leyla, Hussein's wife, the Persian princess, the last
child of Yezdejerd the last of the Sassanides; Zeyneb,
Hussein's sister, the offspring, like himself, of Ali and
Fatima, and the grand-daughter of Mahomet; his
nephew Abdallah, still a little child; finally, his
beautiful daughter Zobeyda. When the piece begins,
the Imam's camp in the desert has already been cut
off from the Euphrates and besieged several days by
the Syrian troops under Ibn-Said and Shemer, and
by the treacherous men of Kufa. The Family of the
Tent were suffering torments of thirst. One of the

children had brought an empty water-bottle, and thrown it, a silent token of distress, before the feet of Abbas, the uncle of Hussein; Abbas had sallied out to cut his way to the river, and had been slain. Afterwards Ali-Akber, Hussein's eldest son, had made the same attempt and met with the same fate. Two younger brothers of Ali-Akber followed his example, and were likewise slain. The Imam Hussein had rushed amidst the enemy, beaten them from the body of Ali-Akber, and brought the body back to his tent; but the river was still inaccessible. At this point the action of the *Marriage of Kassem* begins. Kassem, a youth of sixteen, is burning to go out and avenge his cousin. At one end of the *sakou* is the Imam Hussein seated on his throne; in the middle are grouped all the members of his family; at the other end lies the body of Ali-Akber, with his mother Omm-Leyla, clothed and veiled in black, bending over it. The *kernas* sound, and Kassem, after a solemn appeal from Hussein and his sister Zeyneb to God and to the founders of their house to look upon their great distress, rises and speaks to himself:

Kassem.—"Separate thyself from the women of the harem, Kassem. Consider within thyself for a little; here thou sittest, and presently thou wilt see the body of Hussein, that body like a flower, torn by arrows and lances like thorns, Kassem.

"Thou sawest Ali-Akber's head severed from his body on the field of battle, and yet thou livedst!

"Arise, obey that which is written of thee by thy father; to be slain, that is thy lot, Kassem!

"Go, get leave from the son of Fatima, most honourable among women, and submit thyself to thy fate, Kassem."

Hussein sees him approach. "Alas," he says, "it is the orphan nightingale of the garden of Hassan, my brother!" Then Kassem speaks:

Kassem.—"O God, what shall I do beneath this load of affliction? My eyes are wet with tears, my lips are dried up with thirst. To live is worse than to die. What shall I do, seeing what hath befallen Ali-Akber? If Hussein suffereth me not to go forth, oh misery! For then what shall I do, O God, in the day of the resurrection, when I see my father Hassan? When I see my mother in the day of the resurrection, what shall I do, O God, in my sorrow and shame before her? All my kinsmen are gone to appear before the Prophet: shall not I also one day stand before the Prophet; and what shall I do, O God, in that day?"

Then he addresses the Imam :—

"Hail, threshold of the honour and majesty on high, threshold of heaven, threshold of God! In the roll of martyrs thou art the chief; in the book of creation thy story will live for ever. An orphan, a fatherless child, downcast and weeping, comes to prefer a request to thee."

Hussein bids him tell it, and he answers :—

"O light of the eyes of Mahomet the mighty, O lieutenant of Ali the lion! Abbas has perished, Ali-Akber has suffered martyrdom. O my uncle, thou hast no warriors left, and no standard-bearer! The roses are gone, and gone are their buds; the jessamine is gone, the poppies are gone. I alone, I am still left in the garden of the Faith, a thorn, and miserable. If thou hast any kindness for the orphan, suffer me to go forth and fight."

Hussein refuses. "My child," he says, "thou wast the light of the eyes of the Imam Hassan, thou art my beloved remembrance of him; ask me not this; urge me not, entreat me not; to have lost Ali-Akber is enough."

Kassem answers:—"That Kassem should live and Ali-Akber be martyred—sooner let the earth cover me! O king, be generous to the beggar at thy gate. See how my eyes run over with tears and my lips are dried up with thirst. Cast thine eyes toward the waters of the heavenly Euphrates! I die of thirst; grant me, O thou marked of God, a full pitcher of the water of life! it flows in the Paradise which awaits me."

Hussein still refuses; Kassem breaks forth in complaints and lamentations, his mother comes to him and learns the reason. She then says:—

"Complain not against the Imam, light of my eyes; only by his order can the commission of martyrdom be given. In that commission are sealed two-and-seventy witnesses, all righteous, and among the two-and-seventy is thy name. Know that thy destiny of death is commanded in the writing which thou wearest on thine arm."

This writing is the testament of his father Hassan. He bears it in triumph to the Imam Hussein, who finds

written there that he should, on the death-plain of
Kerbela, suffer Kassem to have his will, but that he
should marry him first to his daughter Zobeyda.
Kassem consents, though in astonishment. "Consider," he says, "there lies Ali-Akber, mangled by
the enemies' hands! Under this sky of ebon blackness, how can joy show her face? Nevertheless if
thou commandest it, what have I to do but obey!
Thy commandment is that of the Prophet, and his
voice is that of God." But Hussein has also to overcome the reluctance of the intended bride and of all
the women of his family.

"Heir of the vicar of God," says Kassem's mother
to the Imam, "bid me die, but speak not to me of a
bridal. If Zobeyda is to be a bride and Kassem a
bridegroom, where is the henna to tinge their hands,
where is the bridal chamber?" "Mother of Kassem,"
answers the Imam solemnly, "yet a few moments,
and in this field of anguish the tomb shall be for
marriage-bed, and the winding-sheet for bridal garment!" All give way to the will of their sacred
Head. The women and children surround Kassem,
sprinkle him with rose-water, hang bracelets and
necklaces on him, and scatter bon-bons around; and
then the marriage procession is formed. Suddenly
drums and trumpets are heard, and the Syrian troops
appear. Ibn-Said and Shemer are at their head.
"The Prince of the Faith celebrates a marriage in
the desert," they exclaim tauntingly; "we will soon
change his festivity into mourning." They pass by,
and Kassem takes leave of his bride. "God keep

thee, my bride," he says, embracing her, "for I must
forsake thee!" "One moment," she says, "remain
in thy place one moment! thy countenance is as the
lamp which giveth us light; suffer me to turn around
thee as the butterfly turneth, gently, gently!" And
making a turn around him, she performs the ancient
Eastern rite of respect from a new-married wife to
her husband. Troubled, he rises to go: "The reins
of my will are slipping away from me!" he murmurs.
She lays hold of his robe: "Take off thy hand," he
cries, "we belong not to ourselves!"

Then he asks the Imam to array him in his winding-sheet. "O nightingale of the divine orchard of
martyrdom," says Hussein, as he complies with his
wish, "I clothe thee with thy winding-sheet, I kiss thy
face; there is no fear, and no hope, but of God!"
Kassem commits his little brother Abdallah to the
Imam's care. Omm-Leyla looks up from her son's
corpse, and says to Kassem: "When thou enterest
the garden of Paradise, kiss for me the head of Ali-
Akber!"

The Syrian troops again appear. Kassem rushes
upon them and they all go off fighting. The Family
of the Tent, at Hussein's command, put the Koran on
their heads and pray, covering themselves with sand.
Kassem reappears victorious. He has slain Azrek, a
chief captain of the Syrians, but his thirst is intolerable. "Uncle," he says to the Imam, who asks him
what reward he wishes for his valour, "my tongue
cleaves to the roof of my mouth; the reward I wish
is *water*." "Thou coverest me with shame, Kassem,"

his uncle answers; "what can I do? Thou askest water; there is no water!"

Kassem.—"If I might but wet my mouth, I could presently make an end of the men of Kufa."

Hussein.—"As I live, I have not one drop of water!"

Kassem.—"Were it but lawful, I would wet my mouth with my own blood."

Hussein.—"Beloved child, what the Prophet forbids, that cannot I make lawful."

Kassem.—"I beseech thee, let my lips be but once moistened, and I will vanquish thine enemies!"

Hussein presses his own lips to those of Kassem, who, refreshed, again rushes forth, and returns bleeding and stuck with darts, to die at the Imam's feet in the tent. So ends the marriage of Kassem.

But the great day is the tenth day of the Moharrem, when comes the death of the Imam himself. The narrative of Gibbon well sums up the events of this great tenth day. "The battle at length expired by the death of the last of the companions of Hussein. Alone, weary, and wounded, he seated himself at the door of his tent. He was pierced in the mouth with a dart. He lifted his hands to heaven—they were full of blood—and he uttered a funeral prayer for the living and the dead. In a transport of despair, his sister issued from the tent, and adjured the general of the Kufians that he would not suffer Hussein to be murdered before his eyes. A tear trickled down the soldier's venerable beard; and the boldest of his men fell back on every side as the dying Imam threw himself among them. The remorseless Shemer—a name detested by the faithful—reproached their cowardice; and the grandson of Mahomet was slain with three and thirty strokes of lances and swords. After they had trampled on his body, they carried his head to the castle of Kufa, and the inhuman Obeidallah (the governor) struck him on the mouth with a cane. 'Alas!' exclaimed an aged Mussulman, 'on those lips have I seen the lips of the Apostle of God!'"

For this catastrophe no one *tazya* suffices; all the companies of actors unite in a vast open space; booths and tents are pitched round the outside circle for the spectators; in the centre is the Imam's camp, and the day ends with its conflagration.

Nor are there wanting pieces which carry on the story beyond the death of Hussein. One which produces an extraordinary effect is *The Christian Damsel.* The carnage is over, the enemy are gone. To the awe-struck beholders, the scene shows the silent plain of Kerbela and the tombs of the martyrs. Their bodies, full of wounds, and with weapons sticking in them still, are exposed to view; but around them all are crowns of burning candles, circles of light, to show that they have entered into glory. At one end of the *sakou* is a high tomb by itself; it is the tomb of the Imam Hussein, and his pierced body is seen stretched out upon it. A brilliant caravan enters, with camels, soldiers, servants, and a young lady on horseback, in European costume, or what passes in Persia for European costume. She halts near the tombs and proposes to encamp. Her servants try to

pitch a tent; but wherever they drive a pole into the
ground, blood springs up, and a groan of horror
bursts from the audience. Then the fair traveller,
instead of encamping, mounts into the *tâgnumâ*, lies
down to rest there, and falls asleep. Jesus Christ
appears to her, and makes known that this is Kerbela, and what has happened here. Meanwhile, an
Arab of the desert, a Bedouin who had formerly received Hussein's bounty, comes stealthily, intent on
plunder, upon the *sakou*. He finds nothing, and in a
paroxysm of brutal fury he begins to ill-treat the
corpses. Blood flows. The feeling of Asiatics about
their dead is well known, and the horror of the audience rises to its height. Presently the ruffian assails
and wounds the corpse of the Imam himself, over
whom white doves are hovering; the voice of Hussein,
deep and mournful, calls from his tomb: "*There is
no God but God!*" The robber flies in terror; the
angels, the prophets, Mahomet, Jesus Christ, Moses,
the Imams, the holy women, all come upon the *sakou*,
press round Hussein, load him with honours. The
Christian damsel wakes, and embraces Islam, the
Islam of the sect of the Shiahs.

Another piece closes the whole story, by bringing
the captive women and children of the Imam's family
to Damascus, to the presence of the Caliph Yezid. It
is in this piece that there comes the magnificent
tableau, already mentioned, of the court of the caliph.
The crown jewels are lent for it, and the dresses of
the ladies of Yezid's court, represented by boys chosen
for their good looks, are said to be worth thousands

and thousands of pounds; but the audience see them without favour, for this brilliant court of Yezid is cruel to the captives of Kerbela. The captives are thrust into a wretched dungeon under the palace walls; but the Caliph's wife had formerly been a slave of Mahomet's daughter Fatima, the mother of Hussein and Zeyneb. She goes to see Zeyneb in prison, her heart is touched, she passes into an agony of repentance, returns to her husband, upbraids him with his crimes, and intercedes for the women of the holy family, and for the children, who keep calling for the Imam Hussein. Yezid orders his wife to be put to death, and sends the head of Hussein to the children. Sekyna, the Imam's youngest daughter, a child of four years old, takes the beloved head in her arms, kisses it, and lies down beside it. Then Hussein appears to her as in life: "Oh! my father," she cries, "where wast thou? I was hungry, I was cold, I was beaten—where wast thou?" But now she sees him again, and is happy. In the vision of her happiness she passes away out of this troublesome life, she enters into rest, and the piece ends with her mother and her aunts burying her.

These are the martyrs of Kerbela; and these are the sufferings which awaken in an Asiatic audience sympathy so deep and serious, transports so genuine of pity, love, and gratitude, that to match them at all one must take the feelings raised at Ammergau. And now, where are we to look, in the subject-matter of the Persian passion-play, for the source of all this emotion?

Count Gobineau suggests that it is to be found in the feeling of patriotism; and that our Indo-European kinsmen, the Persians, conquered by the Semitic Arabians, find in the sufferings of Hussein a portrait of their own martyrdom. "Hussein," says Count Gobineau, " is not only the son of Ali, he is the husband of a princess of the blood of the Persian kings; he, his father Ali, the whole body of Imams taken together, represent the nation, represent Persia, invaded, ill-treated, despoiled, stripped of its inhabitants, by the Arabians. The right which is insulted and violated in Hussein, is identified with the right of Persia. The Arabians, the Turks, the Afghans,—Persia's implacable and hereditary enemies,—recognise Yezid as legitimate caliph; Persia finds therein an excuse for hating them the more, and identifies herself the more with the usurper's victims. It is *patriotism* therefore, which has taken the form, here, of the drama to express itself." No doubt there is much truth in what Count Gobineau thus says; and it is certain that the division of Shiahs and Sunis has its true cause in a division of races, rather than in a difference of religious belief.

But I confess that if the interest of the Persian passion-plays had seemed to me to lie solely in the curious evidence they afford of the workings of patriotic feeling in a conquered people, I should hardly have occupied myself with them at all this length. I believe that they point to something much more interesting. What this is, I cannot do more than simply indicate; but indicate it I will, in conclusion, and then leave the student of human nature to follow it out for himself.

When Mahomet's cousin Jaffer, and others of his first converts, persecuted by the idolaters of Mecca, fled in the year of our era 615, seven years before the Hegira, into Abyssinia, and took refuge with the King of that country, the people of Mecca sent after the fugitives to demand that they should be given up to them. Abyssinia was then already Christian. The king asked Jaffer and his companions what was this new religion for which they had left their country. Jaffer answered : " We were plunged in the darkness of ignorance, we were worshippers of idols. Given over to all our passions, we knew no law but that of the strongest, when God raised up among us a man of our own race, of noble descent, and long held in esteem by us for his virtues. This apostle called us to believe in one God, to worship God only, to reject the superstitions of our fathers, to despise divinities of wood and stone. He commanded us to eschew wickedness, to be truthful in speech, faithful to our engagements, kind and helpful to our relations and neighbours. He bade us respect the chastity of women, and not to rob the orphan. He exhorted us to prayer, alms-giving, and fasting. We believed in his mission, and we accepted the doctrines and the rule of life which he brought to us from God. For this our countrymen have persecuted us ; and now they want to make us return to their idolatry." The king of Abyssinia refused to surrender the fugitives, and then, turning again to Jaffer, after a few more explanations, he picked up a straw from the ground, and said to him : " Between your religion and ours there is not the thickness of this straw difference."

That is not quite so ; yet thus much we may affirm, that Jaffer's account of the religion of Mahomet is a great deal truer than the accounts of it which are commonly current amongst us. Indeed, for the credit of humanity, as more than a hundred millions of men are said to profess the Mahometan religion, one is glad to think so. To popular opinion everywhere, religion is proved by miracles. All religions but a man's own are utterly false and vain ; the authors of them are mere impostors ; and the miracles which are said to attest them, fictitious. We forget that this is a game which two can play at ; although the believer of each religion always imagines the prodigies which attest his own religion to be fenced by a guard granted to them alone. Yet how much more safe is it, as well as more fruitful, to look for the main con- firmation of a religion in its intrinsic correspondence with urgent wants of human nature, in its profound necessity ! Differing religions will then be found to have much in common, but this will be an additional proof of the value of that religion which does most for that which is thus commonly recognised as salutary and necessary. In Christendom one need not go about to establish that the religion of the Hebrews is a better religion than the religion of the Arabs, or that the Bible is a greater book than the Koran. The Bible *grew*, the Koran *was made ;* there lies the im- mense difference in depth and truth between them !

This very inferiority may make the Koran, for certain purposes and for people at a low stage of mental growth, a more powerful instrument than the Bible. From the circumstances of its origin, the Koran has the intensely dogmatic character, it has the perpetual insistence on the motive of future rewards and punishments, the palpable exhibition of paradise and hell, which the Bible has not. Among the little known and little advanced races of the great African continent, the Mahometan missionaries, by reason of the sort of power which this character of the Koran gives, are said to be more successful than ours. Nevertheless even in Africa it will assuredly one day be manifest, that whereas the Bible-people trace themselves to Abraham through Isaac, and the Koran-people trace themselves to Abraham through Ishmael, the difference between the religion of the Bible and the religion of the Koran is almost as the difference between Isaac and Ishmael. I mean that the seriousness about righteousness, which is what the hatred of idolatry really means, and the profound and inexhaustible doctrines that the righteous Eternal loveth righteousness, that there is no peace for the wicked, that the righteous is an everlasting foundation, are exhibited and inculcated in the Old Testament with an authority, majesty, and truth which leave the Koran immeasurably behind, and which, the more mankind grows and gains light, the more will be felt to have no fellows. Mahomet was no doubt acquainted with the Jews and their documents, and gained something from this source for his religion. But his religion is not a mere plagiarism from Judea, any more than it is a mere mass of falsehood. No ; in the seriousness, elevation, and moral energy of himself and of that Semitic race from which he sprang and to which he spoke, Mahomet mainly found that scorn and hatred of idolatry, that sense of the worth and truth of righteousness, judgment, and justice, which make the real greatness of him and his Koran, and which are thus rather an independent testimony to the essential doctrines of the Old Testament, than a plagiarism from them. The world needs righteousness, and the Bible is the grand teacher of it, but for certain times and certain men Mahomet too, in his way, was a teacher of righteousness.

But we know how the Old Testament conception of righteousness ceased with time to have the freshness and force of an intuition, became something petrified, narrow, and formal, needed renewing. We know how Christianity renewed it, carrying into these hard waters of Judaism a sort of warm gulf-stream of tender emotion, due chiefly to qualities which may be summed up as those of inwardness, mildness, and self-renouncement. Mahometanism had no such renewing. It began with a conception of righteousness, lofty indeed, but narrow, and which we may call old Jewish ; and there it remained. It is not a *feeling* religion. No one would say that the virtues of gentleness, mildness, and self-sacrifice were its virtues ; and the more it went on, the more the faults of its original narrow basis became visible, more and more it became fierce and militant, less and less was it amiable. Now, what are Ali, and Hassan, and Hussein and the Imams, but an insurrection of noble and pious natures against this hardness and aridity of the religion round them? an insurrection making its authors seem weak, helpless, and unsuccessful to the world and amidst the struggles of the world, but enabling them to know the joy and peace for which the world thirsts in vain, and inspiring in the heart of mankind an irresistible sympathy. " The twelve Imams," says Gibbon, " Ali, Hassan, Hussein, and the lineal descendants of Hussein, to the ninth generation, without arms, or treasures, or subjects, successively enjoyed the veneration of the people. Their names were often the pretence of sedition and civil war; but these royal saints despised the pomp of the world, submitted to the will of God and the injustice of man, and devoted their innocent lives to the study and practice of religion."

Abnegation and mildness, based on the depth of the inner life, and visited by unmerited misfortune, made the power of the first and famous Imams, Ali, Hassan, and Hussein, over the popular imagination. "O brother," said Hassan, as he was dying of poison, to Hussein who sought to find out and punish his murderer, "O brother, let him alone till he and I meet together before God!" So his father Ali had stood back from his rights instead of snatching at them. So of Hussein himself it was said by his successful rival, the usurping Caliph Yezid: "God loved Hussein, *but he would not suffer him to attain to anything.*" They might attain to nothing, they were too pure,

these great ones of the world as by birth they were;
but the people, which itself also can attain to so little,
loved them all the better on that account, loved them
for their abnegation and mildness, felt that they were
dear to God, that God loved them, and that they and
their lives filled a void in the severe religion of
Mahomet. These saintly self-deniers, these resigned
sufferers, who would not strive nor cry, supplied a
tender and pathetic side in Islam. The conquered
Persians, a more mobile, more impressionable, and
gentler race than their concentrated, narrow, and
austere Semitic conquerors felt the need of it most,
and gave most prominence to the ideals which satisfied
the need; but in Arabs and Turks also, and in all the
Mahometan world, Ali and his sons excite enthusiasm
and affection. Round the central sufferer, Hussein,
has come to group itself everything which is most
tender and touching. His person brings to the
Mussulman's mind the most human side of Mahomet
himself, his fondness for children,—for Mahomet had
loved to nurse the little Hussein on his knee, and
to show him from the pulpit to his people. The
Family of the Tent is full of women and children, and their devotion and sufferings, — blameless
and saintly women, lovely and innocent children.
There, too, are lovers with their story, the beauty
and the love of youth; and all follow the attraction of the pure and resigned Imam, all die for him.
The tender pathos from all these flows into the
pathos from him and enhances it, until finally there
arises for the popular imagination an immense ideal

of mildness and self-sacrifice, melting and overpowering the soul.

Even for us, to whom almost all the names are strange, whose interest in the places and persons is faint, who have them before us for a moment to-day, to see them again, probably, no more for ever,—even for us, unless I err greatly, the power and pathos of this ideal are recognisable. What must they be for those to whom every name is familiar, and calls up the most solemn and cherished associations; who have had their adoring gaze fixed all their lives upon this exemplar of self-denial and gentleness, and who have no other? If it was superfluous to say to English people that the religion of the Koran has not the value of the religion of the Old Testament, still more is it superfluous to say that the religion of the Imams has not the value of Christianity. The character and discourse of Jesus Christ possess, I have elsewhere often said, two signal powers: mildness and sweet reasonableness. The latter, the power which so puts before our view duty of every kind as to give it the force of an intuition, as to make it seem,—to make the total sacrifice of our ordinary self seem,—the most simple, natural, winning, necessary thing in the world, has been hitherto applied with but a very limited range, it is destined to an infinitely wider application, and has a fruitfulness which will yet transform the world. Of this the Imams have nothing, except so far as all mildness and self-sacrifice have in them something of sweet reasonableness and are its indispensable preliminary. This they have, *mildness and self-sacrifice;* and we have seen what an attraction it exercises. Could we ask for a stronger testimony to Christianity? Could we wish for any sign more convincing, that Jesus Christ was indeed, what Christians call him, *the desire of all nations?* So salutary, so necessary is what Christianity contains, that a religion, —a great, powerful, successful religion,—arises without it, and the missing virtue forces its way in! Christianity may say to these Persian Mahometans, with their gaze fondly turned towards the martyred Imams, what in our Bible God says by Isaiah to Cyrus, their great ancestor:—"*I girded thee, though thou hast not known me.*" It is a long way from Kerbela to Calvary; but the sufferers of Kerbela hold aloft to the eyes of millions of our race the lesson so loved by the sufferer of Calvary. For he said: "Learn of me, that I am *mild,* and *lowly of heart;* and ye shall find *rest unto your souls.*"

VIII.

JOUBERT.

WHY should we ever treat of any dead authors but the famous ones? Mainly for this reason: because, from these famous personages, home or foreign, whom we all know so well, and of whom so much has been said, the amount of stimulus which they contain for us has been in a great measure disengaged; people have formed their opinion about them, and do not readily change it. One may write of them afresh, combat received opinions about them, even interest one's readers in so doing; but the interest one's readers receive has to do, in general, rather with the treatment than with the subject; they are susceptible of a lively impression rather of the course of the discussion itself,—its turns, vivacity, and novelty,—than of the genius of the author who is the occasion of it. And yet what is really precious and inspiring, in all that we get from literature, except this sense of an immediate contact with genius itself, and the stimulus towards what is true and excellent which we derive from it? Now in literature, besides the eminent men

of genius who have had their deserts in the way of
fame, besides the eminent men of ability who have
often had far more than their deserts in the way of
fame, there are a certain number of personages who
have been real men of genius,—by which I mean, that
they have had a genuine gift for what is true and
excellent, and are therefore capable of emitting a life-
giving stimulus,—but who, for some reason or other,
in most cases for very valid reasons, have remained
obscure, nay, beyond a narrow circle in their own
country, unknown.   It is salutary from time to time
to come across a genius of this kind, and to extract
his honey.   Often he has more of it for us, as I have
already said, than greater men ; for, though it is by
no means true that from what is new to us there is
most to be learnt, it is yet indisputably true that from
what is new to us we in general learn most.

Of a genius of this kind, Joseph Joubert, I am
now going to speak.   His name is, I believe, almost
unknown in England ; and even in France, his native
country, it is not famous.   M. Sainte-Beuve has given
of him one of his incomparable portraits ; but,—besides
that even M. Sainte-Beuve's writings are far less known
amongst us than they deserve to be,—every country
has its own point of view from which a remarkable
author may most profitably be seen and studied.

Joseph Joubert was born (and his date should be
remarked) in 1754, at Montignac, a little town in
Périgord.   His father was a doctor with small means
and a large family ; and Joseph, the eldest, had his
own way to make in the world.   He was for eight

years, as pupil first, and afterwards as an assistant-
master, in the public school of Toulouse, then managed
by the Jesuits, who seem to have left in him a most
favourable opinion, not only of their tact and address,
but of their really good qualities as teachers and
directors. Compelled by the weakness of his health
to give up, at twenty-two, the profession of teaching,
he passed two important years of his life in hard study,
at home at Montignac; and came in 1778 to try his
fortune in the literary world of Paris, then perhaps
the most tempting field which has ever yet presented
itself to a young man of letters. He knew Diderot,
D'Alembert, Marmontel, Laharpe; he became intimate
with one of the celebrities of the next literary generation, then, like himself, a young man,—Chateaubriand's
friend, the future Grand Master of the University,
Fontanes. But, even then, it began to be remarked
of him, that M. Joubert "*s'inquiétait de perfection bien
plus que de gloire*—cared far more about perfecting
himself than about making himself a reputation."
His severity of morals may perhaps have been rendered
easier to him by the delicacy of his health; but the
delicacy of his health will not by itself account for his
changeless preference of being to seeming, knowing
to showing, studying to publishing; for what terrible
public performers have some invalids been! This
preference he retained all through his life, and it is
by this that he is characterised. "He has chosen,"
Chateaubriand (adopting Epicurus's famous words)
said of him, "*to hide his life*." Of a life which its
owner was bent on hiding there can be but little to

tell.   Yet the only two public incidents of Joubert's
life, slight as they are, do all concerned in them so
much credit that they deserve mention.   In 1790 the
Constituent Assembly made the office of justice of
the peace elective throughout France.   The people of
Montignac retained such an impression of the character
of their young townsman,—one of Plutarch's men of
virtue, as he had lived amongst them, simple, studious,
severe,—that, though he had left them for years, they
elected him in his absence without his knowing anything about it.   The appointment little suited Joubert's
wishes or tastes ; but at such a moment he thought
it wrong to decline it.   He held it for two years, the
legal term, discharging its duties with a firmness and
integrity which were long remembered ; and then,
when he went out of office, his fellow-townsmen re-
elected him.   But Joubert thought that he had now
accomplished his duty towards them, and he went
back to the retirement which he loved.   That seems
to me a little episode of the great French Revolution
worth remembering.   The sage who was asked by the
king, why sages were seen at the doors of kings, but
not kings at the doors of sages, replied, that it was
because sages knew what was good for them, and
kings did not.   But at Montignac the king—for in
1790 the people in France was king with a vengeance
—knew what was good for him, and came to the door
of the sage.

The other incident was this.   When Napoleon, in
1809, reorganised the public instruction of France,
founded the University, and made M. de Fontanes

its Grand Master, Fontanes had to submit to the
Emperor a list of persons to form the council or
governing body of the new University. Third on
his list, after two distinguished names, Fontanes
placed the unknown name of Joubert. "This name,"
he said in his accompanying memorandum to the
Emperor, "is not known as the two first are; and
yet this is the nomination to which I attach most
importance. I have known M. Joubert all my life.
His character and intelligence are of the very highest
order. I shall rejoice if your Majesty will accept
my guarantee for him." Napoleon trusted his Grand
Master, and Joubert became a councillor of the
University. It is something that a man, elevated to
the highest posts of State, should not forget his
obscure friends; or that, if he remembers and places
them, he should regard in placing them their merit
rather than their obscurity. It is more, in the eyes
of those whom the necessities, real or supposed, of a
political system have long familiarised with such
cynical disregard of fitness in the distribution of office,
to see a minister and his master alike zealous, in
giving away places, to give them to the best men to
be found.

Between 1792 and 1809 Joubert had married.
His life was passed between Villeneuve-sur-Yonne,
where his wife's family lived,—a pretty little Bur-
gundian town, by which the Lyons railroad now
passes,—and Paris. Here, in a house in the Rue
St.-Honoré, in a room very high up, and admitting
plenty of the light which he so loved,—a room from

which he saw, in his own words, "a great deal of sky
and very little earth,"—among the treasures of a
library collected with infinite pains, taste, and skill,
from which every book he thought ill of was rigidly
excluded,—he never would possess either a complete
Voltaire or a complete Rousseau,—the happiest hours
of his life were passed. In the circle of one of those
women who leave a sort of perfume in literary history, and who have the gift of inspiring successive
generations of readers with an indescribable regret
not to have known them,—Pauline de Montmorin,
Madame de Beaumont, — he had become intimate
with nearly all which at that time, in the Paris world
of letters or of society, was most attractive and pro-
mising. Amongst his acquaintances one only misses
the names of Madame de Staël and Benjamin Constant. Neither of them was to his taste, and with
Madame de Staël he always refused to become
acquainted; he thought she had more vehemence
than truth, and more heat than light.

Years went on, and his friends became conspicuous
authors or statesmen ; but Joubert remained in the
shade. His constitution was of such fragility that
how he lived so long, or accomplished so much as he
did, is a wonder : his soul had, for its basis of operations, hardly any body at all : both from his stomach
and from his chest he seems to have had constant
suffering, though he lived by rule, and was as ab-
stemious as a Hindoo. Often, after overwork in
thinking, reading, or talking, he remained for days
together in a state of utter prostration,—condemned

to absolute silence and inaction; too happy if the
agitation of his mind would become quiet also, and
let him have the repose of which he stood in so much
need. With this weakness of health, these repeated
suspensions of energy, he was incapable of the prolonged contention of spirit necessary for the creation
of great works. But he read and thought immensely;
he was an unwearied note-taker, a charming letter-
writer; above all, an excellent and delightful talker.
The gaiety and amenity of his natural disposition
were inexhaustible; and his spirit, too, was of
astonishing elasticity; he seemed to hold on to life
by a single thread only, but that single thread was
very tenacious. More and more, as his soul and
knowledge ripened more and more, his friends pressed
to his room in the Rue St.-Honoré; often he received
them in bed, for he seldom rose before three o'clock
in the afternoon; and at his bedroom-door, on his
bad days, Madame Joubert stood sentry, trying, not
always with success, to keep back the thirsty comers
from the fountain which was forbidden to flow. Fontanes did nothing in the University without consult-
ing him, and Joubert's ideas and pen were always at
his friend's service.

When he was in the country, at Villeneuve, the
young priests of his neighbourhood used to resort to
him, in order to profit by his library and by his conversation. He, like our Coleridge, was particularly
qualified to attract men of this kind and to benefit
them: retaining perfect independence of mind, he
was a religious philosopher. As age came on, his

infirmities became more and more overwhelming ; some of his friends, too, died ; others became so immersed in politics, that Joubert, who hated politics, saw them seldomer than of old ; but the moroseness of age and infirmity never touched him, and he never quarrelled with a friend or lost one. From these miseries he was preserved by that quality in him of which I have already spoken ; a quality which is best expressed by a word, not of common use in English,— alas, we have too little in our national character of the quality which this word expresses,—his inborn, his constant amenity. He lived till the year 1824. On the 4th of May in that year he died, at the age of seventy. A day or two after his death M. de Chateaubriand inserted in the *Journal des Débats* a short notice of him, perfect for its feeling, grace, and propriety. *On ne vit dans la mémoire du monde*, he says and says truly, *que par des travaux pour le monde*, —"a man can live in the world's memory only by what he has done for the world." But Chateaubriand used the privilege which his great name gave him to assert, delicately but firmly, Joubert's real and rare merits, and to tell the world what manner of man had just left it.

Joubert's papers were accumulated in boxes and drawers. He had not meant them for publication ; it was very difficult to sort them and to prepare them for it. Madame Joubert, his widow, had a scruple about giving them a publicity which her husband, she felt, would never have permitted. But, as her own end approached, the natural desire to leave of so

remarkable a spirit some enduring memorial, some
memorial to outlast the admiring recollection of the
living who were so fast passing away, made her yield
to the entreaties of his friends, and allow the printing,
but for private circulation only, of a volume of his
fragments. Chateaubriand edited it; it appeared in
1838, fourteen years after Joubert's death. The
volume attracted the attention of those who were
best fitted to appreciate it, and profoundly impressed
them. M. Sainte-Beuve gave of it, in the *Revue des
Deux Mondes*, the admirable notice of which I have
already spoken; and so much curiosity was excited
about Joubert, that the collection of his fragments,
enlarged by many additions, was at last published for
the benefit of the world in general. It has since been
twice reprinted. The first or preliminary chapter
has some fancifulness and affectation in it; the reader
should begin with the second.

I have likened Joubert to Coleridge; and indeed
the points of resemblance between the two men are
numerous. Both of them great and celebrated talkers,
Joubert attracting pilgrims to his upper chamber in
the Rue St.-Honoré, as Coleridge attracted pilgrims
to Mr. Gilman's at Highgate; both of them desultory
and incomplete writers,—here they had an outward
likeness with one another. Both of them passionately
devoted to reading in a class of books, and to thinking
on a class of subjects, out of the beaten line of the
reading and thought of their day; both of them
ardent students and critics of old literature, poetry,
and the metaphysics of religion; both of them curious

explorers of words, and of the latent significance hidden under the popular use of them; both of them, in a certain sense, conservative in religion and politics, by antipathy to the narrow and shallow foolishness of vulgar modern liberalism;—here they had their inward and real likeness.　But that in which the essence of their likeness consisted is this, —that they both had from nature an ardent impulse for seeking the genuine truth on all matters they thought about, and a gift for finding it and recognising it when it was found.　To have the impulse for seeking this truth is much rarer than most people think; to have the gift for finding it is, I need not say, very rare indeed.　By this they have a spiritual relationship of the closest kind with one another, and they become, each of them, a source of stimulus and progress for all of us.

Coleridge had less delicacy and penetration than Joubert, but more richness and power; his production, though far inferior to what his nature at first seemed to promise, was abundant and varied.　Yet in all his production how much is there to dissatisfy us!　How many reserves must be made in praising either his poetry, or his criticism, or his philosophy!　How little either of his poetry, or of his criticism, or of his philosophy, can we expect permanently to stand!　But that which will stand of Coleridge is this: the stimulus of his continual effort,—not a moral effort, for he had no morals,—but of his continual instinctive effort, crowned often with rich success, to get at and to lay bare the real truth of

his matter in hand, whether that matter were literary,
or philosophical, or political, or religious ; and this in
a country where at that moment such an effort was
almost unknown ; where the most powerful minds
threw themselves upon poetry, which conveys truth,
indeed, but conveys it indirectly; and where ordinary minds were so habituated to do without thinking altogether, to regard considerations of established
routine and practical convenience as paramount, that
any attempt to introduce within the domain of these
the disturbing element of thought, they were prompt
to resent as an outrage.   Coleridge's great usefulness
lay in his supplying in England, for many years and
under critical circumstances, by the spectacle of this
effort of his, a stimulus to all minds capable of profit-
ing by it ; in the generation which grew up around
him.   His action will still be felt as long as the need
for it continues.   When, with the cessation of the
need, the action too has ceased, Coleridge's memory,
in spite of the disesteem—nay, repugnance—which
his character may and must inspire, will yet for ever
remain invested with that interest and gratitude
which invests the memory of founders.

M. de Rémusat, indeed, reproaches Coleridge with
his *jugements saugrenus ;* the criticism of a gifted truth-
finder ought not to be *saugrenu*, so on this reproach
we must pause for a moment.   *Saugrenu* is a rather
vulgar French word, but, like many other vulgar
words, very expressive ; used as an epithet for a
judgment, it means something like *impudently absurd*.
The literary judgments of one nation about another

are very apt to be *saugrenus*. It is certainly true, as
M. Sainte-Beuve remarks in answer to Goethe's complaint against the French that they have undervalued
Du Bartas, that as to the estimate of its own authors
every nation is the best judge; the *positive* estimate
of them, be it understood, not, of course, the estimate
of them in comparison with the authors of other
nations. Therefore a foreigner's judgments about
the intrinsic merit of a nation's authors will generally, when at complete variance with that nation's
own, be wrong; but there is a permissible wrongness
in these matters, and to that permissible wrongness
there is a limit. When that limit is exceeded, the
wrong judgment becomes more than wrong, it becomes *saugrenu*, or impudently absurd. For instance,
the high estimate which the French have of Racine
is probably in great measure deserved; or, to take a
yet stronger case, even the high estimate which
Joubert had of the Abbé Delille is probably in great
measure deserved; but the common disparaging
judgment passed on Racine by English readers is not
saugrenu, still less is that passed by them on the
Abbé Delille *saugrenu*, because the beauty of Racine,
and of Delille too, so far as Delille's beauty goes, is
eminently in their language, and this is a beauty
which a foreigner cannot perfectly seize;—this
beauty of diction, *apicibus verborum ligata*, as M.
Sainte-Beuve, quoting Quintilian, says of Chateaubriand's. As to Chateaubriand himself, again, the
common English judgment, which stamps him as a
mere shallow rhetorician, all froth and vanity, is

certainly wrong, one may even wonder that we
English should judge Chateaubriand so wrongly, for
his power goes far beyond beauty of diction; it is a
power, as well, of passion and sentiment, and this
sort of power the English can perfectly well appreciate.   One production of Chateaubriand's, *René*,
is akin to the most popular productions of Byron,
—to the *Childe Harold* or *Manfred*,—in spirit, equal
to them in power, superior to them in form.   But
this work, I hardly know why, is almost unread in
England.   And only consider this criticism of
Chateaubriand's on the true pathetic!   "It is a
dangerous mistake, sanctioned, like so many other
dangerous mistakes, by Voltaire, to suppose that the
best works of imagination are those which draw most
tears.   One could name this or that melodrama, which
no one would like to own having written, and which
yet harrows the feelings far more than the *Æneid*.
The true tears are those which are called forth by
the *beauty* of poetry; there must be as much admiration in them as sorrow.   They are the tears which
come to our eyes when Priam says to Achilles, ἔτλην
δ', οἷ' οὔπω . . .—'And I have endured,—the like
whereof no soul upon the earth hath yet endured,—
to carry to my lips the hand of him who slew my
child;' or when Joseph cries out: 'I am Joseph
your brother, whom ye sold into Egypt.'"   Who
does not feel that the man who wrote that was no
shallow rhetorician, but a born man of genius, with
the true instinct of genius for what is really admirable?   Nay, take these words of Chateaubriand, an

old man of eighty, dying, amidst the noise and bustle of the ignoble revolution of February 1848: "Mon Dieu, mon Dieu, quand donc, quand donc serai-je délivré de tout ce monde, ce bruit; quand donc, quand donc cela finira-t-il?" Who, with any ear, does not feel that those are not the accents of a trumpery rhetorician, but of a rich and puissant nature,—the cry of the dying lion? I repeat it, Chateaubriand is most ignorantly underrated in England; and we English are capable of rating him far more correctly if we knew him better. Still Chateaubriand has such real and great faults, he falls so decidedly beneath the rank of the truly greatest authors, that the depreciatory judgment passed on him in England, though ignorant and wrong, can hardly be said to transgress the limits of permissible ignorance; it is not a *jugement saugrenu.* But when a critic denies genius to a literature which has produced Bossuet and Molière, he passes the bounds; and Coleridge's judgments on French literature and the French genius are undoubtedly, as M. de Rémusat calls them, *saugrenus.*

And yet, such is the impetuosity of our poor human nature, such its proneness to rush to a decision with imperfect knowledge, that his having delivered a *saugrenu* judgment or two in his life by no means proves a man not to have had, in comparison with his fellow-men in general, a remarkable gift for truth, or disqualifies him for being, by virtue of that gift, a source of vital stimulus for us. Joubert had far less smoke and turbid vehemence in him than

Coleridge; he had also a far keener sense of what
was absurd. But Joubert can write to M. Molé (the
M. Molé who was afterwards Louis Philippe's well-
known minister): "As to your Milton, whom the
merit of the Abbé Delille" (the Abbé Delille translated *Paradise Lost*) "makes me admire, and with
whom I have nevertheless still plenty of fault to find,
why, I should like to know, are you scandalised that
I have not enabled myself to read him? I don't
understand the language in which he writes, and I
don't much care to. If he is a poet one cannot put
up with, even in the prose of the younger Racine, am
I to blame for that? If by force you mean beauty
manifesting itself with power, I maintain that the Abbé
Delille has more force than Milton." That, to be
sure, is a petulant outburst in a private letter; it is
not, like Coleridge's, a deliberate proposition in a
printed philosophical essay. But is it possible to
imagine a more perfect specimen of a *saugrenu* judgment? It is even worse than Coleridge's, because it is
saugrenu with reasons. That, however, does not prevent
Joubert from having been really a man of extraordinary
ardour in the search for truth, and of extraordinary
fineness in the perception of it; and so was Coleridge.

Joubert had around him in France an atmosphere
of literary, philosophical, and religious opinion as
alien to him as that in England was to Coleridge.
This is what makes Joubert, too, so remarkable, and
it is on this account that I begged the reader to
remark his date. He was born in 1754; he died in
1824. He was thus in the fulness of his powers at

the beginning of the present century, at the epoch of
Napoleon's consulate.   The French criticism of that
day—the criticism of Laharpe's successors, of Geoffroy and his colleagues in the *Journal des Débats*—
had a dryness very unlike the telling vivacity of the
early Edinburgh reviewers, their contemporaries, but
a fundamental narrowness, a want of genuine insight,
much on a par with theirs.   Joubert, like Coleridge,
has no respect for the dominant oracle ; he treats his
Geoffroy with about as little deference as Coleridge
treats his Jeffrey.   " Geoffroy," he says in an article
in the *Journal des Débats* criticising Chateaubriand's
Génie du Christianisme—" Geoffroy in this article
begins by holding out his paw prettily enough ; but
he ends by a volley of kicks, which lets the whole
world see but too clearly the four iron shoes of the
four-footed animal."   There is, however, in France a
sympathy with intellectual activity for its own sake,
and for the sake of its inherent pleasurableness and
beauty, keener than any which exists in England ;
and Joubert had more effect in Paris,—though his
conversation was his only weapon, and Coleridge
wielded besides his conversation his pen,—than Coleridge had or could have in London.   I mean, a more
immediate, appreciable effect ; an effect not only upon
the young and enthusiastic, to whom the future belongs,
but upon formed and important personages to whom the
present belongs, and who are actually moving society.
He owed this partly to his real advantages over
Coleridge.   If he had, as I have already said, less
power and richness than his English parallel, he had

more tact and penetration. He was more *possible*
than Coleridge; his doctrine was more intelligible
than Coleridge's, more receivable. And yet with
Joubert, the striving after a consummate and attractive clearness of expression came from no mere frivolous dislike of labour and inability for going deep, but
was a part of his native love of truth and perfection.
The delight of his life he found in truth, and in the
satisfaction which the enjoying of truth gives to the
spirit; and he thought the truth was never really and
worthily said, so long as the least cloud, clumsiness,
and repulsiveness hung about the expression of it.

Some of his best passages are those in which he
upholds this doctrine. Even metaphysics he would
not allow to remain difficult and abstract: so long
as they spoke a professional jargon, the language of
the schools, he maintained,—and who shall gainsay
him?—that metaphysics were imperfect; or, at any
rate, had not yet reached their ideal perfection.

"The true science of metaphysics," he says, "consists not in rendering abstract that which is sensible,
but in rendering sensible that which is abstract; apparent that which is hidden; imaginable, if so it may
be, that which is only intelligible; and intelligible,
finally, that which an ordinary attention fails to seize."

And therefore :—

"Distrust, in books on metaphysics, words which
have not been able to get currency in the world, and
are only calculated to form a special language."

Nor would he suffer common words to be employed in a special sense by the schools :—

"Which is the best, if one wants to be useful and to be really understood, to get one's words in the world, or to get them in the schools? I maintain that the good plan is to employ words in their popular sense rather than in their philosophical sense; and the better plan still, to employ them in their natural sense rather than in their popular sense. By their natural sense, I mean the popular and universal acceptation of them brought to that which in this is essential and invariable. To prove a thing by definition proves nothing, if the definition is purely philosophical; for such definitions only bind him who makes them. To prove a thing by definition, when the definition expresses the necessary, inevitable, and clear idea which the world at large attaches to the object, is, on the contrary, all in all; because then what one does is simply to show people what they do really think, in spite of themselves and without knowing it. The rule that one is free to give to words what sense one will, and that the only thing needful is to be agreed upon the sense one gives them, is very well for the mere purposes of argumentation, and may be allowed in the schools where this sort of fencing is to be practised; but in the sphere of the true-born and noble science of metaphysics, and in the genuine world of literature, it is good for nothing. One must never quit sight of realities, and one must employ one's expressions simply as media, —as glasses, through which one's thoughts can be best made evident. I know, by my own experience, how hard this rule is to follow; but I judge of its importance by the failure of every system of metaphysics. Not one of them has succeeded; for the simple reason, that in every one ciphers have been constantly used instead of values, artificial ideas instead of native ideas, jargon instead of idiom."

I do not know whether the metaphysician will ever adopt Joubert's rules; but I am sure that the man of letters, whenever he has to speak of metaphysics, will do well to adopt them. He, at any rate, must remember :—

"It is by means of familiar words that style takes hold of the reader and gets possession of him. It is by means of these that great thoughts get currency and pass for true metal, like gold and silver which have had a recognised stamp put upon them. They beget confidence in the man who, in order to make his thoughts more clearly perceived, uses them; for people feel that such an employment of the language of common human life betokens a man who knows that life and its concerns, and who keeps himself in contact with them. Besides, these words make a style frank and easy. They show that an author has long made the thought or the feeling expressed his mental food; that he has so assimilated them and familiarised them, that the most common expressions suffice him in order to express ideas which have become every-day ideas to him by the length of time they have been in his mind. And lastly, what one says in such words looks more true; for, of all the words in use, none are so clear as those which we call common words; and clearness is so eminently one of

the characteristics of truth, that often it even passes
for truth itself."

These are not, in Joubert, mere counsels of rhetoric;
they come from his accurate sense of perfection, from
his having clearly seized the fine and just idea that
beauty and light are properties of truth, and that
truth is incompletely exhibited if it is exhibited without beauty and light :—

"Be profound with clear terms and not with
obscure terms. What is difficult will at last become
easy; but as one goes deep into things, one must
still keep a charm, and one must carry into these
dark depths of thought, into which speculation has
only recently penetrated, the pure and antique clearness of centuries less learned than ours, but with
more light in them."

And elsewhere he speaks of those "spirits, lovers
of light, who, when they have an idea to put forth,
brood long over it first, and wait patiently till it
shines, as Buffon enjoined, when he defined genius to
be the aptitude for patience; spirits who know by
experience that the driest matter and the dullest
words hide within them the germ and spark of some
brightness, like those fairy nuts in which were found
diamonds if one broke the shell and was the right
person; spirits who maintain that, to see and exhibit
things in beauty, is to see and show things as in their
essence they really are, and not as they exist for the
eye of the careless, who do not look beyond the outside; spirits hard to satisfy, because of a keen-sighted-
ness in them, which makes them discern but too

clearly both the models to be followed and those to be shunned; spirits active though meditative, who cannot rest except in solid truths, and whom only beauty can make happy; spirits far less concerned for glory than for perfection, who, because their art is long and life is short, often die without leaving a monument, having had their own inward sense of life and fruitfulness for their best reward."

No doubt there is something a little too ethereal in all this, something which reminds one of Joubert's physical want of body and substance; no doubt, if a man wishes to be a great author, it is to consider too curiously, to consider as Joubert did; it is a mistake to spend so much of one's time in setting up one's ideal standard of perfection, and in contemplating it. Joubert himself knew this very well: "I cannot build a house for my ideas," said he; "I have tried to do without words, and words take their revenge on me by their difficulty." "If there is a man upon earth tormented by the cursed desire to get a whole book into a page, a whole page into a phrase, and this phrase into one word,—that man is myself." "I can sow, but I cannot build." Joubert, however, makes no claim to be a great author; by renouncing all ambition to be this, by not trying to fit his ideas into a house, by making no compromise with words in spite of their difficulty, by being quite single-minded in his pursuit of perfection, perhaps he is enabled to get closer to the truth of the objects of his study, and to be of more service to us by setting before us ideals, than if he had composed a celebrated work. I doubt whether, in an elaborate work on the philosophy of religion, he would have got his ideas about religion to *shine*, to use his own expression, as they shine when he utters them in perfect freedom. Penetration in these matters is valueless without soul, and soul is valueless without penetration; both of these are delicate qualities, and, even in those who have them, easily lost; the charm of Joubert is, that he has and keeps both. Let us try and show that he does.

"One should be fearful of being wrong in poetry when one thinks differently from the poets, and in religion when one thinks differently from the saints.

"There is a great difference between taking for idols Mahomet and Luther, and bowing down before Rousseau and Voltaire. People at any rate imagined they were obeying God when they followed Mahomet, and the Scriptures when they hearkened to Luther. And perhaps one ought not too much to disparage that inclination which leads mankind to put into the hands of those whom it thinks the friends of God the direction and government of its heart and mind. It is the subjection to irreligious spirits which alone is fatal, and, in the fullest sense of the word, depraving.

"May I say it? It is not hard to know God, provided one will not force oneself to define him.

"Do not bring into the domain of reasoning that which belongs to our innermost feeling. State truths of sentiment, and do not try to prove them. There is a danger in such proofs; for in arguing it is necessary to treat that which is in question as something

problematic : now that which we accustom ourselves
to treat as problematic ends by appearing to us as
really doubtful.   In things that are visible and palpable, never prove what is believed already ; in things
that are certain and mysterious,—mysterious by their
greatness and by their nature,—make people believe
them, and do not prove them ; in things that are
matters of practice and duty, command, and do not
explain.   'Fear God,' has made many men pious ;
the proofs of the existence of God have made many
men atheists.   From the defence springs the attack ;
the advocate begets in his hearer a wish to pick
holes ; and men are almost always led on, from the
desire to contradict the doctor, to the desire to contradict the doctrine.   Make truth lovely, and do not
try to arm her ; mankind will then be far less inclined
to contend with her.

"Why is even a bad preacher almost always heard
by the pious with pleasure ?   *Because he talks to them
about what they love.*   But you who have to expound
religion to the children of this world, you who have
to speak to them of that which they once loved perhaps, or which they would be glad to love,—remember
that they do not love it yet, and to make them love
it take heed to speak with power.

"You may do what you like, mankind will believe
no one but God ; and he only can persuade mankind
who believes that God has spoken to him.   No one
can give faith unless he has faith ; the persuaded persuade, as the indulgent disarm.

"The only happy people in the world are the good

man, the sage, and the saint ; but the saint is happier
than either of the others, so much is man by his nature
formed for sanctity."

The same delicacy and penetration which he here
shows in speaking of the inward essence of religion,
Joubert shows also in speaking of its outward form,
and of its manifestation in the world :—

" Piety is not a religion, though it is the soul of
all religions.   A man has not a religion simply by
having pious inclinations, any more than he has a
country simply by having philanthropy.   A man has
not a country until he is a citizen in a state, until he
undertakes to follow and uphold certain laws, to obey
certain magistrates, and to adopt certain ways of living
and acting.

" Religion is neither a theology nor a theosophy ;
it is more than all this ; it is a discipline, a law, a
yoke, an indissoluble engagement."

Who, again, has ever shown with more truth and
beauty the good and imposing side of the wealth and
splendour of the Catholic Church, than Joubert in
the following passage ?—

" The pomps and magnificence with which the
Church is reproached are in truth the result and the
proof of her incomparable excellence.   From whence,
let me ask, have come this power of hers and these
excessive riches, except from the enchantment into
which she threw all the world ?   Ravished with her
beauty, millions of men from age to age kept loading
her with gifts, bequests, cessions.   She had the talent
of making herself loved, and the talent of making men

happy. It is that which wrought prodigies for her; it is from thence that she drew her power."

"She had the talent of making herself *feared*,"— one should add that too, in order to be perfectly just; but Joubert, because he is a true child of light, can see that the wonderful success of the Catholic Church must have been due really to her good rather than to her bad qualities; to her making herself loved rather than to her making herself feared.

How striking and suggestive, again, is this remark on the Old and New Testaments :—

"The Old Testament teaches the knowledge of good and evil; the Gospel, on the other hand, seems written for the predestinated; it is the book of innocence. The one is made for earth, the other seems made for heaven. According as the one or the other of these books takes hold of a nation, what may be called the *religious humours* of nations differ."

So the British and North American Puritans are the children of the Old Testament, as Joachim of Flora and St. Francis are the children of the New. And does not the following maxim exactly fit the Church of England, of which Joubert certainly never thought when he was writing it ?—"The austere sects excite the most enthusiasm at first; but the temperate sects have always been the most durable."

And these remarks on the Jansenists and Jesuits, interesting in themselves, are still more interesting because they touch matters we cannot well know at first-hand, and which Joubert, an impartial observer, had had the means of studying closely. We are apt

to think of the Jansenists as having failed by reason
of their merits; Joubert shows us how far their failure
was due to their defects :—

"We ought to lay stress upon what is clear in
Scripture, and to pass quickly over what is obscure ;
to light up what in Scripture is troubled, by what is
serene in it ; what puzzles and checks the reason, by
what satisfies the reason. The Jansenists have done
just the reverse. They lay stress upon what is un-
certain, obscure, afflicting, and they pass lightly over
all the rest ; they eclipse the luminous and consoling
truths of Scripture, by putting between us and them
its opaque and dismal truths. For example, 'Many
are called ;' there is a clear truth : 'Few are chosen ;'
there is an obscure truth. 'We are children of wrath ;'
there is a sombre, cloudy, terrifying truth : 'We are
all the children of God ;' 'I came not to call the
righteous, but sinners to repentance ;' there are truths
which are full of clearness, mildness, serenity, light.
The Jansenists trouble our cheerfulness, and shed no
cheering ray on our trouble. They are not, however,
to be condemned for what they say, because what they
say is true ; but they are to be condemned for what
they fail to say, for that is true too,—truer, even, than
the other ; that is, its truth is easier for us to seize,
fuller, rounder, and more complete. Theology, as the
Jansenists exhibit her, has but the half of her disk."

Again :—

"The Jansenists erect 'grace' into a kind of fourth
person of the Trinity. They are, without thinking or
intending it, Quaternitarians. St. Paul and St. Augus-

tine, too exclusively studied, have done all the mischief. Instead of 'grace,' say help, succour, a divine influence, a dew of heaven; then one can come to a right understanding. The word 'grace' is a sort of talisman, all the baneful spell of which can be broken by translating it. The trick of personifying words is a fatal source of mischief in theology."

Once more :—

"The Jansenists tell men to love God; the Jesuits make men love him. The doctrine of these last is full of loosenesses, or, if you will, of errors; still,—singular as it may seem, it is undeniable,—they are the better directors of souls.

"The Jansenists have carried into religion more thought than the Jesuits, and they go deeper; they are faster bound with its sacred bonds. They have in their way of thinking an austerity which incessantly constrains the will to keep the path of duty; all the habits of their understanding, in short, are more Christian. But they seem to love God without affection, and solely from reason, from duty, from justice. The Jesuits, on the other hand, seem to love him from pure inclination; out of admiration, gratitude, tenderness; for the pleasure of loving him, in short. In their books of devotion you find joy, because with the Jesuits nature and religion go hand in hand. In the books of the Jansenists there is a sadness and a moral constraint, because with the Jansenists religion is for ever trying to put nature in bonds.'

The Jesuits have suffered, and deservedly suffered, plenty of discredit from what Joubert gently calls their "loosenesses ;" let them have the merit of their amiability.

The most characteristic thoughts one can quote from any writer are always his thoughts on matters like these ; but the maxims of Joubert on purely literary subjects also, have the same purged and subtle delicacy ; they show the same sedulousness in him to preserve perfectly true the balance of his soul. Let me begin with this, which contains a truth too many people fail to perceive :—

"Ignorance, which in matters of morals extenuates the crime, is itself, in matters of literature, a crime of the first order."

And here is another sentence, worthy of Goethe, to clear the air at one's entrance into the region of literature :—

"With the fever of the senses, the delirium of the passions, the weakness of the spirit ; with the storms of the passing time and with the great scourges of human life,—hunger, thirst, dishonour, diseases, and death,—authors may as long as they like go on making novels which shall harrow our hearts ; but the soul says all the while, 'You hurt me.'"

And again :—

"Fiction has no business to exist unless it is more beautiful than reality. Certainly the monstrosities of fiction may be found in the booksellers' shops ; you buy them there for a certain number of francs, and you talk of them for a certain number of days ; but they have no place in literature, because in literature the one aim of art is the beautiful. Once lose sight of that, and you have the mere frightful reality."

That is just the right criticism to pass on these "monstrosities:" *they have no place in literature*, and those who produce them are not really men of letters. One would think that this was enough to deter from such production any man of genuine ambition. But most of us, alas! are what we must be, not what we ought to be,—not even what we know we ought to be.

The following, of which the first part reminds one of Wordsworth's sonnet, " If thou indeed derive thy light from heaven," excellently defines the true salutary function of literature, and the limits of this function :—

" Whether one is an eagle or an ant, in the intellectual world, seems to me not to matter much ; the essential thing is to have one's place marked there, one's station assigned, and to belong decidedly to a regular and wholesome order. A small talent, if it keeps within its limits and rightly fulfils its task, may reach the goal just as well as a greater one. To accustom mankind to pleasures which depend neither upon the bodily appetites nor upon money, by giving them a taste for the things of the mind, seems to me, in fact, the one proper fruit which nature has meant our literary productions to have. When they have other fruits, it is by accident, and, in general, not for good. Books which absorb our attention to such a degree that they rob us of all fancy for other books, are absolutely pernicious. In this way they only bring fresh crotchets and sects into the world; they multiply the great variety of weights, rules, and measures already existing; they are morally and politically a nuisance."

Who can read these words and not think of the limiting effect exercised by certain works in certain spheres and for certain periods; exercised even by the works of men of genius or virtue,—by the works of Rousseau, the works of Wesley, the works of Swedenborg? And what is it which makes the Bible so admirable a book, to be the one book of those who can have only one, but the miscellaneous character of the contents of the Bible?

Joubert was all his life a passionate lover of Plato; I hope other lovers of Plato will forgive me for saying that their adored object has never been more truly described than he is here :—

"Plato shows us nothing, but he brings brightness with him; he puts light into our eyes, and fills us with a clearness by which all objects afterwards become illuminated. He teaches us nothing; but he prepares us, fashions us, and makes us ready to know all. Somehow or other, the habit of reading him augments in us the capacity for discerning and entertaining whatever fine truths may afterwards present themselves. Like mountain-air, it sharpens our organs, and gives us an appetite for wholesome food."

"Plato loses himself in the void" (he says again); "but one sees the play of his wings, one hears their rustle." And the conclusion is : "It is good to breathe his air, but not to live upon him."

As a pendant to the criticism on Plato, this on the French moralist Nicole is excellent :—

"Nicole is a Pascal without style. It is not what he says which is sublime, but what he thinks; he rises, not by the natural elevation of his own spirit, but by that of his doctrines. One must not look to the form in him, but to the matter, which is exquisite. He ought to be read with a direct view of practice."

English people have hardly ears to hear the praises of Bossuet, and the Bossuet of Joubert is Bossuet at his very best; but this is a far truer Bossuet than the "declaimer" Bossuet of Lord Macaulay, himself a born rhetorician, if ever there was one:—

"Bossuet employs all our idioms, as Homer employed all the dialects. The language of kings, of statesmen, and of warriors; the language of the people and of the student, of the country and of the schools, of the sanctuary and of the courts of law; the old and the new, the trivial and the stately, the quiet and the resounding,—he turns all to his use; and out of all this he makes a style, simple, grave, majestic. His ideas are, like his words, varied,— common and sublime together. Times and doctrines in all their multitude were ever before his spirit, as things and words in all their multitude were ever before it. He is not so much a man as a human nature, with the temperance of a saint, the justice of a bishop, the prudence of a doctor, and the might of a great spirit."

After this on Bossuet, I must quote a criticism on Racine, to show that Joubert did not indiscriminately worship all the French gods of the grand century:—

"Those who find Racine enough for them are poor

souls and poor wits; they are souls and wits which
have never got beyond the callow and boarding-school
stage. Admirable, as no doubt he is, for his skill in
having made poetical the most humdrum sentiments
and the most middling sort of passions, he can yet
stand us in stead of nobody but himself. He is a
superior writer; and, in literature, that at once puts
a man on a pinnacle. But he is not an inimitable
writer."

And again: "The talent of Racine is in his works,
but Racine himself is not there. That is why he
himself became disgusted with them." "Of Racine,
as of his ancients, the genius lay in taste. His elegance is perfect, but it is not supreme, like that of
Virgil." And, indeed, there is something *supreme* in
an elegance which exercises such a fascination as
Virgil's does; which makes one return to his poems
again and again, long after one thinks one has done
with them; which makes them one of those books
that, to use Joubert's words, "lure the reader back to
them, as the proverb says good wine lures back the
wine-bibber." And the highest praise Joubert can
at last find for Racine is this, that he is the Virgil of
the ignorant;—"*Racine est le Virgile des ignorants.*"

Of Boileau, too, Joubert says: "Boileau is a powerful poet, but only in the world of half poetry." How
true is that of Pope also! And he adds: "Neither
Boileau's poetry nor Racine's flows from the fountain-
head." No Englishman, controverting the exaggerated French estimate of these poets, could desire
to use fitter words.

I will end with some remarks on Voltaire and Rousseau, remarks in which Joubert eminently shows his prime merit as a critic,—the soundness and completeness of his judgments. I mean that he has the faculty of judging with all the powers of his mind and soul at work together in due combination; and how rare is this faculty! how seldom is it exercised towards writers who so powerfully as Voltaire and Rousseau stimulate and call into activity a single side in us!

"Voltaire's wits came to their maturity twenty years sooner than the wits of other men, and remained in full vigour thirty years longer. The charm which our style in general gets from our ideas, his ideas get from his style. Voltaire is sometimes afflicted, sometimes strongly moved; but serious he never is. His very graces have an effrontery about them. He had correctness of judgment, liveliness of imagination, nimble wits, quick taste, and a moral sense in ruins. He is the most debauched of spirits, and the worst of him is that one gets debauched along with him. If he had been a wise man, and had had the self-discipline of wisdom, beyond a doubt half his wit would have been gone; it needed an atmosphere of *licence* in order to play freely. Those people who read him every day, create for themselves, by an invincible law, the necessity of liking him. But those people who, having given up reading him, gaze steadily down upon the influences which his spirit has shed abroad, find themselves in simple justice and duty compelled to detest him. It is impossible to be satisfied with him, and impossible not to be fascinated by him."

The literary sense in us is apt to rebel against so severe a judgment on such a charmer of the literary sense as Voltaire, and perhaps we English are not very liable to catch Voltaire's vices, while of some of his merits we have signal need ; still, as the real definitive judgment on Voltaire, Joubert's is undoubtedly the true one. It is nearly identical with that of Goethe. Joubert's sentence on Rousseau is in some respects more favourable :—

"That weight in the speaker (*auctoritas*) which the ancients talk of, is to be found in Bossuet more than in any other French author; Pascal, too, has it, and La Bruyère ; even Rousseau has something of it, but Voltaire not a particle. I can understand how a Rousseau—I mean a Rousseau cured of his faults—might at the present day do much good, and may even come to be greatly wanted ; but under no circumstances can a Voltaire be of any use."

The peculiar power of Rousseau's style has never been better hit off than in the following passage :—

"Rousseau imparted, if I may so speak, *bowels of feeling* to the words he used (*donna des entrailles à tous les mots*), and poured into them such a charm, sweetness so penetrating, energy so puissant, that his writings have an effect upon the soul something like that of those illicit pleasures which steal away our taste and intoxicate our reason."

The final judgment, however, is severe, and justly severe :—

"Life without actions ; life entirely resolved into affections and half-sensual thoughts ; do-nothingness setting up for a virtue ; cowardliness with voluptuousness ; fierce pride with nullity underneath it ; the strutting phrase of the most sensual of vagabonds, who has made his system of philosophy and can give it eloquently forth : there is Rousseau ! A piety in which there is no religion ; a severity which brings corruption with it ; a dogmatism which serves to ruin all authority : there is Rousseau's philosophy ! To all tender, ardent, and elevated natures, I say : Only Rousseau can detach you from religion, and only true religion can cure you of Rousseau."

I must yet find room, before I end, for one at least of Joubert's sayings on political matters ; here, too, the whole man shows himself ; and here, too, the affinity with Coleridge is very remarkable. How true, how true in France especially, is this remark on the contrasting direction taken by the aspirations of the community in ancient and in modern states :—

"The ancients were attached to their country by three things,—their temples, their tombs, and their forefathers. The two great bonds which united them to their government were the bonds of habit and antiquity. With the moderns, hope and the love of novelty have produced a total change. The ancients said *our forefathers*, we say *posterity :* we do not, like them, love our *patria*, that is to say, the country and the laws of our fathers, rather we love the laws and the country of our children ; the charm we are most sensible to is the charm of the future, and not the charm of the past."

And how keen and true is this criticism on the changed sense of the word "liberty" :—

"A great many words have changed their meaning. The word *liberty*, for example, had at bottom among the ancients the same meaning as the word *dominion*. *I would be free* meant, in the mouth of the ancient, *I would take part in governing or administering the State ;* in the mouth of a modern it means, *I would be independent*. The word *liberty* has with us a moral sense ; with them its sense was purely political."

Joubert had lived through the French Revolution, and to the modern cry for liberty he was prone to answer :—

"Let your cry be for free souls rather even than for free men. Moral liberty is the one vitally important liberty, the one liberty which is indispensable ; the other liberty is good and salutary only so far as it favours this. Subordination is in itself a better thing than independence. The one implies order and arrangement ; the other implies only self-sufficiency with isolation. The one means harmony, the other a single tone ; the one is the whole, the other is but the part."

"Liberty ! liberty !" he cries again ; "in all things let us have *justice,* and then we shall have enough liberty."

Let us have justice, and then we shall have enough liberty ! The wise man will never refuse to echo those words ; but then, such is the imperfection of human governments, that almost always, in order to get justice, one has first to secure liberty.

I do not hold up Joubert as a very astonishing and powerful genius, but rather as a delightful and edifying genius. I have not cared to exhibit him as a sayer of brilliant epigrammatic things, such things as " Notre vie est du vent tissu . . . . les dettes abrégent la vie . . . . celui qui a de l'imagination sans érudition a des ailes et n'a pas de pieds (*Our life is woven wind . . . . debts take from life . . . . the man of imagination without learning has wings and no feet*)," though for such sayings he is famous. In the first place, the French language is in itself so favourable a vehicle for such sayings, that the making them in it has the less merit; at least half the merit ought to go, not to the maker of the saying, but to the French language. In the second place, the peculiar beauty of Joubert is not there; it is not in what is exclusively intellectual,—it is in the union of *soul* with intellect, and in the delightful, satisfying result which this union produces. "Vivre, c'est penser et sentir son âme . . . . le bonheur est de sentir son âme bonne . . . . toute vérité nue et crue n'a pas assez passé par l'âme . . . . les hommes ne sont justes qu'envers ceux qu'ils aiment (*The essence of life lies in thinking and being conscious of one's soul . . . . happiness is the sense of one's soul being good . . . . if a truth is nude and crude, that is a proof it has not been steeped long enough in the soul ; . . . . man cannot even be just to his neighbour, unless he loves him*) ;" it is much rather in sayings like these that Joubert's best and innermost nature

manifests itself. He is the most prepossessing and
convincing of witnesses to the good of loving light.
Because he sincerely loved light, and did not prefer
to it any little private darkness of his own, he found
light; his eye was single, and therefore his whole
body was full of light. And because he was full of
light, he was also full of happiness. In spite of his
infirmities, in spite of his sufferings, in spite of his
obscurity, he was the happiest man alive; his life
was as charming as his thoughts. For certainly it is
natural that the love of light, which is already, in
some measure, the possession of light, should irradiate
and beatify the whole life of him who has it. There
is something unnatural and shocking where, as in the
case of Coleridge, it does not. Joubert pains us by
no such contradiction; "the same penetration of
spirit which made him such delightful company to his
friends, served also to make him perfect in his own
personal life, by enabling him always to perceive and
do what was right;" he loved and sought light till
he became so habituated to it, so accustomed to the
joyful testimony of a good conscience, that, to use his
own words, "he could no longer exist without this,
and was obliged to live without reproach if he would
live without misery."

Joubert was not famous while he lived, and he will
not be famous now that he is dead. But, before we
pity him for this, let us be sure what we mean, in literature, by *famous*. There are the famous men of genius
in literature,— the Homers, Dantes, Shakspeares:
of them we need not speak; their praise is for ever

and ever. Then there are the famous men of ability
in literature : their praise is in their own generation.
And what makes this difference ? The work of the
two orders of men is at the bottom the same,—*a criticism of life.* The end and aim of all literature, if one
considers it attentively, is, in truth, nothing but that.
But the criticism which the men of genius pass upon
human life is permanently acceptable to mankind ;
the criticism which the men of ability pass upon
human life is transitorily acceptable. Between Shakspeare's criticism of human life and Scribe's the difference is there ;—the one is permanently acceptable,
the other transitorily. Whence then, I repeat, this
difference ? It is that the acceptableness of Shak
speare's criticism depends upon its inherent truth: the
acceptableness of Scribe's upon its suiting itself, by
its subject-matter, ideas, mode of treatment, to the
taste of the generation that hears it. But the taste
and ideas of one generation are not those of the next.
This next generation in its turn arrives ;—first its
sharpshooters, its quick-witted, audacious light troops ;
then the elephantine main body. The imposing array
of its predecessor it confidently assails, riddles it with
bullets, passes over its body. It goes hard then with
many once popular reputations, with many authorities
once oracular. Only two kinds of authors are safe in
the general havoc. The first kind are the great
abounding fountains of truth, whose criticism of life
is a source of illumination and joy to the whole human
race for ever,—the Homers, the Shakspeares. These
are the sacred personages, whom all civilised warfare

respects. The second are those whom the out-skir-
mishers of the new generation, its forerunners,—quick-
witted soldiers, as I have said, the select of the army,
—recognise, though the bulk of their comrades behind might not, as of the same family and character
with the sacred personages, exercising like them an
immortal function, and like them inspiring a permanent
interest. They snatch them up, and set them in a
place of shelter, where the on-coming multitude may
not overwhelm them. These are the Jouberts. They
will never, like the Shakspeares, command the homage of the multitude ; but they are safe ; the multitude will not trample them down. Except these two
kinds, no author is safe. Let us consider, for example,
Joubert's famous contemporary, Lord Jeffrey. All
his vivacity and accomplishment avail him nothing ;
of the true critic he had in an eminent degree no
quality, except one,—curiosity. Curiosity he had,
but he had no gift for truth ; he cannot illuminate
and rejoice us ; no intelligent out-skirmisher of the
new generation cares about him, cares to put him in
safety ; at this moment we are all passing over his
body. Let us consider a greater than Jeffrey, a critic
whose reputation still stands firm,—will stand, many
people think, for ever,—the great apostle of the
Philistines, Lord Macaulay. Lord Macaulay was, as
I have already said, a born rhetorician ; a splendid
rhetorician doubtless, and, beyond that, an *English*
rhetorician also, an *honest* rhetorician ; still, beyond
the apparent rhetorical truth of things he never could
penetrate ; for their vital truth, for what the French

call the *vraie vérité*, he had absolutely no organ;
therefore his reputation, brilliant as it is, is not secure.
Rhetoric so good as his excites and gives pleasure;
but by pleasure alone you cannot permanently bind
men's spirits to you. Truth illuminates and gives
joy, and it is by the bond of joy, not of pleasure, that
men's spirits are indissolubly held. As Lord Macaulay's own generation dies out, as a new generation
arrives, without those ideas and tendencies of its predecessor which Lord Macaulay so deeply shared and
so happily satisfied, will he give the same pleasure?
and, if he ceases to give this, has he enough of light
in him to make him last? Pleasure the new generation will get from its own novel ideas and tendencies;
but light is another and a rarer thing, and must be
treasured wherever it can be found. Will Macaulay
be saved, in the sweep and pressure of time, for his
light's sake, as Johnson has already been saved by
two generations, Joubert by one? I think it very
doubtful. But for a spirit of any delicacy and dignity, what a fate, if he could foresee it! to be an
oracle for one generation, and then of little or no
account for ever. How far better, to pass with scant
notice through one's own generation, but to be singled
out and preserved by the very iconoclasts of the next,
then in their turn by those of the next, and so, like
the lamp of life itself, to be handed on from one
generation to another in safety! This is Joubert's
lot, and it is a very enviable one. The new men of
the new generations, while they let the dust deepen
on a thousand Laharpes, will say of him: "He lived

in the Philistine's day, in a place and time when almost every idea current in literature had the mark of Dagon upon it, and not the mark of the children of light. Nay, the children of light were as yet hardly so much as heard of : the Canaanite was then in the land. Still, there were even then a few, who, nourished on some secret tradition, or illumined, perhaps, by a divine inspiration, kept aloof from the reigning superstitions, never bowed the knee to the gods of Canaan ; and one of these few was called *Joubert*."

SPINOZA AND THE BIBLE.

" By the sentence of the angels, by the decree of the saints, we anathematise, cut off, curse, and execrate Baruch Spinoza, in the presence of these sacred books with the six hundred and thirteen precepts which are written therein, with the anathema wherewith Joshua anathematised Jericho ; with the cursing wherewith Elisha cursed the children ; and with all the cursings which are written in the Book of the Law : cursed be he by day, and cursed by night ; cursed when he lieth down, and cursed when he riseth up ; cursed when he goeth out, and cursed when he cometh in ; the Lord pardon him never ; the wrath and fury of the Lord burn upon this man, and bring upon him all the curses which are written in the Book of the Law. The Lord blot out his name under heaven. The Lord set him apart for destruction from all the tribes of Israel, with all the curses of the firmament which are written in the Book of this Law. . . . There shall no man speak to him, no man write to him, no man show him any kindness, no man stay

under the same roof with him, no man come nigh
him."

With these amenities, the current compliments of
theological parting, the Jews of the Portuguese synagogue at Amsterdam took in 1656 (and not in 1660,
as has till now been commonly supposed) their leave
of their erring brother, Baruch or Benedict Spinoza.
They remained children of Israel, and he became a
child of modern Europe.

That was in 1656, and Spinoza died in 1677, at
the early age of forty-four. Glory had not found
him out. His short life—a life of unbroken diligence,
kindliness, and purity—was passed in seclusion. But
in spite of that seclusion, in spite of the shortness of
his career, in spite of the hostility of the dispensers
of renown in the 18th century,—of Voltaire's disparagement and Bayle's detraction,—in spite of the
repellent form which he has given to his principal
work, in spite of the exterior semblance of a rigid
dogmatism alien to the most essential tendencies of
modern philosophy, in spite, finally, of the immense
weight of disfavour cast upon him by the long-
repeated charge of atheism, Spinoza's name has
silently risen in importance, the man and his work
have attracted a steadily increasing notice, and bid
fair to become soon what they deserve to become,—
in the history of modern philosophy the central point
of interest. An avowed translation of one of his
works,—his *Tractatus Theologico-Politicus*,—has at last
made its appearance in English. It is the principal
work which Spinoza published in his lifetime ; his

book on ethics, the work on which his fame rests, is posthumous.

The English translator has not done his task well. Of the character of his version there can, I am afraid, be no doubt ; one such passage as the following is decisive :—

"I confess that, *while with them* (the theologians) *I have never been able sufficiently to admire the unfathomed mysteries of Scripture, I have still found them giving utterance to nothing but Aristotelian and Platonic speculations*, artfully dressed up and cunningly accommodated to Holy Writ, lest the speakers should show themselves too plainly to belong to the sect of the Grecian heathens.   *Nor was it enough for these men to discourse with the Greeks ; they have further taken to raving with the Hebrew prophets.*"

This professes to be a translation of these words of Spinoza : "Fateor, eos nunquam satis mirari potuisse Scripturæ profundissima mysteria ; attamen præter Aristotelicorum vel Platonicorum speculationes nihil docuisse video, atque his, ne gentiles sectari viderentur, Scripturam accommodaverunt.   Non satis his fuit cum Graecis insanire, sed prophetas cum iisdem deliravisse voluerunt."   After one such specimen of a translator's force, the experienced reader has a sort of instinct that he may as well close the book at once, with a smile or a sigh, according as he happens to be a follower of the weeping or of the laughing philosopher.   If, in spite of this instinct, he persists in going on with the English version of the *Tractatus Theologico-Politicus*, he will find many more such specimens. It is not, however, my intention to fill my space with these, or with strictures upon their author. I prefer to remark, that he renders a service to literary history by pointing out, in his preface, how " to Bayle may be traced the disfavour in which the name of Spinoza was so long held;" that, in his observations on the system of the Church of England, he shows a laudable freedom from the prejudices of ordinary English Liberals of that advanced school to which he clearly belongs; and lastly, that, though he manifests little familiarity with Latin, he seems to have considerable familiarity with philosophy, and to be well able to follow and comprehend speculative reasoning. Let me advise him to unite his forces with those of some one who has that accurate knowledge of Latin which he himself has not, and then, perhaps, of that union a really good translation of Spinoza will be the result. And, having given him this advice, let me again turn, for a little, to the *Tractatus Theologico-Politicus* itself.

This work, as I have already said, is a work on the interpretation of Scripture, — it treats of the Bible. What was it exactly which Spinoza thought about the Bible and its inspiration? That will be, at the present moment, the central point of interest for the English readers of his Treatise. Now, it is to be observed, that just on this very point the Treatise, interesting and remarkable as it is, will fail to satisfy the reader. It is important to seize this notion quite firmly, and not to quit hold of it while one is reading Spinoza's work. The scope of that work is this.

Spinoza sees that the life and practice of Christian nations professing the religion of the Bible, are not the due fruits of the religion of the Bible ; he sees only hatred, bitterness, and strife, where he might have expected to see love, joy, and peace in believing ; and he asks himself the reason of this. The reason is, he says, that these people misunderstand their Bible. Well, then, is his conclusion, I will write a *Tractatus Theologico-Politicus.* I will show these people, that, taking the Bible for granted, taking it to be all which it asserts itself to be, taking it to have all the authority which it claims, it is not what they imagine it to be, it does not say what they imagine it to say. I will show them what it really does say, and I will show them that they will do well to accept this real teaching of the Bible, instead of the phantom with which they have so long been cheated. I will show their governments that they will do well to remodel the national churches, to make of them institutions informed with the spirit of the true Bible, instead of institutions informed with the spirit of this false phantom.

The comments of men, Spinoza said, had been foisted into the Christian religion ; the pure teaching of God had been lost sight of. He determined, therefore, to go again to the Bible, to read it over and over with a perfectly unprejudiced mind, and to accept nothing as its teaching which it did not clearly teach. He began by constructing a method, or set of conditions indispensable for the adequate interpretation of Scripture. These conditions are such, he

points out, that a perfectly adequate interpretation of
Scripture is now impossible.   For example, to understand any prophet thoroughly, we ought to know the
life, character, and pursuits of that prophet, under
what circumstances his book was composed, and in
what state and through what hands it has come down
to us ; and, in general, most of this we cannot now
know.   Still, the main sense of the Books of Scripture may be clearly seized by us.   Himself a Jew
with all the learning of his nation, and a man of the
highest natural powers, Spinoza had in the difficult
task of seizing this sense every aid which special
knowledge or pre-eminent faculties could supply.

In what then, he asks, does Scripture, interpreted
by its own aid, and not by the aid of Rabbinical
traditions or Greek philosophy, allege its own divinity
to consist ?   In a revelation given by God to the
prophets.   Now all knowledge is a divine revelation ;
but prophecy, as represented in Scripture, is one of
which the laws of human nature, considered in themselves alone, cannot be the cause.   Therefore nothing
must be asserted about it, except what is clearly
declared by the prophets themselves ; for they are
our only source of knowledge on a matter which does
not fall within the scope of our ordinary knowing
faculties.   But ignorant people, not knowing the
Hebrew genius and phraseology, and not attending to
the circumstances of the speaker, often imagine the
prophets to assert things which they do not.

The prophets clearly declare themselves to have
received the revelation of God through the means of

words and images;—not, as Christ, through immediate communication of the mind with the mind of
God. Therefore the prophets excelled other men by
the power and vividness of their representing and
imagining faculty, not by the perfection of their
mind. This is why they perceived almost everything
through figures, and express themselves so variously,
and so improperly, concerning the nature of God.
Moses imagined that God could be seen, and attributed to him the passions of anger and jealousy;
Micaiah imagined him sitting on a throne, with the
host of heaven on his right and left hand; Daniel as
an old man, with a white garment and white hair;
Ezekiel as a fire; the disciples of Christ thought they
saw the Spirit of God in the form of a dove; the
apostles in the form of fiery tongues.

Whence, then, could the prophets be certain of the
truth of a revelation which they received through the
imagination, and not by a mental process?—for only
an idea can carry the sense of its own certainty along
with it, not an imagination. To make them certain
of the truth of what was revealed to them, a reasoning process came in; they had to rely on the testimony of a sign; and (above all) on the testimony of
their own conscience, that they were good men, and
spoke for God's sake. Either testimony was incomplete without the other. Even the good prophet
needed for his message the confirmation of a sign;
but the bad prophet, the utterer of an immoral
doctrine, had no certainty for his doctrine, no truth
in it, even though he confirmed it by a sign. The

testimony of a good conscience was, therefore, the
prophet's grand source of certitude. Even this, however, was only a moral certitude, not a mathematical;
for no man can be perfectly sure of his own goodness.

The power of imagining, the power of feeling
what goodness is, and the habit of practising goodness, were therefore the sole essential qualifications
of a true prophet. But for the purpose of the
message, the revelation, which God designed him to
convey, these qualifications were enough. The sum
and substance of this revelation was simply: *Believe
in God, and lead a good life.* To be the organ of this
revelation, did not make a man more learned; it left
his scientific knowledge as it found it. This explains
the contradictory and speculatively false opinions
about God, and the laws of nature, which the patriarchs, the prophets, the apostles entertained. Abraham and the patriarchs knew God only as *El Sadai*,
the power which gives to every man that which
suffices him; Moses knew him as *Jehovah*, a self-
existent being, but imagined him with the passions of
a man. Samuel imagined that God could not repent
of his sentences; Jeremiah, that he could. Joshua,
on a day of great victory, the ground being white
with hail, seeing the daylight last longer than usual,
and imaginatively seizing this as a special sign of the
help divinely promised to him, declared that the sun
was standing still. To be obeyers of God themselves,
and inspired leaders of others to obedience and good
life, did not make Abraham and Moses metaphysi-
cians, or Joshua a natural philosopher. His revelation

no more changed the speculative opinions of each
prophet, than it changed his temperament or style.
The wrathful Elisha required the natural sedative of
music, before he could be the messenger of good
fortune to Jehoram. The high-bred Isaiah and
Nahum have the style proper to their condition, and
the rustic Ezekiel and Amos the style proper to
theirs. We are not therefore bound to pay heed to
the speculative opinions of this or that prophet, for
in uttering these he spoke as a mere man : only in
exhorting his hearers to obey God and lead a good
life was he the organ of a divine revelation.

To know and love God is the highest blessedness
of man, and of all men alike ; to this all mankind are
called, and not any one nation in particular. The
divine law, properly so named, is the method of life
for attaining this height of human blessedness : this
law is universal, written in the heart, and one for all
mankind. Human law is the method of life for
attaining and preserving temporal security and prosperity : this law is dictated by a lawgiver, and every
nation has its own. In the case of the Jews, this
law was dictated, by revelation, through the prophets ;
its fundamental precept was to obey God and to keep
his commandments, and it is therefore, in a secondary
sense, called divine ; but it was, nevertheless, framed
in respect of temporal things only. Even the truly
moral and divine precept of this law, to practise for
God's sake justice and mercy towards one's neighbour, meant for the Hebrew of the Old Testament
his Hebrew neighbour only, and had respect to the

concord and stability of the Hebrew commonwealth
The Jews were to obey God and to keep his commandments, that they might continue long in the land
given to them, and that it might be well with them
there. Their election was a temporal one, and lasted
only so long as their State. It is now over; and the
only election the Jews now have is that of the *pious*,
the *remnant* which takes place, and has always taken
place, in every other nation also. Scripture itself
teaches that there is a universal divine law, that this
is common to all nations alike, and is the law which
truly confers eternal blessedness. Solomon, the wisest
of the Jews, knew this law, as the few wisest men in
all nations have ever known it; but for the mass of
the Jews, as for the mass of mankind everywhere,
this law was hidden, and they had no notion of its
moral action, its *vera vita* which conducts to eternal
blessedness, except so far as this action was enjoined
upon them by the prescriptions of their temporal law.
When the ruin of their State brought with it the ruin
of their temporal law, they would have lost altogether
their only clue to eternal blessedness.

Christ came when that fabric of the Jewish State,
for the sake of which the Jewish law existed, was
about to fall; and he proclaimed the universal divine
law. A certain moral action is prescribed by this
law, as a certain moral action was prescribed by the
Jewish law: but he who truly conceives the universal
divine law conceives God's decrees adequately as
eternal truths, and for him moral action has liberty
and self-knowledge; while the prophets of the Jewish

law inadequately conceived God's decrees as mere
rules and commands, and for them moral action had
no liberty and no self-knowledge.   Christ, who beheld
the decrees of God as God himself beholds them,—
as eternal truths,—proclaimed the love of God and
the love of our neighbour as *commands*, only because
of the ignorance of the multitude : to those to whom
it was "given to know the mysteries of the kingdom
of God," he announced them, as he himself perceived
them, as eternal truths.   And the apostles, like Christ,
spoke to many of their hearers "as unto carnal not
spiritual ; " presented to them, that is, the love of God
and their neighbour as a divine command authenticated
by the life and death of Christ, not as an eternal idea
of reason carrying its own warrant along with it.
The presentation of it as this latter their hearers
"were not able to bear."   The apostles, moreover,
though they preached and confirmed their doctrine by
signs as prophets, wrote their Epistles, not as prophets,
but as doctors and reasoners.   The essentials of their
doctrine, indeed, they took not from reason, but, like
the prophets, from fact and revelation ; they preached
belief in God and goodness of life as a catholic religion
existing by virtue of the passion of Christ, as the prophets had preached belief in God and goodness of life
as a national religion existing by virtue of the Mosaic
covenant : but while the prophets announced their
message in a form purely dogmatical, the apostles
developed theirs with the forms of reasoning and
argumentation, according to each apostle's ability and
way of thinking, and as they might best commend

their message to their hearers; and for their reasonings they themselves claim no divine authority, submitting them to the judgment of their hearers. Thus each apostle built essential religion on a non-essential foundation of his own, and, as St. Paul says, avoided building on the foundations of another apostle, which might be quite different from his own. Hence the discrepancies between the doctrine of one apostle and another,—between that of St. Paul, for example, and that of St. James; but these discrepancies are in the non-essentials not given to them by revelation, and not in essentials. Human churches, seizing these discrepant non-essentials as essentials, one maintaining one of them, another another, have filled the world with unprofitable disputes, have "turned the Church into an academy, and religion into a science, or rather a wrangling," and have fallen into endless schism.

What, then, are the essentials of religion according both to the Old and to the New Testament? Very few and very simple. The precept to love God and our neighbour. The precepts of the first chapter of Isaiah: "Wash you, make you clean; put away the evil of your doings from before mine eyes; cease to do evil; learn to do well; seek judgment; relieve the oppressed; judge the fatherless; plead for the widow." The precepts of the Sermon on the Mount, which add to the foregoing the injunction that we should cease to do evil and learn to do well, not to our brethren and fellow-citizens only, but to all mankind. It is by following these precepts that belief in God is to be shown: if we believe in him, we shall keep his com-

mandment; and this is his commandment, that we
love one another. It is because it contains these precepts that the Bible is properly called the Word of
God, in spite of its containing much that is mere
history, and, like all history, sometimes true, some
times false; in spite of its containing much that is
mere reasoning, and, like all reasoning, sometimes
sound, sometimes hollow. These precepts are also
the precepts of the universal divine law written in
our hearts; and it is only by this that the divinity of
Scripture is established;—by its containing, namely,
precepts identical with those of this inly-written and
self-proving law. This law was in the world, as St.
John says, before the doctrine of Moses or the doctrine
of Christ. And what need was there, then, for these
doctrines? Because the world at large "knew not"
this original divine law, in which precepts are ideas,
and the belief in God the knowledge and contempla-
tion of him. Reason gives us this law, reason tells
us that it leads to eternal blessedness, and that those
who follow it have no need of any other. But reason
could not have told us that the moral action of the
universal divine law,—followed not from a sense of
its intrinsic goodness, truth, and necessity, but simply
in proof of obedience (for both the Old and New
Testament are but one long discipline of obedience),
simply because it is so commanded by Moses in virtue
of the covenant, simply because it is so commanded
by Christ in virtue of his life and passion,—can lead
to eternal blessedness, which means, for reason, eternal
knowledge. Reason could not have told us this, and

this is what the Bible tells us. This is that "thing which had been kept secret since the foundation of the world." It is thus that by means of the foolishness of the world God confounds the wise, and with things that are not brings to nought things that are. Of the truth of the promise thus made to obedience without knowledge, we can have no mathematical certainty; for we can have a mathematical certainty only of things deduced by reason from elements which she in herself possesses. But we can have a moral certainty of it; a certainty such as the prophets had themselves, arising out of the goodness and pureness of those to whom this revelation has been made, and rendered possible for us by its contradicting no principles of reason. It is a great comfort to believe it; because "as it is only the very small minority who can pursue a virtuous life by the sole guidance of reason, we should, unless we had this testimony of Scripture, be in doubt respecting the salvation of nearly the whole human race."

It follows from this that philosophy has her own independent sphere, and theology hers, and that neither has the right to invade and try to subdue the other. Theology demands perfect obedience, philosophy perfect knowledge: the obedience demanded by theology and the knowledge demanded by philosophy are alike saving. As speculative opinions about God, theology requires only such as are indispensable to the reality of this obedience; the belief that God is, that he is a rewarder of them that seek him, and that the proof of seeking him is a good life. These

are the fundamentals of faith, and they are so clear
and simple that none of the inaccuracies provable in
the Bible narrative the least affect them, and they
have indubitably come to us uncorrupted. He who
holds them may make, as the patriarchs and prophets
did, other speculations about God most erroneous,
and yet their faith is complete and saving. Nay,
beyond these fundamentals, speculative opinions are
pious or impious, not as they are true or false, but as
they confirm or shake the believer in the practice of
obedience. The truest speculative opinion about the
nature of God is impious if it makes its holder re-
bellious; the falsest speculative opinion is pious if it
makes him obedient. Governments should never render
themselves the tools of ecclesiastical ambition by pro-
mulgating as fundamentals of the national Church's
faith more than these, and should concede the fullest
liberty of speculation.

But the multitude, which respects only what
astonishes, terrifies, and overwhelms it, by no means
takes this simple view of its own religion. To the
multitude, religion seems imposing only when it is
subversive of reason, confirmed by miracles, conveyed
in documents materially sacred and infallible, and
dooming to damnation all without its pale. But this
religion of the multitude is not the religion which a
true interpretation of Scripture finds in Scripture.
Reason tells us that a miracle,—understanding by a
miracle a breach of the laws of nature,—is impossible,
and that to think it possible is to dishonour God; for
the laws of nature are the laws of God, and to say

that God violates the laws of nature is to say that he violates his own nature. Reason sees, too, that miracles can never attain their professed object,— that of bringing us to a higher knowledge of God; since our knowledge of God is raised only by perfecting and clearing our conceptions, and the alleged design of miracles is to baffle them. But neither does Scripture anywhere assert, as a general truth, that miracles are possible. Indeed, it asserts the contrary; for Jeremiah declares that Nature follows an invariable order. Scripture, however, like Nature herself, does not lay down speculative propositions (*Scriptura definitiones non tradit, ut nec etiam natura*). It relates matters in such an order and with such phraseology as a speaker (often not perfectly instructed himself) who wanted to impress his hearers with a lively sense of God's greatness and goodness would naturally employ; as Moses, for instance, relates to the Israelites the passage of the Red Sea without any mention of the east wind which attended it, and which is brought accidentally to our knowledge in another place. So that to know exactly what Scripture means in the relation of each seeming miracle, we ought to know (besides the tropes and phrases of the Hebrew language) the circumstances, and also,— since every one is swayed in his manner of presenting facts by his own preconceived opinions, and we have seen what those of the prophets were,—the preconceived opinions of each speaker. But this mode of interpreting Scripture is fatal to the vulgar notion of its verbal inspiration, of a sanctity and absolute truth

in all the words and sentences of which it is com·
posed.   This vulgar notion is, indeed, a palpable
error.   It is demonstrable from the internal testimony
of the Scriptures themselves, that the books from the
first of the Pentateuch to the last of Kings were put
together, after the first destruction of Jerusalem, by
a compiler (probably Ezra) who designed to relate
the history of the Jewish people from its origin to
that destruction; it is demonstrable, moreover, that
the compiler did not put his last hand to the work,
but left it with its extracts from various and conflict-
ing sources sometimes unreconciled, left it with errors
of text and unsettled readings.   The prophetic books
are mere fragments of the prophets, collected by the
Rabbins where they could find them, and inserted in
the Canon according to their discretion.   They, at
first, proposed to admit neither the Book of Proverbs
nor the Book of Ecclesiastes into the Canon, and only
admitted them because there were found in them
passages which commended the law of Moses.   Ezekiel
also they had determined to exclude; but one of
their number remodelled him, so as to procure his
admission.   The Books of Ezra, Nehemiah, Esther,
and Daniel are the work of a single author, and were
not written till after Judas Maccabeus had restored
the worship of the Temple.   The Book of Psalms
was collected and arranged at the same time.   Before
this time, there was no Canon of the sacred writings,
and the great synagogue, by which the Canon was
fixed, was first convened after the Macedonian conquest of Asia.   Of that synagogue none of the pro·

phets were members; the learned men who composed
it were guided by their own fallible judgment. In
like manner the uninspired judgment of human coun-
cils determined the Canon of the New Testament.

Such, reduced to the briefest and plainest terms
possible, stripped of the developments and proofs
with which he delivers it, and divested of the metaphysical language in which much of it is clothed by
him, is the doctrine of Spinoza's treatise on the interpretation of Scripture. By the whole scope and
drift of its argument, by the spirit in which the subject is throughout treated, his work undeniably is
most interesting and stimulating to the general culture
of Europe. There are errors and contradictions in
Scripture; and the question which the general culture
of Europe, well aware of this, asks with real interest
is: What then? What follows from all this? What
change is it, if true, to produce in the relations of
mankind to the Christian religion? If the old theory
of Scripture inspiration is to be abandoned, what
place is the Bible henceforth to hold among books?
What is the new Christianity to be like? How are
governments to deal with National Churches founded
to maintain a very different conception of Christianity?
Spinoza addresses himself to these questions. All
secondary points of criticism he touches with the
utmost possible brevity. He points out that Moses
could never have written: "And the Canaanite was
then in the land," because the Canaanite was in the
land still at the death of Moses. He points out that

Moses could never have written : "There arose not a prophet since in Israel like unto Moses." He points out how such a passage as, "These are the kings that reigned in Edom *before there reigned any king over the children of Israel*," clearly indicates an author writing not before the times of the Kings. He points out how the account of Og's iron bedstead : "Only Og the king of Bashan remained of the remnant of giants ; behold, his bedstead was a bedstead of iron ; is it not in Rabbath of the children of Ammon ?"— probably indicates an author writing after David had taken Rabbath, and found there "abundance of spoil," amongst it this iron bedstead, the gigantic relic of another age. He points out how the language of this passage, and of such a passage as that in the Book of Samuel : "Beforetime in Israel, when a man went to inquire of God, thus he spake : Come and let us go to the seer ; for he that is now called prophet was aforetime called seer"—is certainly the language of a writer describing the events of a long-past age, and not the language of a contemporary. But he devotes to all this no more space than is absolutely necessary. He apologises for delaying over such matters so long : *non est cur circa hæc diu detinear—nolo tædiosâ lectione lectorem detinere.* For him the interesting question is, not whether the fanatical devotee of the letter is to continue, for a longer or for a shorter time, to believe that Moses sate in the land of Moab writing the description of his own death, but what he is to believe when he does not believe this. Is he to take for the guidance

of his life a great gloss put upon the Bible by theologians, who, "not content with going mad themselves
with Plato and Aristotle, want to make Christ and
the prophets go mad with them too,"—or the Bible
itself? Is he to be presented by his national church
with metaphysical formularies for his creed, or with
the real fundamentals of Christianity? If with the
former, religion will never produce its due fruits. A
few elect will still be saved; but the vast majority of
mankind will remain without grace and without good
works, hateful and hating one another. Therefore
he calls urgently upon governments to make the
national church what it should be. This is the conclusion of the whole matter for him; a fervent appeal
to the State, to save us from the untoward generation
of metaphysical Article-makers. And therefore,
anticipating Mr. Gladstone, he called his book *The
Church in its Relations with the State.*

Such is really the scope of Spinoza's work. He
pursues a great object, and pursues it with signal
ability. But it is important to observe that he
nowhere distinctly gives his own opinion about the
Bible's fundamental character. He takes the Bible as
it stands, as he might take the phenomena of nature,
and he discusses it as he finds it. Revelation differs
from natural knowledge, he says, not by being more
divine or more certain than natural knowledge, but
by being conveyed in a different way; it differs from
it because it is a knowledge "of which the laws of
human nature considered in themselves alone cannot
be the cause." What is really its cause, he says, we

need not here inquire (*verum nec nobis jam opus est pro-
pheticæ cognitionis causam scire*), for we take Scripture,
which contains this revelation, as it stands, and do not
ask how it arose (*documentorum causas nihil curamus*).

Proceeding on this principle, Spinoza leaves the
attentive reader somewhat baffled and disappointed,
clear, as is his way of treating his subject, and remarkable as are the conclusions with which he presents us. He starts, we feel, from what is to him
a hypothesis, and we want to know what he really
thinks about this hypothesis. His greatest novelties
are all within limits fixed for him by this hypothesis.
He says that the voice which called Samuel was an
imaginary voice; he says that the waters of the Red
Sea retreated before a strong wind; he says that the
Shunammite's son was revived by the natural heat of
Elisha's body; he says that the rainbow which was
made a sign to Noah appeared in the ordinary course
of nature. Scripture itself, rightly interpreted, says,
he affirms, all this. But he asserts that the divine
voice which uttered the commandments on Mount
Sinai was a real voice, *vera vox*. He says, indeed, that
this voice could not really give to the Israelites that
proof which they imagined it gave to them of the
existence of God, and that God on Sinai was dealing
with the Israelites only according to their imperfect
knowledge. Still he asserts the divine voice to have
been a real one; and for this reason, that we do
violence to Scripture if we do not admit it to have
been a real one (*nisi Scripturæ vim inferre velimus,
omnino concedendum est, Israëlitas veram vocem audivisse*).

The attentive reader wants to know what Spinoza himself thought about this *vera vox* and its possibility; he is much more interested in knowing this than in knowing what Spinoza considered Scripture to affirm about the matter.

The feeling of perplexity thus caused is not diminished by the language of the chapter on miracles. In this chapter Spinoza broadly affirms a miracle to be an impossibility. But he himself contrasts the method of demonstration *à priori,* by which he claims to have established this proposition, with the method which he has pursued in treating of prophetic revelation. "This revelation," he says, "is a matter out of human reach, and therefore I was bound to take it as I found it." *Monere volo, me aliâ prorsus methodo circa miracula processisse, quam circa prophetiam . . . quod etiam consulto feci, quia de prophetiâ, quandoquidem ipsa captum humanum superat et quæstio mere theologica est, nihil affirmare, neque etiam scire poteram in quo ipsa potissimum constiterit, nisi ex fundamentis revelatis.* The reader feels that Spinoza, proceeding on a hypothesis, has presented him with the assertion of a miracle, and afterwards, proceeding *à priori,* has presented him with the assertion that a miracle is impossible. He feels that Spinoza does not adequately reconcile these two assertions by declaring that any event really miraculous, if found recorded in Scripture, must be "a spurious addition made to Scripture by sacrilegious men." Is, then, he asks the *vera vox* of Mount Sinai in Spinoza's opinion a spurious addition made to Scripture by sacrilegious men; or, if not, how is it not miraculous?

Spinoza, in his own mind, regarded the Bible as a vast collection of miscellaneous documents, many of them quite disparate and not at all to be harmonised with others; documents of unequal value and of varying applicability, some of them conveying ideas salutary for one time, others for another. But in the *Tractatus Theologico-Politicus* he by no means always deals in this free spirit with the Bible. Sometimes he chooses to deal with it in the spirit of the veriest worshipper of the letter; sometimes he chooses to treat the Bible as if all its parts were (so to speak) equipollent; to snatch an isolated text which suits his purpose, without caring whether it is annulled by the context, by the general drift of Scripture, or by other passages of more weight and authority. The great critic thus becomes voluntarily as uncritical as Exeter Hall. The Epicurean Solomon, whose *Ecclesiastes* the Hebrew doctors, even after they had received it into the canon, forbade the young and weak-minded among their community to read, Spinoza quotes as of the same authority with the severe Moses; he uses promiscuously, as documents of identical force, without discriminating between their essentially different character, the softened cosmopolitan teaching of the prophets of the captivity and the rigid national teaching of the instructors of Israel's youth. He is capable of extracting, from a chance expression of Jeremiah, the assertion of a speculative idea which Jeremiah certainly never entertained, and from which he would have recoiled in dismay,—the idea, namely, that miracles are impos-

sible; just as the ordinary Englishman can extract
from God's words to Noah, *Be fruitful and multiply*,
an exhortation to himself to have a large family.
Spinoza, I repeat, knew perfectly well what this
verbal mode of dealing with the Bible was worth:
but he sometimes uses it because of the hypothesis
from which he set out; because of his having agreed
"to take Scripture as it stands, and not to ask how it
arose."

No doubt the sagacity of Spinoza's rules for
Biblical interpretation, the power of his analysis of
the contents of the Bible, the interest of his reflec-
tions on Jewish history, are, in spite of this, very
great, and have an absolute worth of their own, independent of the silence or ambiguity of their author
upon a point of cardinal importance. Few candid
people will read his rules of interpretation without
exclaiming that they are the very dictates of good
sense, that they have always believed in them; and
without adding, after a moment's reflection, that
they have passed their lives in violating them. And
what can be more interesting, than to find that perhaps the main cause of the decay of the Jewish polity
was one of which from our English Bible, which entirely mistranslates the 26th verse of the 20th chapter
of Ezekiel, we hear nothing,—the perpetual reproach
of impurity and rejection cast upon the mass of the
Hebrew nation by the exclusive priesthood of the
tribe of Levi? What can be more suggestive, after
Mr. Mill and Dr. Stanley have been telling us how
great an element of strength to the Hebrew nation

was the institution of prophets, than to hear from the
ablest of Hebrews how this institution seems to him
to have been to his nation one of her main elements
of weakness?   No intelligent man can read the
Tractatus Theologico-Politicus without being profoundly
instructed by it : but neither can he read it without
feeling that, as a speculative work, it is, to use a
French military expression, *in the air;* that, in a certain
sense, it is in want of a base and in want of supports ;
that this base and these supports are, at any rate, not
to be found in the work itself, and, if they exist, must
be sought for in other works of the author.

The genuine speculative opinions of Spinoza, which
the *Tractatus Theologico-Politicus* but imperfectly re-
veals, may in his Ethics and in his Letters be found
set forth clearly.   It is, however, the business of
criticism to deal with every independent work as with
an independent whole, and, instead of establishing
between the *Tractatus Theologico-Politicus* and the
Ethics of Spinoza a relation which Spinoza himself
has not established,—to seize, in dealing with the
Tractatus Theologico-Politicus, the important fact that
this work has its source, not in the axioms and definition of the Ethics, but in a hypothesis.   The Ethics
are not yet translated into English, and I have not
here to speak of them.   Then will be the right time
for criticism to try and seize the special character and
tendencies of that remarkable work, when it is dealing with it directly.   The criticism of the Ethics is
far too serious a task to be undertaken incidentally,
and merely as a supplement to the criticism of the

Tractatus Theologico-Politicus. Nevertheless, on certain governing ideas of Spinoza, which receive their systematic expression, indeed, in the Ethics, and on which the *Tractatus Theologico-Politicus* is not formally based, but which are yet never absent from Spinoza's mind in the composition of any work, which breathe through all his works, and fill them with a peculiar effect and power, I have a word or two to say.

A philosopher's real power over mankind resides not in his metaphysical formulas, but in the spirit and tendencies which have led him to adopt those formulas. Spinoza's critic, therefore, has rather to bring to light that spirit and those tendencies of his author, than to exhibit his metaphysical formulas. Propositions about substance pass by mankind at large like the idle wind, which mankind at large regards not; it will not even listen to a word about these propositions, unless it first learns what their author was driving at with them, and finds that this object of his is one with which it sympathises, one, at any rate, which commands its attention. And mankind is so far right that this object of the author is really, as has been said, that which is most important, that which sets all his work in motion, that which is the secret of his attraction for other minds, which, by different ways, pursue the same object.

Mr. Maurice, seeking for the cause of Goethe's great admiration for Spinoza, thinks that he finds it in Spinoza's Hebrew genius. " He spoke of God," says Mr. Maurice, " as an actual being, to those who had fancied him a name in a book. The child of the

circumcision had a message for Lessing and Goethe
which the pagan schools of philosophy could not
bring." This seems to me, I confess, fanciful. An
intensity and impressiveness, which came to him
from his Hebrew nature, Spinoza no doubt has ; but
the two things which are most remarkable about him,
and by which, as I think, he chiefly impressed
Goethe, seem to me not to come to him from his
Hebrew nature at all,—I mean his denial of final
causes, and his stoicism, a stoicism not passive, but
active. For a mind like Goethe's,—a mind profoundly impartial and passionately aspiring after the
science, not of men only, but of universal nature,—
the popular philosophy which explains all things by
reference to man, and regards universal nature as
existing for the sake of man, and even of certain
classes of men, was utterly repulsive. Unchecked,
this philosophy would gladly maintain that the
donkey exists in order that the invalid Christian may
have donkey's milk before breakfast ; and such views
of nature as this were exactly what Goethe's whole
soul abhorred. Creation, he thought, should be
made of sterner stuff ; he desired to rest the donkey's
existence on larger grounds. More than any philosopher who has ever lived, Spinoza satisfied him here.
The full exposition of the counter-doctrine to the
popular doctrine of final causes is to be found in the
Ethics ; but this denial of final causes was so essential an element of all Spinoza's thinking that we
shall, as has been said already, find it in the work
with which we are here concerned, the *Tractatus*

Theologico-Politicus, and, indeed, permeating that work
and all his works.   From the *Tractatus Theologico-
Politicus* one may take as good a general statement of
this denial as any which is to be found in the Ethics :—

"Deus naturam dirigit, prout ejus leges univer-
sales, non autem prout humanæ naturæ particulares
leges exigunt, adeoque Deus non solius humani
generis, sed totius naturæ rationem habet. (*God
directs nature, according as the universal laws of nature,
but not according as the particular laws of human nature
require ; and so God has regard, not of the human race
only, but of entire nature.*)"

And, as a pendant to this denial by Spinoza of
final causes, comes his stoicism :—

"Non studemus, ut natura nobis, sed contra ut nos
naturæ pareamus. (*Our desire is not that nature may
obey us, but, on the contrary, that we may obey nature.*)"

Here is the second source of his attractiveness for
Goethe ; and Goethe is but the eminent representative of a whole order of minds whose admiration has
made Spinoza's fame.   Spinoza first impresses Goethe
and any man like Goethe, and then he composes him ;
first he fills and satisfies his imagination by the width
and grandeur of his view of nature, and then he
fortifies and stills his mobile, straining, passionate,
poetic temperament by the moral lesson he draws
from his view of nature.   And a moral lesson not of
mere resigned acquiescence, not of melancholy quietism, but of joyful activity within the limits of man's
true sphere :—

"Ipsa hominis essentia est conatus quo unusquis-

que suum esse conservare conatur. . . . Virtus hominis est ipsa hominis essentia, quatenus a solo conatu
suum esse conservandi definitur. . . . Felicitas in eo
consistit quod homo suum esse conservare potest. . . .
Lætitia est hominis transitio ad majorem perfectionem
. . . Tristitia est hominis transitio ad minorem perfectionem. (*Man's very essence is the effort wherewith
each man strives to maintain his own being. . . . Man's
virtue is this very essence, so far as it is defined by this
single effort to maintain his own being. . . . Happiness
consists in a man's being able to maintain his own being.
. . . Joy is man's passage to a greater perfection. . . .
Sorrow is man's passage to a lesser perfection.*)"

It seems to me that by neither of these, his grand
characteristic doctrines, is Spinoza truly Hebrew or
truly Christian. His denial of final causes is essentially alien to the spirit of the Old Testament, and his
cheerful and self-sufficing stoicism is essentially alien
to the spirit of the New. The doctrine that "God
directs nature, not according as the particular laws of
human nature, but according as the universal laws of
nature require," is at utter variance with that Hebrew
mode of representing God's dealings, which makes
the locusts visit Egypt to punish Pharaoh's hardness
of heart, and the falling dew avert itself from the
fleece of Gideon. The doctrine that "all sorrow is a
passage to a lesser perfection" is at utter variance
with the Christian recognition of the blessedness of
sorrow, working "repentance to salvation not to be
repented of;" of sorrow, which, in Dante's words,
"remarries us to God."

Spinoza's repeated and earnest assertions that the love of God is man's *summum bonum* do not remove the fundamental diversity between his doctrine and the Hebrew and Christian doctrines. By the love of God he does not mean the same thing which the Hebrew and Christian religions mean by the love of God. He makes the love of God to consist in the knowledge of God; and, as we know God only through his manifestation of himself in the laws of all nature, it is by knowing these laws that we love God, and the more we know them the more we love him. This may be true, but this is not what the Christian means by the love of God. Spinoza's ideal is the intellectual life; the Christian's ideal is the religious life. Between the two conditions there is all the difference which there is between the being in love, and the following, with delighted comprehension, a reasoning of Plato. For Spinoza, undoubtedly, the crown of the intellectual life is a transport, as for the saint the crown of the religious life is a transport; but the two transports are not the same.

This is true; yet it is true, also, that by thus crowning the intellectual life with a sacred transport, by thus retaining in philosophy, amid the discontented murmurs of all the army of atheism, the name of God, Spinoza maintains a profound affinity with that which is truest in religion, and inspires an indestructible interest. One of his admirers, M. Van Vloten, has recently published at Amsterdam a supplementary volume to Spinoza's works, containing the interesting document of Spinoza's sentence of excommunication.

from which I have already quoted, and containing, besides, several lately found works alleged to be Spinoza's, which seem to me to be of doubtful authenticity, and, even if authentic, of no great importance. M. Van Vloten (who, let me be permitted to say in passing, writes a Latin which would make one think that the art of writing Latin must be now a lost art in the country of Lipsius) is very anxious that Spinoza's unscientific retention of the name of God should not afflict his readers with any doubts as to his perfect scientific orthodoxy :—

"It is a great mistake," he cries, "to disparage Spinoza as merely one of the dogmatists before Kant. By keeping the name of God, while he did away with his person and character, he has done himself an injustice. Those who look to the bottom of things will see, that, long ago as he lived, he had even then reached the point to which the post-Hegelian philosophy and the study of natural science has only just brought our own times. Leibnitz expressed his apprehension lest those who did away with final causes should do away with God at the same time. But it is in his having done away with final causes, *and with God along with them*, that Spinoza's true merit consists."

Now it must be remarked that to use Spinoza's denial of final causes in order to identify him with the Coryphæi of atheism, is to make a false use of Spinoza's denial of final causes, just as to use his assertion of the all-importance of loving God to identify him with the saints would be to make a false use of

his assertion of the all-importance of loving God. He
is no more to be identified with the post-Hegelian philosophers than he is to be identified with St. Augustine.
Unction, indeed, Spinoza's writings have not; that
name does not precisely fit any quality which they
exhibit. And yet, so all-important in the sphere of
religious thought is the power of edification, that in
this sphere a great fame like Spinoza's can never be
founded without it. A court of literature can never
be very severe to Voltaire: with that inimitable wit
and clear sense of his, he cannot write a page in
which the fullest head may not find something
suggestive: still, because, handling religious ideas,
he yet, with all his wit and clear sense, handles
them wholly without the power of edification, his
fame as a great man is equivocal. Strauss has treated
the question of Scripture miracles with an acuteness
and fulness which even to the most informed minds
is instructive; but because he treats it almost wholly
without the power of edification, his fame as a serious
thinker is equivocal. But in Spinoza there is not a
trace either of Voltaire's passion for mockery or of
Strauss's passion for demolition. His whole soul was
filled with desire of the love and knowledge of God,
and of that only. Philosophy always proclaims herself
on the way to the *summum bonum;* but too often on
the road she seems to forget her destination, and
suffers her hearers to forget it also. Spinoza never
forgets his destination: "The love of God is man's
highest happiness and blessedness, and the final end
and aim of all human actions;"—"The supreme re-

ward for keeping God's Word is that Word itself—
namely, to know him and with free will and pure
and constant heart love him:" these sentences are
the keynote to all he produced, and were the inspiration of all his labours. This is why he turns so
sternly upon the worshippers of the letter,—the
editors of the *Masora*, the editor of the *Record*,—
because their doctrine imperils our love and knowledge of God. "What!" he cries, "our knowledge
of God to depend upon these perishable things, which
Moses can dash to the ground and break to pieces
like the first tables of stone, or of which the originals
can be lost like the original book of the Covenant,
like the original book of the Law of God, like the
book of the Wars of God! . . . which can come
to us confused, imperfect, mis-written by copyists,
tampered with by doctors! And you accuse others
of impiety! It is you who are impious, to believe
that God would commit the treasure of the true
record of himself to any substance less enduring than
the heart!"

And Spinoza's life was not unworthy of this elevated
strain. A philosopher who professed that knowledge
was its own reward, a devotee who professed that the
love of God was its own reward, this philosopher and
this devotee believed in what he said. Spinoza led a
life the most spotless, perhaps, to be found among the
lives of philosophers; he lived simple, studious, even-
tempered, kind; declining honours, declining riches,
declining notoriety. He was poor, and his admirer
Simon de Vries sent him two thousand florins;—he

refused them.   The same friend left him his fortune;
—he returned it to the heir.   He was asked to dedi-
cate one of his works to the magnificent patron of
letters in his century, Louis the Fourteenth;—he
declined.   His great work, his Ethics, published after
his death, he gave injunctions to his friends to publish
anonymously, for fear he should give his name to a
school.   Truth, he thought, should bear no man's
name.   And finally, — "Unless," he said, "I had
known that my writings would in the end advance
the cause of true religion, I would have suppressed
them,—*tacuissem.*"   It was in this spirit that he lived;
and this spirit gives to all he writes not exactly unction,
—I have already said so,—but a kind of sacred solemnity.   Not of the same order as the saints, he yet
follows the same service : *Doubtless thou art our Father,
though Abraham be ignorant of us, and Israel acknowledge
us not.*

Therefore he has been, in a certain sphere, edifying,
and has inspired in many powerful minds an interest
and an admiration such as no other philosopher has
inspired since Plato.   The lonely precursor of German
philosophy, he still shines when the light of his successors is fading away; they had celebrity, Spinoza
has fame.   Not because his peculiar system of philosophy has had more adherents than theirs; on the
contrary, it has had fewer.   But schools of philosophy
arise and fall; their bands of adherents inevitably
dwindle; no master can long persuade a large body
of disciples that they give to themselves just the same
account of the world as he does; it is only the very

young and the very enthusiastic who can think themselves sure that they possess the whole mind of Plato,
or Spinoza, or Hegel, at all. The very mature and
the very sober can even hardly believe that these
philosophers possessed it themselves enough to put it
all into their works, and to let us know entirely how
the world seemed to them. What a remarkable
philosopher really does for human thought, is to
throw into circulation a certain number of new and
striking ideas and expressions, and to stimulate with
them the thought and imagination of his century or
of after-times. So Spinoza has made his distinction
between adequate and inadequate ideas a current
notion for educated Europe. So Hegel seized a single
pregnant sentence of Heracleitus, and cast it, with a
thousand striking applications, into the world of
modern thought. But to do this is only enough to
make a philosopher noteworthy; it is not enough to
make him great. To be great, he must have something in him which can influence character, which is
edifying; he must, in short, have a noble and lofty
character himself, a character,—to recur to that much-
criticised expression of mine, — *in the grand style.*
This is what Spinoza had; and because he had it, he
stands out from the multitude of philosophers, and
has been able to inspire in powerful minds a feeling
which the most remarkable philosophers, without this
grandiose character, could not inspire. "There is no
possible view of life but Spinoza's," said Lessing.
Goethe has told us how he was calmed and edified by
him in his youth, and how he again went to him for

support in his maturity.   Heine, the man (in spite of his faults) of truest genius that Germany has produced since Goethe,—a man with faults, as I have said, immense faults, the greatest of them being that he could reverence so little, — reverenced Spinoza.   Hegel's influence ran off him like water : "I have seen Hegel," he cries, "seated with his doleful air of a hatching hen upon his unhappy eggs, and I have heard his dismal clucking.—How easily one can cheat oneself into thinking that one understands everything, when one has learnt only how to construct dialectical formulas ! "   But of Spinoza, Heine said : "His life was a copy of the life of his divine kinsman, Jesus Christ."

And therefore, when M. Van Vloten violently presses the parallel with the post-Hegelians, one feels that the parallel with St. Augustine is the far truer one.   Compared with the soldier of irreligion M. Van Vloten would have him to be, Spinoza is religious. "It is true," one may say to the wise and devout Christian, "Spinoza's conception of beatitude is not yours, and cannot satisfy you, but whose conception of beatitude would you accept as satisfying ?   Not even that of the devoutest of your fellow-Christians. Fra Angelico, the sweetest and most inspired of devout souls, has given us, in his great picture of the Last Judgment, his conception of beatitude.   The elect are going round in a ring on long grass under laden fruit-trees; two of them, more restless than the others, are flying up a battlemented street,—a street blank with all the ennui of the Middle Ages.   Across a gulf is visible, for the delectation of the saints, a blazing caldron in which Beelzebub is sousing the damned. This is hardly more your conception of beatitude than Spinoza's is. But 'in my Father's house are many mansions;' only, to reach any one of these mansions, there are needed the wings of a genuine sacred transport, of an 'immortal longing.'" These wings Spinoza had; and, because he had them, his own language about himself, about his aspirations and his course, is true: his foot is in the *vera vita*, his eye on the beatific vision.

MARCUS AURELIUS.

MR. MILL says, in his book on Liberty, that "Christian morality is in great part merely a protest against
paganism; its ideal is negative rather than positive,
passive rather than active." He says, that, in certain
most important respects, "it falls far below the best
morality of the ancients." Now, the object of
systems of morality is to take possession of human
life, to save it from being abandoned to passion or
allowed to drift at hazard, to give it happiness by
establishing it in the practice of virtue; and this
object they seek to attain by prescribing to human
life fixed principles of action, fixed rules of conduct.
In its uninspired as well as in its inspired moments,
in its days of languor and gloom as well as in its
days of sunshine and energy, human life has thus
always a clue to follow, and may always be making
way towards its goal. Christian morality has not
failed to supply to human life aids of this sort. It
has supplied them far more abundantly than many
of its critics imagine. The most exquisite document

after those of the New Testament, of all the documents the Christian spirit has ever inspired,—the
Imitation,—by no means contains the whole of Christian morality; nay, the disparagers of this morality
would think themselves sure of triumphing if one
agreed to look for it in the *Imitation* only. But even
the *Imitation* is full of passages like these : " Vita
sine proposito languida et vaga est ; "—" Omni die
renovare debemus propositum nostrum, dicentes: nunc
hodiè perfectè incipiamus, quia nihil est quod hactenus
fecimus ;"—"Secundum propositum nostrum est cursus
profectûs nostri ; "—" Raro etiam unum vitium perfectè vincimus, et ad *quotidianum* profectum non ac-
cendimur;"—"Semper aliquid certi proponendum est ;"
—"Tibi ipsi violentiam frequenter fac : " (*A life without a purpose is a languid, drifting thing ;—Every day
we ought to renew our purpose, saying to ourselves : This
day let us make a sound beginning, for what we have
hitherto done is nought ;—Our improvement is in proportion to our purpose ;—We hardly ever manage to get completely rid even of one fault, and do not set our hearts on
daily improvement ;—Always place a definite purpose
before thee ;—Get the habit of mastering thine inclination.*)
These are moral precepts, and moral precepts of the
best kind. As rules to hold possession of our conduct, and to keep us in the right course through outward troubles and inward perplexity, they are equal
to the best ever furnished by the great masters of
morals—Epictetus or Marcus Aurelius.

But moral rules, apprehended as ideas first, and
then rigorously followed as laws, are, and must be,

for the sage only. The mass of mankind have neither
force of intellect enough to apprehend them clearly as
ideas, nor force of character enough to follow them
strictly as laws. The mass of mankind can be carried
along a course full of hardship for the natural man,
can be borne over the thousand impediments of the
narrow way, only by the tide of a joyful and bound-
ing emotion. It is impossible to rise from reading
Epictetus or Marcus Aurelius without a sense of constraint and melancholy, without feeling that the
burden laid upon man is well-nigh greater than he
can bear. Honour to the sages who have felt this,
and yet have borne it ! Yet, even for the sage, this
sense of labour and sorrow in his march towards the
goal constitutes a relative inferiority ; the noblest
souls of whatever creed, the pagan Empedocles as
well as the Christian Paul, have insisted on the necessity of an inspiration, a joyful emotion, to make
moral action perfect ; an obscure indication of this
necessity is the one drop of truth in the ocean of
verbiage with which the controversy on justification
by faith has flooded the world. But, for the ordinary
man, this sense of labour and sorrow constitutes an
absolute disqualification ; it paralyses him ; under the
weight of it, he cannot make way towards the goal at
all. The paramount virtue of religion is, that it has
lighted up morality ; that it has supplied the emotion
and inspiration needful for carrying the sage along
the narrow way perfectly, for carrying the ordinary
man along it at all. Even the religions with most
dross in them have had something of this virtue ; but

the Christian religion manifests it with unexampled splendour. "Lead me, Zeus and Destiny!" says the prayer of Epictetus, "whithersoever I am appointed to go; I will follow without wavering; even though I turn coward and shrink, I shall have to follow all the same." The fortitude of that is for the strong, for the few; even for them the spiritual atmosphere with which it surrounds them is bleak and gray. But, "Let thy loving spirit lead me forth into the land of righteousness;"—"The Lord shall be unto thee an everlasting light, and thy God thy glory;"— "Unto you that fear my name shall the sun of right-eousness arise with healing in his wings," says the Old Testament; "Born, not of blood, nor of the will of the flesh, nor of the will of man, but of God;"— "Except a man be born again, he cannot see the kingdom of God;"—"Whatsoever is born of God, overcometh the world," says the New. The ray of sunshine is there, the glow of a divine warmth;—the austerity of the sage melts away under it, the paralysis of the weak is healed; he who is vivified by it renews his strength; "all things are possible to him;" "he is a new creature."

Epictetus says: "Every matter has two handles, one of which will bear taking hold of, the other not. If thy brother sin against thee, lay not hold of the matter by this, that he sins against thee; for by this handle the matter will not bear taking hold of. But rather lay hold of it by this, that he is thy brother, thy born mate; and thou wilt take hold of it by what will bear handling." Jesus, being asked whether a man is bound to forgive his brother as often as seven times, answers : "I say not unto thee, until seven times, but until seventy times seven." Epictetus here suggests to the reason grounds for forgiveness of injuries which Jesus does not ; but it is vain to say that Epictetus is on that account a better moralist than Jesus, if the warmth, the emotion, of Jesus's answer fires his hearer to the practice of forgiveness of injuries, while the thought in Epictetus's leaves him cold. So with Christian morality in general : its distinction is not that it propounds the maxim, "Thou shalt love God and thy neighbour," with more development, closer reasoning, truer sincerity, than other moral systems ; it is that it propounds this maxim with an inspiration which wonderfully catches the hearer and makes him act upon it. It is because Mr. Mill has attained to the perception of truths of this nature, that he is,—instead of being, like the school from which he proceeds, doomed to sterility,— a writer of distinguished mark and influence, a writer deserving all attention and respect ; it is (I must be pardoned for saying) because he is not sufficiently leavened with them, that he falls just short of being a great writer.

That which gives to the moral writings of the Emperor Marcus Aurelius their peculiar character and charm, is their being suffused and softened by something of this very sentiment whence Christian morality draws its best power. Mr. Long has recently published in a convenient form a translation of these writings, and has thus enabled English readers to judge Marcus Aurelius for themselves; he has rendered his countrymen a real service by so doing. Mr. Long's reputation as a scholar is a sufficient guarantee of the general fidelity and accuracy of his translation; on these matters, besides, I am hardly entitled to speak, and my praise is of no value. But that for which I and the rest of the unlearned may venture to praise Mr. Long is this; that he treats Marcus Aurelius's writings, as he treats all the other remains of Greek and Roman antiquity which he touches, not as a dead and dry matter of learning, but as documents with a side of modern applicability and living interest, and valuable mainly so far as this side in them can be made clear; that as in his notes on Plutarch's Roman Lives he deals with the modern epoch of Cæsar and Cicero, not as food for schoolboys, but as food for men, and men engaged in the current of contemporary life and action, so in his remarks and essays on Marcus Aurelius he treats this truly modern striver and thinker not as a Classical Dictionary hero, but as a present source from which to draw "example of life, and instruction of manners." Why may not a son of Dr. Arnold say, what might naturally here be said by any other critic, that in this lively and fruitful way of considering the men and affairs of ancient Greece and Rome, Mr. Long resembles Dr. Arnold?

One or two little complaints, however, I have against Mr. Long, and I will get them off my mind at once. In the first place, why could he not have found gentler and juster terms to describe the trans-

lation of his predecessor, Jeremy Collier,—the re-
doubtable enemy of stage plays,—than these: "a
most coarse and vulgar copy of the original?" As a
matter of taste, a translator should deal leniently
with his predecessor; but putting that out of the
question, Mr. Long's language is a great deal too
hard. Most English people who knew Marcus
Aurelius before Mr. Long appeared as his intro-
ducer, knew him through Jeremy Collier. And
the acquaintance of a man like Marcus Aurelius is
such an imperishable benefit, that one can never
lose a peculiar sense of obligation towards the man
who confers it. Apart from this claim upon one's
tenderness, however, Jeremy Collier's version deserves respect for its genuine spirit and vigour,
the spirit and vigour of the age of Dryden. Jeremy
Collier too, like Mr. Long, regarded in Marcus
Aurelius the living moralist, and not the dead
classic; and his warmth of feeling gave to his style
an impetuosity and rhythm which from Mr. Long's
style (I do not blame it on that account) are absent.
Let us place the two side by side. The impressive
opening of Marcus Aurelius's fifth book, Mr. Long
translates thus :—

"In the morning when thou risest unwillingly,
let this thought be present: I am rising to the
work of a human being. Why then am I dissatisfied if I am going to do the things for which I
exist and for which I was brought into the world?
Or have I been made for this, to lie in the bed-
clothes and keep myself warm?—But this is more

pleasant.—Dost thou exist then to take thy pleasure, and not at all for action or exertion?"

Jeremy Collier has :—

"When you find an unwillingness to rise early in the morning, make this short speech to yourself: "I am getting up now to do the business of a man ; and am I out of humour for going about that which I was made for, and for the sake of which I was sent into the world? Was I then designed for nothing but to doze and batten beneath the counterpane? I thought action had been the end of your being.'"

In another striking passage, again, Mr. Long has :—

"No longer wonder at hazard ; for neither wilt thou read thy own memoirs, nor the acts of the ancient Romans and Hellenes, and the selections from books which thou wast reserving for thy old age. Hasten then to the end which thou hast before thee, and, throwing away idle hopes, come to thine own aid, if thou carest at all for thyself, while it is in thy power."

Here his despised predecessor has :—

"Don't go too far in your books and overgrasp yourself. Alas, you have no time left to peruse your diary, to read over the Greek and Roman history : come, don't flatter and deceive yourself ; look to the main chance, to the end and design of reading, and mind life more than notion : I say, if you have a kindness for your person, drive at the practice and help yourself, for that is in your own power."

It seems to me that here for style and force Jeremy Collier can (to say the least) perfectly stand comparison with Mr. Long. Jeremy Collier's real defect as a translator is not his coarseness and vulgarity, but his imperfect acquaintance with Greek; this is a serious defect, a fatal one; it rendered a translation like Mr. Long's necessary. Jeremy Collier's work will now be forgotten, and Mr. Long stands master of the field; but he may be content, at any rate, to leave his predecessor's grave unharmed, even if he will not throw upon it, in passing, a handful of kindly earth.

Another complaint I have against Mr. Long is, that he is not quite idiomatic and simple enough. It is a little formal, at least, if not pedantic, to say *Ethic* and *Dialectic*, instead of *Ethics* and *Dialectics*, and to say "*Hellenes* and Romans" instead of "*Greeks* and Romans." And why, too,—the name of Antoninus being preoccupied by Antoninus Pius, —will Mr. Long call his author Marcus *Antoninus* instead of Marcus *Aurelius?* Small as these matters appear, they are important when one has to deal with the general public, and not with a small circle of scholars; and it is the general public that the translator of a short masterpiece on morals, such as is the book of Marcus Aurelius, should have in view; his aim should be to make Marcus Aurelius's work as popular as the *Imitation*, and Marcus Aurelius's name as familiar as Socrates's. In rendering or naming him, therefore, punctilious accuracy of phrase is not so much to be sought as accessibility and cur

rency ; everything which may best enable the Emperor and his precepts *volitare per ora virûm*. It is
essential to render him in language perfectly plain
and unprofessional, and to call him by the name by
which he is best and most distinctly known. The
translators of the Bible talk of *pence* and not *denarii*,
and the admirers of Voltaire do not celebrate him
under the name of Arouet.

But, after these trifling complaints are made, one
must end, as one began, in unfeigned gratitude to
Mr. Long for his excellent and substantial reproduc-
tion in English of an invaluable work. In general
the substantiality, soundness, and precision of Mr.
Long's rendering are (I will venture, after all, to give
my opinion about them) as conspicuous as the living
spirit with which he treats antiquity ; and these
qualities are particularly desirable in the translator of
a work like that of Marcus Aurelius, of which the
language is often corrupt, almost always hard and
obscure. Any one who wants to appreciate Mr. Long's
merits as a translator may read, in the original and
in Mr. Long's translation, the seventh chapter of the
tenth book ; he will see how, through all the dubious-
ness and involved manner of the Greek, Mr. Long has
firmly seized upon the clear thought which is certainly
at the bottom of that troubled wording, and, in distinctly rendering this thought, has at the same time
thrown round its expression a characteristic shade of
painfulness and difficulty which just suits it. And
Marcus Aurelius's book is one which, when it is rendered so accurately as Mr. Long renders it, even those

who know Greek tolerably well may choose to read
rather in the translation than in the original.   For not
only are the contents here incomparably more valuable
than the external form, but this form, the Greek of a
Roman, is not exactly one of those styles which have a
physiognomy, which are an essential part of their
author, which stamp an indelible impression of him on
the reader's mind.   An old Lyons commentator finds,
indeed, in Marcus Aurelius's Greek, something characteristic, something specially firm and imperial ; but I
think an ordinary mortal will hardly find this : he will
find crabbed Greek, without any great charm of distinct
physiognomy.   The Greek of Thucydides and Plato
has this charm, and he who reads them in a translation, however accurate, loses it, and loses much in
losing it ; but the Greek of Marcus Aurelius, like the
Greek of the New Testament, and even more than
the Greek of the New Testament, is wanting in it.
If one could be assured that the English Testament
were made perfectly accurate, one might be almost
content never to open a Greek Testament again ; and,
Mr. Long's version of Marcus Aurelius being what it
is, an Englishman who reads to live, and does not
live to read, may henceforth let the Greek original
repose upon its shelf.

The man whose thoughts Mr. Long has thus faithfully reproduced, is perhaps the most beautiful figure
in history.   He is one of those consoling and hope-
inspiring marks, which stand for ever to remind our
weak and easily discouraged race how high human
goodness and perseverance have once been carried,

and may be carried again. The interest of mankind is peculiarly attracted by examples of signal goodness in high places; for that testimony to the worth of goodness is the most striking which is borne by those to whom all the means of pleasure and self-indulgence lay open, by those who had at their command the kingdoms of the world and the glory of them. Marcus Aurelius was the ruler of the grandest of empires; and he was one of the best of men. Besides him, history presents one or two sovereigns eminent for their goodness, such as Saint Louis or Alfred. But Marcus Aurelius has, for us moderns, this great superiority in interest over Saint Louis or Alfred, that he lived and acted in a state of society modern by its essential characteristics, in an epoch akin to our own, in a brilliant centre of civilisation. Trajan talks of "our enlightened age" just as glibly as the *Times* talks of it. Marcus Aurelius thus becomes for us a man like ourselves, a man in all things tempted as we are. Saint Louis inhabits an atmosphere of mediæval Catholicism, which the man of the nineteenth century may admire, indeed, may even passionately wish to inhabit, but which, strive as he will, he cannot really inhabit. Alfred belongs to a state of society (I say it with all deference to the *Saturday Review* critic who keeps such jealous watch over the honour of our Saxon ancestors) half barbarous. Neither Alfred nor Saint Louis can be morally and intellectually as near to us as Marcus Aurelius.

The record of the outward life of this admirable man has in it little of striking incident. He was

born at Rome on the 26th of April, in the year 121
of the Christian era.   He was nephew and son-in-law
to his predecessor on the throne, Antoninus Pius.
When Antoninus died, he was forty years old, but
from the time of his earliest manhood he had assisted
in administering public affairs.   Then, after his uncle's
death in 161, for nineteen years he reigned as emperor.
The barbarians were pressing on the Roman frontier,
and a great part of Marcus Aurelius's nineteen years
of reign was passed in campaigning.   His absences
from Rome were numerous and long.   We hear of
him in Asia Minor, Syria, Egypt, Greece ; but, above
all, in the countries on the Danube, where the war
with the barbarians was going on,— in Austria,
Moravia, Hungary.   In these countries much of his
Journal seems to have been written ; parts of it are
dated from them ; and there, a few weeks before his
fifty-ninth birthday, he fell sick and died.[1]   The
record of him on which his fame chiefly rests is
the record of his inward life,—his *Journal*, or *Com-
mentaries*, or *Meditations*, or *Thoughts*, for by all these
names has the work been called.   Perhaps the most
interesting of the records of his outward life is that
which the first book of this work supplies, where he
gives an account of his education, recites the names
of those to whom he is indebted for it, and enumerates
his obligations to each of them.   It is a refreshing
and consoling picture, a priceless treasure for those,
who, sick of the " wild and dreamlike trade of blood
and guile," which seems to be nearly the whole of

---

[1] He died on the 17th of March, A.D. 180.

what history has to offer to our view, seek eagerly for
that substratum of right thinking and well-doing
which in all ages must surely have somewhere existed
for without it the continued life of humanity would
have been impossible. "From my mother I learnt
piety and beneficence, and abstinence not only from
evil deeds but even from evil thoughts; and further,
simplicity in my way of living, far removed from the
habits of the rich." Let us remember that, the next
time we are reading the sixth satire of Juvenal.
"From my tutor I learnt"(hear it, ye tutors of princes!)
"endurance of labour, and to want little, and to work
with my own hands, and not to meddle with other
people's affairs, and not to be ready to listen to slander."
The vices and foibles of the Greek sophist or rhetorician—the *Græculus esuriens*—are in everybody's mind;
but he who reads Marcus Aurelius's account of his
Greek teachers and masters, will understand how it
is that, in spite of the vices and foibles of individual
Græculi, the education of the human race owes to
Greece a debt which can never be overrated. The
vague and colourless praise of history leaves on the
mind hardly any impression of Antoninus Pius : it is
only from the private memoranda of his nephew that
we learn what a disciplined, hard-working, gentle,
wise, virtuous man he was; a man who, perhaps, interests mankind less than his immortal nephew only
because he has left in writing no record of his inner
life,—*caret quia vate sacro.*

Of the outward life and circumstances of Marcus
Aurelius, beyond these notices which he has himself

supplied, there are few of much interest and importance.   There is the fine anecdote of his speech when
he heard of the assassination of the revolted Avidius
Cassius, against whom he was marching ; *he was sorry*,
he said, *to be deprived of the pleasure of pardoning him.*
And there are one or two more anecdotes of him
which show the same spirit.   But the great record
for the outward life of a man who has left such a
record of his lofty inward aspirations as that which
Marcus Aurelius has left, is the clear consenting voice
of all his contemporaries,—high and low, friend and
enemy, pagan and Christian,—in praise of his sincerity,
justice, and goodness.   The world's charity does not
err on the side of excess, and here was a man occupying the most conspicuous station in the world, and
professing the highest possible standard of conduct ;—
yet the world was obliged to declare that he walked
worthily of his profession.   Long after his death, his
bust was to be seen in the houses of private men
through the wide Roman empire.   It may be the
vulgar part of human nature which busies itself with
the semblance and doings of living sovereigns, it is
its nobler part which busies itself with those of the
dead ; these busts of Marcus Aurelius, in the homes
of Gaul, Britain, and Italy, bear witness, not to the
inmates' frivolous curiosity about princes and palaces,
but to their reverential memory of the passage of a
great man upon the earth.

Two things, however, before one turns from the
outward to the inward life of Marcus Aurelius, force
themselves upon one's notice, and demand a word of

comment; he persecuted the Christians, and he had
for his son the vicious and brutal Commodus. The
persecution at Lyons, in which Attalus and Pothinus
suffered, the persecution at Smyrna, in which Polycarp
suffered, took place in his reign. Of his humanity,
of his tolerance, of his horror of cruelty and violence,
of his wish to refrain from severe measures against
the Christians, of his anxiety to temper the severity
of these measures when they appeared to him indispensable, there is no doubt : but, on the one hand, it
is certain that the letter, attributed to him, directing
that no Christian should be punished for being a
Christian, is spurious ; it is almost certain that his
alleged answer to the authorities of Lyons, in which
he directs that Christians persisting in their profession
shall be dealt with according to law, is genuine. Mr.
Long seems inclined to try and throw doubt over
the persecution at Lyons, by pointing out that the
letter of the Lyons Christians relating it, alleges it
to have been attended by miraculous and incredible
incidents. "A man," he says, "can only act consist-
ently by accepting all this letter or rejecting it all,
and we cannot blame him for either." But it is contrary to all experience to say that because a fact is
related with incorrect additions, and embellishments,
therefore it probably never happened at all ; or that
it is not, in general, easy for an impartial mind to
distinguish between the fact and the embellishments.
I cannot doubt that the Lyons persecution took place,
and that the punishment of Christians for being
Christians was sanctioned by Marcus Aurelius. But

then I must add that nine modern readers out of ten,
when they read this, will, I believe, have a perfectly
false notion of what the moral action of Marcus
Aurelius, in sanctioning that punishment, really was.
They imagine Trajan, or Antoninus Pius, or Marcus
Aurelius, fresh from the perusal of the Gospel, fully
aware of the spirit and holiness of the Christian saints
ordering their extermination because he loved darkness rather than light.   Far from this, the Christianity
which these emperors aimed at repressing was, in
their conception of it, something philosophically contemptible, politically subversive, and morally abominable.   As men, they sincerely regarded it much as
well-conditioned people, with us, regard Mormonism ;
as rulers, they regarded it much as Liberal statesmen,
with us, regard the Jesuits.   A kind of Mormonism,
constituted as a vast secret society, with obscure aims
of political and social subversion, was what Antoninus
Pius and Marcus Aurelius believed themselves to be
repressing when they punished Christians.   The early
Christian apologists again and again declare to us
under what odious imputations the Christians lay,
how general was the belief that these imputations
were well-grounded, how sincere was the horror which
the belief inspired.   The multitude, convinced that
the Christians were atheists who ate human flesh and
thought incest no crime, displayed against them a
fury so passionate as to embarrass and alarm their
rulers.   The severe expressions of Tacitus, *exitiabilis
superstitio — odio humani generis convicti*, show how
deeply the prejudices of the multitude imbued the

educated class also.   One asks oneself with astonishment how a doctrine so benign as that of Jesus Christ
can have incurred misrepresentation so monstrous.
The inner and moving cause of the misrepresentation
lay, no doubt, in this,—that Christianity was a new
spirit in the Roman world, destined to act in that
world as its dissolvent; and it was inevitable that
Christianity in the Roman world, like democracy in
the modern world, like every new spirit with a similar
mission assigned to it, should at its first appearance
occasion an instinctive shrinking and repugnance in
the world which it was to dissolve.   The outer and
palpable causes of the misrepresentation were, for the
Roman public at large, the confounding of the Christians with the Jews, that isolated, fierce, and stubborn
race, whose stubbornness, fierceness, and isolation,
real as they were, the fancy of a civilised Roman yet
further exaggerated; the atmosphere of mystery and
novelty which surrounded the Christian rites; the
very simplicity of Christian theism.   For the Roman
statesman, the cause of mistake lay in that character
of secret assemblages which the meetings of the
Christian community wore, under a State-system as
jealous of unauthorised associations as is the State-
system of modern France.

A Roman of Marcus Aurelius's time and position
could not well see the Christians except through the
mist of these prejudices.   Seen through such a mist,
the Christians appeared with a thousand faults not
their own; but it has not been sufficiently remarked
that faults really their own many of them assuredly

appeared with besides, faults especially likely to strike such an observer as Marcus Aurelius, and to confirm him in the prejudices of his race, station, and rearing. We look back upon Christianity after it has proved what a future it bore within it, and for us the sole representatives of its early struggles are the pure and devoted spirits through whom it proved this; Marcus Aurelius saw it with its future yet unshown, and with the tares among its professed progeny not less conspicuous than the wheat. Who can doubt that among the professing Christians of the second century, as among the professing Christians of the nineteenth, there was plenty of folly, plenty of rabid nonsense, plenty of gross fanaticism? who will even venture to affirm that, separated in great measure from the intellect and civilisation of the world for one or two centuries, Christianity, wonderful as have been its fruits, had the development perfectly worthy of its inestimable germ? Who will venture to affirm that, by the alliance of Christianity with the virtue and intelligence of men like the Antonines,—of the best product of Greek and Roman civilisation, while Greek and Roman civilisation had yet life and power,— Christianity and the world, as well as the Antonines themselves, would not have been gainers? That alliance was not to be. The Antonines lived and died with an utter misconception of Christianity; Christianity grew up in the Catacombs, not on the Palatine. And Marcus Aurelius incurs no moral reproach by having authorised the punishment of the Christians; he does not thereby become in the least

what we mean by a *persecutor*. One may concede
that it was impossible for him to see Christianity as
it really was;—as impossible as for even the moderate
and sensible Fleury to see the Antonines as they
really were;—one may concede that the point of
view from which Christianity appeared something
anti-civil and anti-social, which the State had the
faculty to judge and the duty to suppress, was inevitably his. Still, however, it remains true that
this sage, who made perfection his aim and reason his
law, did Christianity an immense injustice and rested
in an idea of State-attributes which was illusive.
And this is, in truth, characteristic of Marcus Aurelius,
that he is blameless, yet, in a certain sense, unfortunate; in his character, beautiful as it is, there
is something melancholy, circumscribed, and ineffectual.

For of his having such a son as Commodus, too,
one must say that he is not to be blamed on that
account, but that he is unfortunate. Disposition and
temperament are inexplicable things; there are
natures on which the best education and example are
thrown away; excellent fathers may have, without
any fault of theirs, incurably vicious sons. It is to be
remembered, also, that Commodus was left, at the
perilous age of nineteen, master of the world; while
his father, at that age, was but beginning a twenty
years' apprenticeship to wisdom, labour, and self-
command, under the sheltering teachership of his
uncle Antoninus. Commodus was a prince apt to be
led by favourites; and if the story is true which says

that he left, all through his reign, the Christians un-
troubled, and ascribes this lenity to the influence of
his mistress Marcia, it shows that he could be led to
good as well as to evil.   But for such a nature to be
left at a critical age with absolute power, and wholly
without good counsel and direction, was the more
fatal.   Still one cannot help wishing that the example
of Marcus Aurelius could have availed more with his
own only son.   One cannot but think that with such
virtue as his there should go, too, the ardour which
removes mountains, and that the ardour which removes mountains might have even won Commodus.
The word *ineffectual* again rises to one's mind ; Marcus
Aurelius saved his own soul by his righteousness, and
he could do no more.   Happy they who can do this !
but still happier, who can do more !

Yet, when one passes from his outward to his inward life, when one turns over the pages of his
Meditations,—entries jotted down from day to day,
amid the business of the city or the fatigues of the
camp, for his own guidance and support, meant for
no eye but his own, without the slightest attempt at
style, with no care, even, for correct writing, not to
be surpassed for naturalness and sincerity,—all disposition to carp and cavil dies away, and one is overpowered by the charm of a character of such purity,
delicacy, and virtue.   He fails neither in small things
nor in great ; he keeps watch over himself both that
the great springs of action may be right in him, and
that the minute details of action may be right also.
How admirable in a hard-tasked ruler, and a ruler,

too, with a passion for thinking and reading, is such a memorandum as the following :—

"Not frequently nor without necessity to say to any one, or to write in a letter, that I have no leisure ; nor continually to excuse the neglect of duties required by our relation to those with whom we live, by alleging urgent occupation."

And, when that ruler is a Roman emperor, what an "idea" is this to be written down and meditated by him : -

"Tne idea of a polity in which there is the same law for all, a polity administered with regard to equal rights and equal freedom of speech, and the idea of a kingly government which respects most of all the freedom of the governed."

And, for all men who "drive at practice," what practical rules may not one accumulate out of these *Meditations* :—

"The greatest part of what we say or do being unnecessary, if a man takes this away, he will have more leisure and less uneasiness. Accordingly, on every occasion a man should ask himself : 'Is this one of the unnecessary things ?' Now a man should take away not only unnecessary acts, but also unnecessary thoughts, for thus superfluous acts will not follow after."

And again :—

"We ought to check in the series of our thoughts everything that is without a purpose and useless, but most of all the over curious feeling and the malignant ; and a man should use himself to think of those

things only about which if one should suddenly ask,
'What hast thou now in thy thoughts?' with perfect
openness thou mightest immediately answer, 'This or
That;' so that from thy words it should be plain that
everything in thee is simple and benevolent, and such
as befits a social animal, and one that cares not for
thoughts about sensual enjoyments, or any rivalry
or envy and suspicion, or anything else for which thou
wouldst blush if thou shouldst say thou hadst it in
thy mind."

So, with a stringent practicalness worthy of
Franklin, he discourses on his favourite text, *Let
nothing be done without a purpose.* But it is when he
enters the region where Franklin cannot follow him,
when he utters his thoughts on the ground-motives
of human action, that he is most interesting; that he
becomes the unique, the incomparable Marcus Aurelius.
Christianity uses language very liable to be misunderstood when it seems to tell men to do good, not, certainly, from the vulgar motives of worldly interest, or
vanity, or love of human praise, but "that their
Father which seeth in secret may reward them
openly." The motives of reward and punishment
have come, from the misconception of language of
this kind, to be strangely overpressed by many Christian moralists, to the deterioration and disfigurement
of Christianity. Marcus Aurelius says, truly and
nobly :—

"One man, when he has done a service to another,
is ready to set it down to his account as a favour con-
ferred. Another is not ready to do this, but still in

his own mind he thinks of the man as his debtor, and he knows what he has done. A third in a manner does not even know what he has done, *but he is like a vine which has produced grapes, and seeks for nothing more after it has once produced its proper fruit.* As a horse when he has run, a dog when he has caught the game, a bee when it has made its honey, so a man when he has done a good act, does not call out for others to come and see, but he goes on to another act, as a vine goes on to produce again the grapes in season. Must a man, then, be one of these, who in a manner acts thus without observing it ? Yes."

And again :—

"What more dost thou want when thou hast done a man a service ? Art thou not content that thou hast done something conformable to thy nature, and dost thou seek to be paid for it, *just as if the eye demanded a recompense for seeing, or the feet for walking ?*"

Christianity, in order to match morality of this strain, has to correct its apparent offers of external reward, and to say : *The kingdom of God is within you.*

I have said that it is by its accent of emotion that the morality of Marcus Aurelius acquires a special character, and reminds one of Christian morality. The sentences of Seneca are stimulating to the intellect ; the sentences of Epictetus are fortifying to the character ; the sentences of Marcus Aurelius find their way to the soul. I have said that religious emotion has the power to *light up* morality : the emotion of Marcus Aurelius does not quite light up his morality, but it suffuses it; it has not power to melt the clouds of effort and austerity quite away, but it shines through them and glorifies them; it is a spirit, not so much of gladness and elation, as of gentleness and sweetness; a delicate and tender sentiment, which is less than joy and more than resignation. He says that in his youth he learned from Maximus, one of his teachers, "cheerfulness in all circumstances as well as in illness; *and a just admixture in the moral character of sweetness and dignity:*" and it is this very admixture of sweetness with his dignity which makes him so beautiful a moralist. It enables him to carry even into his observation of nature, a delicate penetration, a sympathetic tenderness, worthy of Wordsworth; the spirit of such a remark as the following has hardly a parallel, so far as my knowledge goes, in the whole range of Greek and Roman literature :—

"Figs, when they are quite ripe, gape open; and in the ripe olives the very circumstance of their being near to rottenness adds a peculiar beauty to the fruit. And the ears of corn bending down, and the lion's eyebrows, and the foam which flows from the mouth of wild boars, and many other things,—though they are far from being beautiful, in a certain sense,—still, because they come in the course of nature, have a beauty in them, and they please the mind; so that if a man should have a feeling and a deeper insight with respect to the things which are produced in the universe, there is hardly anything which comes in the

course of nature which will not seem to him to be in
a manner disposed so as to give pleasure."

But it is when his strain passes to directly moral
subjects that his delicacy and sweetness lend to it
the greatest charm.   Let those who can feel the
beauty of spiritual refinement read this, the reflection of an emperor who prized mental superiority
highly :—

"Thou sayest, 'Men cannot admire the sharpness
of thy wits.'   Be it so; but there are many other
things of which thou canst not say, 'I am not formed
for them by nature.'   Show those qualities, then,
which are altogether in thy power,—sincerity, gravity,
endurance of labour, aversion to pleasure, contentment
with thy portion and with few things, benevolence,
frankness, no love of superfluity, freedom from trifling,
magnanimity.   Dost thou not see how many qualities
thou art at once able to exhibit, as to which there is
no excuse of natural incapacity and unfitness, and yet
thou still remainest voluntarily below the mark?   Or
art thou compelled, through being defectively furnished by nature, to murmur, and to be mean, and
to flatter, and to find fault with thy poor body, and
to try to please men, and to make great display, and
to be so restless in thy mind?   No, indeed; but thou
mightest have been delivered from these things long
ago.   Only, if in truth thou canst be charged with
being rather slow and dull of comprehension, thou
must exert thyself about this also, not neglecting nor
yet taking pleasure in thy dulness."

The same sweetness enables him to fix his mind,

when he sees the isolation and moral death caused by sin, not on the cheerless thought of the misery of this condition, but on the inspiriting thought that man is blest with the power to escape from it :—

"Suppose that thou hast detached thyself from the natural unity,—for thou wast made by nature a part, but now thou hast cut thyself off,—yet here is this beautiful provision, that it is in thy power again to unite thyself. God has allowed this to no other part, —after it has been separated and cut asunder, to come together again. But consider the goodness with which he has privileged man ; for he has put it in his power, when he has been separated, to return and to be united and to resume his place."

It enables him to control even the passion for retreat and solitude, so strong in a soul like his, to which the world could offer no abiding city :—

"Men seek retreat for themselves, houses in the country, seashores, and mountains ; and thou, too, art wont to desire such things very much. But this is altogether a mark of the most common sort of men, for it is in thy power whenever thou shalt choose to retire into thyself. For nowhere either with more quiet or more freedom from trouble does a man retire than into his own soul, particularly when he has within him such thoughts that by looking into them he is immediately in perfect tranquillity. Constantly, then, give to thyself this retreat, and renew thyself ; and let thy principles be brief and fundamental, which, as soon as thou shalt recur to them, will be sufficient to cleanse the soul completely, and to send

thee back free from all discontent with the things to
which thou returnest."

Against this feeling of discontent and weariness,
so natural to the great for whom there seems nothing
left to desire or to strive after, but so enfeebling to
them, so deteriorating, Marcus Aurelius never ceased
to struggle. With resolute thankfulness he kept in
remembrance the blessings of his lot; the true blessings of it, not the false :—

"I have to thank Heaven that I was subjected to
a ruler and a father (Antoninus Pius) who was able
to take away all pride from me, and to bring me to
the knowledge that it is possible for a man to live in
a palace without either guards, or embroidered dresses,
or any show of this kind; but that it is in such a
man's power to bring himself very near to the fashion
of a private person, without being for this reason
either meaner in thought or more remiss in action
with respect to the things which must be done for
public interest. . . . I have to be thankful that my
children have not been stupid nor deformed in body;
that I did not make more proficiency in rhetoric,
poetry, and the other studies, by which I should perhaps have been completely engrossed, if I had seen
that I was making great progress in them; . . . that
I knew Apollonius, Rusticus, Maximus; . . . that I
received clear and frequent impressions about living
according to nature, and what kind of a life that is,
so that, so far as depended on Heaven, and its gifts,
help, and inspiration, nothing hindered me from forth-
with living according to nature, though I still fall short

of it through my own fault, and through not observing
the admonitions of Heaven, and, I may almost say, its
direct instructions ; that my body has held out so long
in such a kind of life as mine ; that though it was my
mother's lot to die young, she spent the last years of
her life with me ; that whenever I wished to help any
man in his need, I was never told that I had not the
means of doing it ; that, when I had an inclination to
philosophy, I did not fall into the hands of a sophist."

And, as he dwelt with gratitude on these helps and
blessings vouchsafed to him, his mind (so, at least, it
seems to me) would sometimes revert with awe to the
perils and temptations of the lonely height where he
stood, to the lives of Tiberius, Caligula, Nero, Domi-
tian, in their hideous blackness and ruin ; and then
he wrote down for himself such a warning entry as
this, significant and terrible in its abruptness :—

" A black character, a womanish character, a stubborn character, bestial, childish, animal, stupid, counter-
feit, scurrilous, fraudulent, tyrannical ! "

Or this :—

" About what am I now employing my soul ?　On
every occasion I must ask myself this question, and
enquire, What have I now in this part of me which
they call the ruling principle, and whose soul have I
now ?—that of a child, or of a young man, or of a
weak woman, or of a tyrant, or of one of the lower
animals in the service of man, or of a wild beast ? "

The character he wished to attain he knew well,
and beautifully he has marked it, and marked, too,
his sense of shortcoming :—

"When thou hast assumed these names,—good, modest, true, rational, equal-minded, magnanimous,— take care that thou dost not change these names ; and, if thou shouldst lose them, quickly return to them. If thou maintainest thyself in possession of these names without desiring that others should call thee by them, thou wilt be another being, and wilt enter on another life.　For to continue to be such as thou hast hitherto been, and to be torn in pieces and defiled in such a life, is the character of a very stupid man, and one overfond of his life, and like those half-devoured fighters with wild beasts, who though covered with wounds and gore still entreat to be kept to the following day, though they will be exposed in the same state to the same claws and bites. Therefore fix thyself in the possession of these few names : and if thou art able to abide in them, abide as if thou wast removed to the Happy Islands."

For all his sweetness and serenity, however, man's point of life " between two infinities " (of that expression Marcus Aurelius is the real owner) was to him anything but a Happy Island, and the performances on it he saw through no veils of illusion.　Nothing is in general more gloomy and monotonous than declamations on the hollowness and transitoriness of human life and grandeur : but here, too, the great charm of Marcus Aurelius, his emotion, comes in to relieve the monotony and to break through the gloom ; and even on this eternally used topic he is imaginative, fresh, and striking :—

"Consider, for example, the times of Vespasian

Thou wilt see all these things, people marrying, bringing up children, sick, dying, warring, feasting, trafficking, cultivating the ground, flattering, obstinately arrogant, suspecting, plotting, wishing for somebody to die, grumbling about the present, loving, heaping up treasure, desiring to be consuls or kings. Well then that life of these people no longer exists at all. Again, go to the times of Trajan. All is again the same. Their life too is gone. But chiefly thou shouldst think of those whom thou hast thyself known distracting themselves about idle things, neglecting to do what was in accordance with their proper constitution, and to hold firmly to this and to be content with it."

Again :—

"The things which are much valued in life are empty, and rotten, and trifling; and people are like little dogs, biting one another, and little children quarrelling, crying, and then straightway laughing. But fidelity, and modesty, and justice, and truth, are fled

'Up to Olympus from the wide-spread earth.'

What then is there which still detains thee here?"

And once more :—

"Look down from above on the countless herds of men, and their countless solemnities, and the infinitely varied voyagings in storms and calms, and the differences among those who are born, who live together, and die. And consider too the life lived by others in olden time, and the life now lived among barbarous nations, and how many know not even thy name, and

how many will soon forget it, and how they who perhaps now are praising thee will very soon blame thee,
and that neither a posthumous name is of any value,
nor reputation, nor anything else."

He recognised, indeed, that (to use his own words)
"the prime principle in man's constitution is the
social;" and he laboured sincerely to make not only
his acts towards his fellow-men, but his thoughts also,
suitable to this conviction :—

"When thou wishest to delight thyself, think of
the virtues of those who live with thee; for instance,
the activity of one, and the modesty of another, and
the liberality of a third, and some other good quality
of a fourth."

Still, it is hard for a pure and thoughtful man to
live in a state of rapture at the spectacle afforded to
him by his fellow-creatures; above all it is hard,
when such a man is placed as Marcus Aurelius was
placed, and has had the meanness and perversity of
his fellow-creatures thrust, in no common measure,
upon his notice,—has had, time after time, to experience how "within ten days thou wilt seem a god to
those to whom thou art now a beast and an ape."
His true strain of thought as to his relations with his
fellow-men is rather the following. He has been
enumerating the higher consolations which may support a man at the approach of death, and he goes
on :—

"But if thou requirest also a vulgar kind of comfort which shall reach thy heart, thou wilt be made
best reconciled to death by observing the objects from

which thou art going to be removed, and the morals
of those with whom thy soul will no longer be mingled.
For it is no way right to be offended with men, but
it is thy duty to care for them and to bear with them
gently ; and yet to remember that thy departure will
not be from men who have the same principles as
thyself.   For this is the only thing, if there be any,
which could draw us the contrary way and attach us
to life, to be permitted to live with those who have
the same principles as ourselves.   But now thou seest
how great is the distress caused by the difference of
those who live together, so that thou mayest say :
'Come quick, O death, lest perchance I too should
forget myself.'"

*O faithless and perverse generation ! how long shall I
be with you ? how long shall I suffer you ?* Sometimes
this strain rises even to passion :—

"Short is the little which remains to thee of life.
Live as on a mountain.   Let men see, let them know,
a real man, who lives as he was meant to live.   If
they cannot endure him, let them kill him.   For that
is better than to live as men do."

It is remarkable how little of a merely local and
temporary character, how little of those *scoriæ* which
a reader has to clear away before he gets to the precious ore, how little that even admits of doubt or
question, the morality of Marcus Aurelius exhibits.
Perhaps as to one point we must make an exception.
Marcus Aurelius is fond of urging as a motive for
man's cheerful acquiescence in whatever befalls him,
that "whatever happens to every man *is for the in-*

terest of the universal ;" that the whole contains nothing *which is not for its advantage ;* that everything which happens to a man is to be accepted, "even if it seems disagreeable, *because it leads to the health of the universe."* And the whole course of the universe, he adds, has a providential reference to man's welfare : "*all other things have been made for the sake of rational beings.*" Religion has in all ages freely used this language, and it is not religion which will object to Marcus Aurelius's use of it ; but science can hardly accept as severely accurate this employment of the terms *interest* and *advantage.* To a sound nature and a clear reason the proposition that things happen " for the interest of the universal," as men conceive of interest, may seem to have no meaning at all, and the proposition that " all things have been made for the sake of rational beings " may seem to be false. Yet even to this language, not irresistibly cogent when it is thus absolutely used, Marcus Aurelius gives a turn which makes it true and useful, when he says : "The ruling part of man can make a material for itself out of that which opposes it, as fire lays hold of what falls into it, and rises higher by means of this very material ;"—when he says : "What else are all things except exercises for the reason ? Persevere then until thou shalt have made all things thine own, as the stomach which is strengthened makes all things its own, as the blazing fire makes flame and brightness out of everything that is thrown into it ;"—when he says : "Thou wilt not cease to be miserable till thy mind is in such a condition, that, what luxury is to those who enjoy

pleasure, such shall be to thee, in every matter which
presents itself, the doing of the things which are
conformable to man's constitution; for a man ought
to consider as an enjoyment everything which it is in
his power to do according to his own nature,—and it
is in his power everywhere." In this sense it is, indeed, most true that "all things have been made for
the sake of rational beings;" that "all things work
together for good."

In general, however, the action Marcus Aurelius
prescribes is action which every sound nature must
recognise as right, and the motives he assigns are
motives which every clear reason must recognise as
valid. And so he remains the especial friend and
comforter of all clear-headed and scrupulous, yet pure-
hearted and upward striving men, in those ages most
especially that walk by sight, not by faith, but yet
have no open vision. He cannot give such souls,
perhaps, all they yearn for, but he gives them much;
and what he gives them, they can receive.

Yet no, it is not for what he thus gives them that
such souls love him most! it is rather because of the
emotion which lends to his voice so touching an accent,
it is because he too yearns as they do for something
unattained by him. What an affinity for Christianity
had this persecutor of the Christians! The effusion
of Christianity, its relieving tears, its happy self-
sacrifice, were the very element, one feels, for which
his soul longed; they were near him, they brushed
him, he touched them, he passed them by. One feels,
too, that the Marcus Aurelius one reads must still

have remained, even had Christianity been fully
known to him, in a great measure himself; he would
have been no Justin;—but how would Christianity
have affected him? in what measure would it have
changed him? Granted that he might have found,
like the *Alogi* of modern times, in the most beautiful
of the Gospels, the Gospel which has leavened Christendom most powerfully, the Gospel of St. John, too
much Greek metaphysics, too much *gnosis;* granted
that this Gospel might have looked too like what he
knew already to be a total surprise to him: what,
then, would he have said to the Sermon on the Mount,
to the twenty-sixth chapter of St. Matthew? What
would have become of his notions of the *exitiabilis
superstitio,* of the "obstinacy of the Christians"?
Vain question! yet the greatest charm of Marcus
Aurelius is that he makes us ask it. We see him
wise, just, self-governed, tender, thankful, blameless;
yet, with all this, agitated, stretching out his arms for
something beyond,—*tendentemque manus ripæ ulterioris
amore.*

THE END.

Printed in Great Britain by R. & R. CLARK, LIMITED, *Edinburgh.*